Copernicus®

*Marketing Consulting
and Research*

Three University Park
95 Sawyer Road, Suite 130
Waltham, MA 02453

Kevin J. Clancy, Ph.D., and
Peter C. Krieg are Chairman and
President respectively of Copernicus
Marketing Consulting and Research.
Copernicus is in the business of
transforming companies, helping to
develop, plan, and implement
marketing strategies that change
brand trajectories, careers, sometimes
entire companies and even industries.

For more information:

(781) 392-2500
www.copernicusmarketing.com
www.useyourheadnow.com

YOUR GUT IS STILL
NOT SMARTER
THAN YOUR HEAD

YOUR GUT IS STILL NOT SMARTER THAN YOUR HEAD

How Disciplined, Fact-Based
Marketing Can Drive Extraordinary
Growth and Profits

Kevin Clancy
Peter Krieg

John Wiley & Sons, Inc.

Published by John Wiley & Sons, Inc., Hoboken, New Jersey.

Published simultaneously in Canada.

Wiley Bicentennial Logo: Richard J. Pacifico

For general information on our other products and services or for technical support, please contact our Customer Care Department within the United States at (800) 762-2974, outside the United States at (317) 572–3993 or fax (317) 572–4002.

Wiley also publishes its books in a variety of electronic formats. Some content that appears in print may not be available in electronic books. For more information about Wiley products, visit our web site at www.wiley.com.

Library of Congress Cataloging-in-Publication Data:
Clancy, Kevin J., 1942-
  Your gut is still not smarter than your head : how disciplined, fact-based marketing can drive extraordinary growth and profits / Kevin Clancy.
       p. cm.
  ISBN 978–0–471–97993–7 (cloth)
1. Marketing—Decision making. 2. Marketing—Management. 3. Product management.
  I. Title.
  HF5415.135.C55 2007
  658.8—dc22
                                                        2007002401

Printed in the United States of America.

10 9 8 7 6 5 4 3 2 1

We dedicate this book to our supportive, intelligent, forward-thinking, and, thankfully, numerous clients. There are too many to mention here, but they know who they are. They have infused our work—and this book—with their insights, curiosity, and desire for excellence. They used their heads and not (just) their guts. And we had a great time in the process.

We would also like to thank our colleagues at Copernicus, particularly Ami Bowen, and the members of the Copernicus Board of Advisors for their many contributions in the way of ideas, analysis, and war stories from the world of marketing consulting and research. You enrich our professional and personal lives and make us smarter.

No one makes us smarter than the brilliant Wally Wood, a talented consultant and business writer who helped conceptualize, research, write, and edit our evolving manuscript over the two years that we worked on this project. We also acknowledge and thank our agent, Richard Curtis, and our editor at John Wiley & Sons, Richard Narramore.

The spirit of the late Robert Shulman can be seen and heard throughout the pages of this book. Robert was our former partner at Yankelovich Clancy Shulman and, later, Copernicus; our coauthor on previous books; and above all, a dear friend. He was truly a force majeure—pushing clients and colleagues to be better, to think better, and to do better. He was a man who had more innovative ideas in an average week than some of us have in a lifetime. He was a presence in any room, which feels emptier now without him. He may be gone but he will never be forgotten.

And to our wives and children, we are forever indebted for your patience and encouragement. You make us better people.

Contents

SECTION III
HOW TO FINALLY MAKE IT ALL WORK TOGETHER
203

SECTION I

Why You Should Be Unhappy with Your Marketing Even if You're Not

1

Nothing Is More Important than Marketing

Peter Drucker once noted the only purpose of a business is to find and keep customers. If there are no customers, there is no business. And the only purpose of marketing is to find customers for businesses. Therefore, marketing is at the heart of every business. However, by *marketing* we don't mean silly advertising, golf outings, or buy-one-get-one-free loss leaders. We mean solving people's problems with products and services at a profit.

Because the business's purpose is to find and keep customers, all company activities that touch customers directly or indirectly fall within marketing's purview. So marketing is about research and development (R&D), distribution, pricing, advertising, direct marketing, and sales. It is about public relations, the company web site, and sports and event sponsorship. And in the sophisticated company of tomorrow, the chief marketing officer (CMO) will be responsible for all of these functions.

In these companies, the CMOs will still make marketing decisions based in part on creativity, judgment, and experience—to a modest extent by using their gut—but experience will be supplemented, buttressed, or balanced by careful analysis of unimpeachable data. That is, facts.

We've helped companies large and small improve their marketing through analysis of hard data, by using their heads rather than their instincts. Yet we see too many marketers making their decisions with their gut rather than their heads. Consider what happened to Interstate Bakeries.

In early 2001, senior executives at Interstate Bakeries faced a dismal business outlook. The country's largest wholesale baker—known for brands like Wonder, Home Pride, Sunbeam Breads, Dolly Madison, Hostess Twinkies, Ding-Dongs, Drake's Coffee Cakes, and more— carried a heavy debt load, many of its 60 factories were outmoded and inefficient, and competition for shelf space and market share was fierce.

Perhaps worse, consumers were increasingly concerned their kids were eating too many Twinkies and other junk foods, leading to childhood obesity, and they themselves had started counting carbohydrates, adopting the Atkins diet, and dropping bread from their meals. The situation appeared dire as Interstate's management looked for a way to reverse a string of annual losses.

This was, we believe, a situation crying for better marketing. If consumer tastes are changing, develop products that satisfy the new tastes. If kids are eating too many Twinkies, Ho-Hos, and Ding-Dongs, start marketing to adults. Reposition the snacks as a quick pickup or as a reward for getting through a difficult day. Interstate's management could have tried a number of alternative marketing strategies.

Interstate's management, apparently using their gut rather than their head, saw the challenge as a financial issue. It's expensive to keep fresh bread on store shelves: Three days out of the oven and bread becomes noticeably stale. That's one reason why Interstate had all those factories; you can't take a lot of time shipping bread around the countryside, so the bakery has to be close to the retail outlet.

Company chemists had discovered a way to extend the shelf life of Zingers, a Dolly Madison crumb cake. New additives made Zingers, and subsequently the entire Hostess products line, stay soft and fresh-looking longer without compromising taste. Rather than restock store shelves every week, drivers would have to restock them only every other week, cutting delivery costs.

At the same time, an industry supplier had developed enzymes that promised a longer life for bread as well. Increasing bread's shelf life meant the company could reduce spoilage and waste—a big savings. Longer shelf life would mean Interstate could close inefficient bakeries and would require fewer deliveries to the same number of stores—a colossal savings. "Our extended-shelf-life program will continue to play a significant role in cost control," proclaimed Charles Sullivan, Interstate's chairman and chief executive officer (CEO) at the time. Executives promised Wall Street "cost cutting like never before" as James Elsesser, a legendary cost cutter at Ralston-Purina, took over for Sullivan and continued to support the shelf-life plan.

Unfortunately, the company didn't give the significant customer-side implications a second thought as they forged ahead with the plan. First, from a strategic point of view, the idea of bread having a longer shelf life was unlikely to appeal to consumers who were increasingly looking for fresh, right-out-of-the-oven baked goods. Interstate's own retailers—major supermarket chains—were adding bakeries to their stores to meet this demand. So there was no added value to consumers for a product with a longer shelf life thanks to additives and enzymes. In fact, there was nothing that would further—and positively—differentiate Interstate's brands or give customers a compelling reason to buy them and keep buying them.

Most importantly, however, increasing product shelf life meant meddling with a recipe that consumers loved. Although the taste and appearance of Twinkies and other snacks didn't seem to be affected by the additives, bread was another story. Once the new recipe went into production, it worked inconsistently. Loaves sometimes turned out gummy and doughy, and the center often caved in. Customers started complaining: "I've been eating Merita bread [an Interstate brand] for decades," but "the taste seems to have changed," wrote one anonymous consumer on the web. "Whatever has happened or is happening we do not like it and have gone to another brand," wrote another.[1]

The product's taste was not the only problem. Before the shelf-life plan, delivery people would remove damaged goods and spruce up retail shelves so the products didn't look picked over. But when the company cut the number of deliveries, the Interstate store shelves looked disheveled or were empty for days at a time. Not only did the product look and taste yucky in many cases, it looked worse on messy or empty shelves, which pleased neither retailers nor customers. The company eventually acknowledged it had cut service too deeply and began restoring driver routes, but the damage was already done to retailer and consumer relationships.

With the cost-cutting program a flop and other problems coming to a head, Interstate filed for bankruptcy and CEO Elsesser resigned at the end of September 2004. Analysts said the current food fads had little to do with the company's troubles. "It exacerbates their sales issues," said one, "but it's not the critical issue at all."[2] The critical issues were high labor costs and—especially—lack of innovation. Other analysts responded to the bankruptcy filing with the strong suggestion that "the company's highest priority ought to be improved marketing and increased sales, rather than cost cutting." The problem with having cost cutters in charge, rather than marketers, is that they don't distinguish between an unnecessary and a necessary expense. They fail to recognize that certain costs are vital to supporting a brand's positioning, maintaining product quality, sustaining customer loyalty, or all three.

In retrospect (and speaking as total outsiders), we think Interstate had several marketing alternatives. The company could have rolled out new products: a multigrain bread, a new favorite among consumers and the bread industry's hottest product, for instance. It could have launched a reinvigorating ad campaign for Twinkies and Ding-Dongs. Indeed, postbankruptcy research found that 53 percent of households that purchase Twinkies have no children; adult males who grab Ho-Hos, Ding-Dongs, and fruit pies at convenience stores represent a major market segment. Instead, management looked for a financial panacea, and their brands, their employees, their stockholders (the stock went from $16 a share to $2.05 in six months), and their customers have suffered the consequences.[3]

Why Marketing Is in Trouble

The Interstate Bakeries example may be a case in which a company ignored marketing with catastrophic results, but Interstate is certainly not alone in disregarding marketing. Companies take two routes to grow today: mergers and acquisitions or marketing. Our research shows that 8 out of 10 U.S. companies are not growing organically by more than 2 percent or 3 percent per year—that is, through their marketing efforts, R&D, and new products. The rest are holding their own or actually declining.

Growth through mergers and acquisitions is often short-lived and illusory. As Gary Hamel, chairman of Strategos and director of the Woodside Institute, noted, "a spate of academic research has demonstrated the mega-mergers are as likely to destroy shareholder wealth as to create it. In most cases, the costs of integration, both direct and indirect, overwhelm the anticipated economies. As management's attention turns inward, customers lose out and market share wanes."[4]

One indication of the lack of growth is falling market share. As we look across a broad range of consumer and business offerings, the shares of the market leaders are declining in most product categories. Compare the shares of the top 10 brands in almost any product category, say ten years ago and at the end of 2006, and you'll see the average has declined.

Market shares fall for a number of reasons. Poor marketing is perhaps the most important and the one the company can most easily affect and improve. CEOs and chief financial officers (CFOs) talking to analysts about their businesses always blame the problems on outside forces, on exogenous variables: Consumer tastes are changing, demographics are changing, new technologies have been introduced. It's not *our* fault. They almost never mention the inadequate marketing.

Look at some U.S. marketing icons: Coca-Cola, Budweiser, MasterCard, McDonald's, General Motors. The problem, from our perspective, is clearly marketing. Coca-Cola hasn't had a successful new advertising campaign since the kids were singing "I'd like to give world a Coke" a quarter century ago. Coke hasn't had a really successful Coca-Cola line extension, or new product other than water, since it launched Diet Coke many years ago.

General Motors is another example. We've watched GM's market share erode over the past twenty years. We've seen their brands decline in value (and one, Oldsmobile, discontinued). They've had very few exciting new products in twenty years. Their automobiles are inferior to the Japanese brands, to the German brands, and increasingly to the South Korean brands. They have had to resort to price promotions like the "General Motors Employee Discount for Everyone" to sell their cars, which, of course, affects sales for months after. It may be convenient to blame the corporation's problems on exogenous factors, but somebody has to look in the mirror and recognize that bad management decision making is the key to the problem.

A summer 2006 study undertaken by Copernicus and Greenfield Online of a nationally representative sample of 1,133 men and women found that far more brands are being transformed into commodities than commodities into brands. In 48 of the 51 categories in which the most marketing money is spent, brand equity—consumer perceptions of what distinguishes a brand from a commodity—is declining. This is particularly true for bottled water, credit cards, gas stations, and large office-supply stores. Table 1.1 shows the results of the study. At the one extreme, not surprisingly, most people see little difference between Aquafina and Dasani. At the other, they see considerable differences between Dunkin' Donuts and Starbucks.

Our work with business-to-business clients in industries ranging from cement to medical instruments, industrial gases to computers, printing services to insurance reveals a similar slide toward

Table 1.1 The Extent of Brand Commoditization*

Aquafina/Dasani	75
Visa/MasterCard	74
ExxonMobil/Shell	73
MetLife/Prudential	72
Office Depot/Staples	72
E-Trade/TDAmeritrade	70
Home Depot/Lowe's	70
Expedia/Travelocity	68
Gillette/Schick	67
DirecTV/Dish Network	65
Cialis/Viagra	64
Crest/Colgate	62
Allegra/Claritin	63
Nexium/Prevacid	63
Walgreens/CVS	62
Vytorin/Crestor	62
Folgers/Maxwell House	62
Fidelity/Charles Schwab	62
Red Bull/Monster	62
Purina/Pedigree	61
Bank of America/Wachovia	61
Best Buy/Circuit City	61
Lay's/Ruffles	60
Pampers/Huggies	59
UPS/FedEx	58
Carnival Cruise Lines/Royal Caribbean	57
Aflac/MetLife	56
Maybelline/Revlon	55
Budweiser/Miller	55
Toyota/Nissan	55

(continued)

Table 1.1   *(Continued)*

Cadillac/Lincoln	54
Verizon/Cingular	53
JCPenney/Sears	53
Sony/Philips	53
Tylenol/Advil	52
Nike/Adidas	52
Pantene/Garnier	50
Southwest Airlines/American Airlines	50
Canon/Kodak	50
McDonald's/Burger King	49
Google/Yahoo!	49
Mercedes-Benz/BMW	49
Tide/All	48
Olay/L'Oréal	47
Coke/Pepsi	46
Dell/HP	46
Ford/Chevrolet	45
State Farm/Geico	44
AOL/PeoplePC	43
Wal-Mart/Target	40
Dunkin' Donuts/Starbucks	28

*Percentage of consumers in the target market who perceive no difference or only a slight difference between the two brands in each pair.

commoditization. As perceived product differences disappear, a low price becomes increasingly important. Why, the consumer asks, should I pay more for essentially the same product? Why indeed? Table 1.2 shows the importance of price as opposed to product features and benefits in driving purchase behavior in the same 51 product categories. Note the strong correlation between the importance

Table 1.2 The Importance of Price versus Product Features and Benefits*

Bottled water	74
A gas station	71
Booking travel online	70
Airline tickets	69
A new credit card	68
Automobile insurance	60
Purchasing/leasing a vehicle	58
Wireless phone service plan	54
An office supply retail store	52
A satellite TV provider	52
A cruise line vacation package	51
A discount retail store	50
An online trading site	50
A new bank account	50
Disability insurance	48
An express package delivery service	48
Life insurance	47
An Internet service provider	46
A home improvement retail store	46
An electronics retail store	46
A financial planning services firm	45
A drugstore	43
A department store	42
Prescription medication	41
Disposable baby diapers	39
Home entertainment equipment	37
A personal computer	37
A pair of athletic shoes	36
An energy drink	35

(continued)

Table 1.2   (*Continued*)

A digital camera	35
A razor or blades	33
A laundry detergent	31
Packaged ground coffee	30
Allergy medication	29
Potato chips	28
Toothpaste	28
Women's cosmetics	28
Shampoo	26
Pet food	25
A fast-food restaurant	25
Antiaging cream/lotion	25
A cola soft drink	25
A coffee/bakery shop	24
Beer for at-home consumption	20

*Percentage who agree "When thinking about the last purchase you made in the category, would you say price is very important? You strive to pay the lowest price or lowest fees."

of price on Table 1.2 and the level of commoditization shown in Table 1.1. Generally speaking, the more commoditized a category is perceived to be, the greater the value of a low price.

This slide into commoditization is preventable by sound marketing, by using the techniques we'll be discussing in the chapters ahead. Marketers who fail to communicate product differences, brand benefits, or brand equities in their advertising and sales efforts will see their brands lose ground. Many television commercials, for example, are nothing more than 27 seconds of entertainment with three seconds of the brand name tagged on at the end. Apparently, somebody made a conscious decision that entertaining, brand-personality type advertising is more effective than communicating anything useful about the product.

But not only are existing brands becoming commodities, new products and services continue to fail at an appalling rate. According to AC Nielsen BASES, 93 percent of the estimated all-new consumer products fail within the first three years. Yes, more than nine out of every ten new products do not make it.

High-revenue-potential new products fail at or soon after launch for several key reasons. According to a 2004 Deloitte Touche Tomahtsu study of 650 companies in North America and Europe, these reasons include insufficient information on customer needs (i.e., an inadequate and substandard level of marketing research); supplier capabilities; a reluctance to allocate appropriate spending on R&D; and a disjointed approach to innovation across product, customer, and supply chain operations.[5]

Despite the fact that many (perhaps most) senior executives consider genuinely new products (although not necessarily truly authentic innovations) to be the number one driver of revenue growth, the marketing department is often willing to go along with the belief of nonmarketers that it's easier and cheaper—not to mention far less risky—to launch a line extension, a product or service that builds on the cachet of an existing brand. Often, the marketing department initiates the launch with inadequate research to determine the level of consumer interest and preference for the new product. There is little or no test marketing to assess the probabilities of target trial and repeat purchase (if these have even been defined) or tests of media effectiveness. If the results of focus groups look good, the company launches the product and begins spending on the promotion campaign.

Unfortunately, product and concept test databases have shown repeatedly that line extensions are far more likely to fail than truly new products. Generally, consumers want uniqueness and distinctiveness in their new products, including line extensions. Equity in the parent brand, however strong, does not automatically translate into consumer acceptance of the extension. Also, they often fail to bring new users into the category or customers from other brands. Cherry Coke attracts Coke drinkers almost exclusively. As a consequence, they tend to cannibalize the parent brand and do not produce the net incremental sales required to make the extension profitable. Exceptions to these generalities exist, and we'll talk about them in Chapter 6.

Under these circumstances, marketing departments are guilty of negligence on at least two counts. First, they fail to press for support for genuinely new products having a higher probability of success and return on investment (ROI). Second, they fail to provide adequate research that demonstrates the new product or line extension's probability of success or failure. Granted, senior management may not want to spend the money to develop genuinely new products or to pay for adequate research, but a responsible marketing executive will at least make the case that it is in the firm's best interests to do so.

The Trouble with Measuring Marketing Return on Investment

Marketing is also in difficulty with senior management because after years of justifiably claiming that it was hard to impossible to measure marketing effectiveness, today's new data sources, technologies, and tools have made it possible to link marketing investments directly to market share, sales, and profits. And the results are embarrassing.

We have collected performance data on more than 500 marketing programs for consumer and business-to-business (B2B) products and services. The results are not good. Some 84 percent of these programs fail to have a positive ROI. This issue concerns us so much that we asked Marketing Management Analytics (MMA) to ransack its databases to tease out the effects of advertising. MMA is the largest ROI analytics firm in the United States. It discovered that advertising for established consumer packaged goods returns only 54 cents for every dollar invested. Other product categories return 87 cents—better, but still a losing proposition.

We and MMA are not alone. A 2004 Deutsche Bank study of packaged goods brands found that just 18 percent of television advertising campaigns generated a positive ROI in the short term; less than half (45 percent) saw any ROI payoff over the long run. And according to Dominique Hanssens, the director of the Marketing

Science Institute and former professor at the University of California, Los Angeles's Anderson School of Management, the advertising elasticity coefficient for advertising for established products and services is 0.01, which means you would have to increase the ad budget by 100 percent (double it) to see a 1 percent increase in sales.

This means that if Anheuser-Busch had doubled the approximately $550 million the company spent on television, print, radio, outdoor, and Internet advertising in 2006, the firm would likely have enjoyed a 1 percent increase in net revenues from its current base of $15 billion. In other words, the firm would have spent $1.1 billion to make an incremental $150 million. Before you cancel your advertising, however, read Chapters 7 and 8 for some better ideas.

Often when MMA reports these dismal results, clients respond that MMA has only measured short-term effects, whereas the corporate objective is to build brand equity in the long term. Yet in addition to the 2006 study discussed earlier, four different studies suggest that brand equity for leading brands is declining. Stated differently, more than halfway through the first decade of this new century, most marketers are building neither sales nor brand equity.

If this isn't bad enough, consider that customer satisfaction averages just 74 percent, not just in our database but in the American Customer Satisfaction Index, produced by the University of Michigan;[6] most new-customer acquisition efforts fail to reach breakeven (i.e., it costs more to acquire a customer than the customer returns to the company); most promotional programs have proved to be unprofitable; and direct marketing response rates have been declining for thirty years. Looking at all the evidence, it's clear that most marketing programs are failures and that most brands are in trouble.

Most Executives Don't Know How Bad It Is

Most CEOs, CFOs, and even some CMOs are unaware of these terrible findings. Most are unaware of marketing's dismal performance. After all, if they were aware, it would be illogical (if not insane) to keep running programs that don't work. But those company executives who have seriously studied marketing program performance now recognize that what they've been doing for years doesn't work and are looking for ways to reverse the findings. Often they blame television advertising, frequently the largest-dollar item in the marketing budget. They argue that TV audiences are shrinking and consumers are giving less attention to those ads to which they are exposed. Surely, they say, there must be more effective media.

Their confidence in traditional media shattered (for good reason), marketers are responding by reallocating substantial dollars to nontraditional media. Unfortunately, there is very little data on the effectiveness of nontraditional media. In fact, measurement is today where measurement of traditional media was in the 1960s. Nontraditional media include sports and event sponsorships, Internet advertising, electronic outdoor billboards, simulated word-of-mouth buzz, and plastering logos and ads on every possible space (subway turnstile bars, office water jugs, turnpike toll booths).

Even though there is little information about nontraditional media's performance, with less clutter and, in many cases, lower costs—not to mention lots of hype—they appear to some marketers to be a more attractive (i.e., safer) investment. Our own experience, as an aside, is that nontraditional forms of media are no more powerful than the traditional forms, but that's a story for Chapter 7.

By installing measurement systems and buying what they hope is more effective media, marketers may feel they are making the practice more accountable. But using supporting elements of marketing accountability to improve performance is like fighting cancer with a thermometer and aspirin—it doesn't get anyone closer to a cure.

If marketers would turn their attention beyond measurement and media for just a moment and take a big-picture look at why the numbers are so bad, they'd see that their marketing strategies are flawed. With the help of the new measurement systems, marketers are evaluating with ever-increasing precision the impact of ill-defined targeting, weak positioning, unprofitably configured products and services, mediocre advertising campaigns, giveaway promotions, poorly allocated marketing dollars, and more.

Let's Address the Trouble

What can a company do about these problems? How can it improve its organic growth, growth that comes from selling its products (or services) to new customers; from selling more products to existing customers; from selling new, more profitable products to existing and new customers; or all three?

Can you do it with the sales department? We don't think so. At the companies we see, the salespeople are working flat out. "Go sell more," even if doable, does not address the company's basic problems. Without a compelling story, the salespeople's future efforts will be no better than they are right now.

Can you do it with new products and services? Yes, if they're successful. But as we just pointed out, most new products and services fail. We know from our experience that superior research improves targeting, positioning, new offerings, and more. We'll talk about each of these points in detail in coming chapters, but we see a chicken/egg issue here.

If the marketing is ineffective, most new products and services will (and do) fail. But if new products routinely fail, the CEO and the CFO want to know why they should give resources to a department that's not adding value. Why give those people even more responsibility, thereby perpetuating an ineffective department? At many companies, the marketing department's responsibilities are already exceedingly limited.

Marketing guru Philip Kotler related an exchange he had with the vice president of marketing for a major airline. Kotler asked the VP what his job involved. Did he control pricing? "Not really. That's the yield management department." Did he control where and how often the airline flies or the classes of service it offers? "No, that's the flight scheduling department." Did he control the services provided to customers by the airline on the ground? "Not really. That's the operations department." So, Kotler asked, what *did* he control? "Well," the VP replied, "I run advertising and the frequent-flyer program."[7]

Marketing is misunderstood in many, perhaps most, organizations. Senior executives—indeed, most managers in other departments—often equate marketing with advertising. They do not understand how the marketing function can contribute value to the enterprise that leads to organic growth. Yet as we have repeatedly seen, when CEOs, CFOs, and other top managers *do* understand marketing's potential, they lead their companies to greater revenues, profits, and growth than their less astute competitors.

Procter & Gamble (P&G) had been a marketing powerhouse until the 1990s, when it seemed to lose its way. It spent more than ten years integrating acquisitions and moving into emerging markets. In 1993, to compete with cheaper, private-label competitors, it cut 13,000 jobs, closed 30 factories, and took a $1.5 billion charge against earnings to pay for the restructuring. That clearly was not the answer to its problems because in July 1999, six months after Durk Jager took over as CEO, he announced that P&G was cutting 15,000 more jobs, closing more factories, and taking a $1.9 billion charge against earnings. Meanwhile, P&G had lost its sales lead in toothpaste (Crest), diapers (Pampers, Luvs), and soap (Ivory).

Jager told a *Fortune* reporter, "The core business is innovation. If we innovate well, we will ultimately win. If we innovate poorly, we won't win. To innovate, you have to go away from the norm. You have to be rebellious or nonconventional. You have to do things differently." All that may be true, but P&G needed to rededicate itself to improving its marketing. It has done so under A. G. Lafley, who became president and CEO in June 2000, and Jim Stengel, who became global marketing officer in 2001.

They have been changing the way the company thinks about the women who buy its products. "P&G has always aimed its marketing at women," says *The Wall Street Journal*. "But it used to develop consumer goods in its labs and market them based on the product's best technical feature. Its market research tended to be about the pros and cons of specific products. These days, employees spend hours with women, watching them do laundry, clean the floor, apply makeup and diaper their children. They look for nuisances that a new product might solve. Then, they return to the labs determined to address the feature women care about most." As Lafley told P&G executives at a recent meeting, "We discovered that women don't care about our technology and they couldn't care less what machine a product is made on. They want to hear that we understand them."[8] As P&G's marketing efforts have improved, the company's earnings have increased, on average, 17 percent each year since Lafley became CEO, to more than $7.3 billion.

But it is not only multibillion dollar corporations that can benefit from effective marketing; much smaller firms can benefit as well. (Indeed, a case can be made that because of size, inertia, and complexity, it is more difficult for a giant corporation to become a marketing force than a small company.) McCue Corporation has become the retail industry's recognized leader in protective and decorative bumper and shopping carts. Founder David McCue spent 11 years working in sales, product design, and marketing for a manufacturer of equipment for the retail industry. During his supermarket visits, he realized that the shopping carts were beating up the retail fixtures, and the more shopping carts per store, the more likely the aisles, counters, and displays had a beat-up look. His marketing strategy was simple: Start with a target that would be responsive to a new shopping cart (large food retailers) and solve their problem.

As a two-man company, McCue produced its first marketing brochure before it had its first product. The positioning and message was so strong, McCue began selling its first product and was able to contract with a manufacturer's rep company. Two years later, Wal-Mart began buying McCue products for its stores, and as McCue has grown, it has been able to develop more products to solve the problems of chain drug stores, supermarkets, and discount stores in trying to keep the stores clean, neat, and attractive. The marketing has been effective; McCue Corp. has now been listed twice on *Inc.* magazine's ranking of 50 fast-growing private companies.

Unfortunately, too many senior managers see marketing as a line-item expense—advertising, lead generation, customer loyalty programs—and unrelated to creating revenues or profits. The marketing budget is frequently the first expense to cut when management feels pressure to show a short-term profit. Executives under pressure often feel that spending more money on marketing—that is, on advertising—is a waste; hiring more salespeople who can begin to generate revenue immediately is a better investment. Given marketing's sad record, they are often correct.

Managers at entrepreneurial and medium-size companies tend to think that marketing is mainly advertising and, therefore, is relevant mainly to companies with large advertising budgets. They also feel that marketing is only tactical, not strategic; it's something you do for a specific product to get the word out. They do not believe that marketing people command a set of skills and processes on which the organization can depend to grow the entire business.

Many people in business see marketing as about *creating* needs, not *fulfilling* needs. They feel marketing is a qualitative discipline, more art than science, whereas business is quantitative. Moreover, they believe marketing usually cannot measure precisely the results of plans and programs; it therefore cannot be held accountable for decisions and action plans. When marketers *can* measure results (an ability that grows almost daily), they are often pitiful (as we've seen). Finally, we find a widespread belief among top executives that marketing is not needed to create new business concepts and products; R&D can do this very well without marketing's help. They also believe that if the product is good enough, you don't need marketing to sell it. As the heavenly voice told Kevin Costner in *Field of Dreams*, "If you build it, he will come."

What Kind of Company Have We Got?

Marketers may have learned in marketing management classes that sales is one of the elements under the marketing umbrella. The books say that sales should be part of a promotion process managed by the marketing department. Yet the reality in many organizations is that sales, not marketing, is in power because everyone recognizes that without sales no one gets paid. It's clear what salespeople do, and in every organization the outcome from the sales department is the same: sales put money in the bank. Senior managers can tie budgets to quantifiable sales quotas. A sales rep who breaks records gets a bonus; one who falls short gets replaced, and it's obvious who the star is and who the goat is.

No one would argue that the sales force is unimportant. A recent Accenture survey of 200 corporate executives rated each of 11 principal corporate functions in terms of their value contribution to the overall company (where 1 = no contribution and 5 = very significant contribution). These executives gave sales a rating of 4.4 and marketing a 3.7. Moreover, 61 percent said that sales makes a "very significant" value contribution, whereas only 23 percent said marketing does so.[9]

Sales reps routinely want new products, something fresh to tell prospects and customers. Many senior executives also believe that introducing new products and services is an effective way to obtain revenue growth. They need new products because most existing products are growing outmoded. The 2004 Deloitte Touche Tomahtsu study cited earlier found executives saying that new product revenue will increase from 21 percent of total revenue in 1998 to 35 percent in 2007. So the formula seems to be: Give the salespeople more new products to sell and the company will grow.

Marketing, however, is not the same as selling. As marketing professor Theodore Levitt wrote, "Selling focuses on the needs of the seller, marketing on the needs of the buyer. Selling is preoccupied with the seller's need to convert his product into cash, marketing with the idea of satisfying the needs of the customer by means of the product and the whole cluster of things associated with creating, delivering, and finally consuming it."[10] Selling is getting rid of what we've got; marketing is learning what people want and helping them get it.

We find that companies tend to be either sales-driven or marketing-driven. Although the marketing concept was developed by a number of scholars and businesspeople in the mid-1950s, and although a number of scholars have found in the last fifty years that companies that embrace the concept achieve superior performance, we still find top managers who believe marketing should support the sales department (with brochures, collateral, advertising, and leads) rather than believing that the sales function is one element in a comprehensive marketing program.

In summer 2006, Copernicus and *Brandweek* magazine surveyed 256 senior marketing executives at *Fortune* 1,000 companies to determine if the company they worked for was primarily sales or marketing directed. The 42 questions ranged from simple self-report measures such as "My company is more of a sales-driven company than a marketing-driven company" and its converse, "My company is more of a marketing-driven company than a sales-driven company," to more sophisticated measures that tapped into how respondents described their companies on six different dimensions (four items each).

We were surprised to discover how much importance our respondents place on the sales function: 49 percent said that they worked for a sales-oriented company in contrast to 31 percent who said they worked for a marketing-oriented company. Some 51 percent said that CEOs come from the ranks of the sales department, whereas only 22 percent said they come from marketing. These findings are particularly interesting because the respondents were all marketing executives and suggest that in many companies they see themselves as second-class managers. See Table 1.3 for selected findings from the study.

A sales-oriented culture is not limited to large companies. We find many small and medium companies are sales-driven. For instance, an entrepreneur identifies a problem and creates a solution. Because those with the problem are identifiable (supermarkets with battered fixtures, convenience stores that need plus-size staff uniforms), the entrepreneur has defined a target market. Because the new product solves a problem, the positioning is obvious. Because the positioning and target market are obvious, the advertising approach and the media to use are usually not difficult to create and select.

This works well as long as the company is small and close to its customers. When the organization grows to the point at which these marketing decisions are not obvious, however, a formal marketing effort becomes essential. Regrettably, there are senior executives even in major corporations who believe you need marketing only when your product is no good.

Sales are important. Every profit-making organization (and some nonprofits—think Girl Scout Cookies) has to have sales. The weaker the organization's marketing, however, the less efficient the

Table 1.3 Sales versus Marketing*

Between just marketing and sales, I would say that more CEOs come from sales than from marketing.	51
There are sales-oriented companies and marketing-oriented companies. Ours is a sales-oriented company.	49
Chief marketing officers should be responsible for both marketing and sales in their organizations.	47
In our organization, any sales plan needs to have buy-in from marketing management before it wins approval from top management.	38
There are sales-oriented companies and marketing-oriented companies. Ours is a marketing-oriented company.	31

*Percentage who strongly or somewhat agree.

sales effort tends to be. Salespeople generally do not have the time or inclination to provide much market research. (Why should they? It's not their job.) Salespeople are inclined to make the easiest sales they can—the low-hanging fruit syndrome. These may not be the sales the company needs to make for growth and profitability, however. We find sales-driven companies tend to be less efficient and profitable than marketing-driven firms. Over and over, we see sales-focused companies either out of stock and unable to fill orders or dumping inventory at fire-sale prices because they misjudged demand.

Effective marketing makes all organizations—those selling consumer products and services, those selling B2B products and services, large companies and small, profit-making and nonprofits—more efficient. For a profit-making company, that means a better return; for a nonprofit organization, it means a more effective use of resources and delivery of services.

What This Book Is About

It's obvious to us that effective marketing leads to superior company results. We have seen it transform a brand's trajectory, an executive's career, even an entire company for the better. Whether you market breakfast cereal or automotive parts, business insurance or museum memberships, the principles and ideas we discuss in the chapters ahead will help you improve your marketing. The principles apply to consumer products and services and to B2B products and services; they apply to profit-making organizations and to nonprofits alike. So the real question should be: How can we make the organization's marketing efforts more effective?

We'll begin in a moment to talk about the problems of intuitive decision-making, exactly why your gut is not smarter than your head—assuming your head has access to fact-based information and is not bedazzled by the research technique of the week. We then show you how to look at your products or service in the broad market situation, how to do a marketing decision audit.

The next seven chapters describe how to identify market targets that are the most profitable, how to craft a strong positioning, how to develop product/service offerings that have consumer appeal and are profitable, how to make sense of all the changes in traditional and nontraditional media, how to improve the impact and return on your advertising investments, the problems we see with sport sponsorships, and how to work with the sales department.

The book concludes with how to improve marketing plans, how to get the marketing plan implemented (never easy when you want to break with a pedestrian past to do something that can transform a brand, but we have some suggestions), an explanation of customer equity (as opposed to brand equity), and how to measure marketing's return on investment.

But first, let's talk about making major marketing decisions from the gut and the eccentric research that companies have used (or are still using) on which to base their decisions.

2

More Marketing Decisions Are Made with Guts than Brains

Marketing from his gut, Gary Heavin's first business effort did not go well. Once his firm collapsed into bankruptcy, Heavin spent six months in jail for failure to pay child support and reflected on the failure. But today he heads the world's fastest-growing franchise operation. Gary and Diane, his second wife, through their research identified a huge untapped target market, solved a serious problem for time- and cash-strapped women, and positioned their health club to set it apart from all others.

Heavin was a premed student in college, waiting tables at a pizza parlor and working as a roughneck on oil rigs to pay his way. After two years, he dropped out of college, went to work in a health club in Houston, and ultimately saved enough money to buy the money-losing club. He slept on the club's floor because he couldn't afford an apartment. In ten years, with the help of his brothers David and

Paul, Heavin turned Women's World of Fitness into a regional chain of 14 fitness centers. He got married, had two children, and bought an airplane.

Rather than marketing from the head, however, the brothers relied on their gut instincts and increased the size of their clubs even though business was dropping off. Without adequate research, they entered markets that turned out to be too small to support a full-scale health club. In 1986, the business failed and Heavin, $5 million in debt, declared bankruptcy. His wife divorced him, he lost custody of his children, and got slammed for nonpayment of child support.

Shortly before he went to jail, he married Diane, who had a background in marketing and was a fitness enthusiast. Together, they planned an original marketing concept that became the model for Curves, a hugely successful franchise operation. As he told us, "You make a lot of mistakes and the hard lessons of experience, but you learn from those mistakes and don't repeat them. And that seems to be a lot of things that cause people to stumble. They repeat their mistakes, which is amazing to me."[1] For his new venture, Heavin used his brain rather than his gut.

Rather than offer a full-service health club with a gym, weight room, lockers and showers, sauna, and pool for relatively affluent 24-to-39-year-old fitness buffs, their strategy was to offer something less elaborate. "We looked around at the things that were really essential," says Heavin. For example, "the women in my conventional gyms didn't actually use the shower. It turns out that women don't want to do their hair and makeup; they would rather just go home and do it. They don't like to shower in public, in front of each other." So they eliminated the shower when they designed a Curves facility.

The Heavins realized that their target market was not coming for the equipment as such. "The idea of a gym is the more equipment you had, the more business you had," says Heavin. But this is not true for women. "Women were really looking for a community of support, so we created a line of equipment that was really efficient, wasn't real glamorous, but gave them what they needed. We made sure our emphasis was on the culture, not on more equipment."

They also wanted to make Curves comfortable for their target market, women who wanted the exercise but who did not go to a conventional gym because they didn't want to be stared at by men when not looking their best. "We knew that most of our sisters, mothers, and grandmothers weren't going to the gym because the gym environments were intimidating."

By focusing on what consumers wanted and what they really needed, the Heavins designed a more efficient business model. "We knew if we could get rid of showers and all this fancy equipment, we could reduce this thing down to 1,500 square feet and go to smaller towns," he remembers. He noticed, too, that the women in their target market rarely work out in the middle of the day. "They come in the morning if they are housewives and they come in after work if they have a job. So most Curves facilities are closed during the middle of the day," he explains. As a result, the club workweek for a franchisee could be reduced to 40 hours, which makes the job and the staffing much easier. "We ended up with such an efficient business model that we could go into much smaller towns—towns that before Curves, couldn't have quality women's fitness facilities. In fact, we went into the smaller towns first, because we didn't have competition and it was easy to get the word out and build membership right away."

The Heavins opened the first Curves in 1991 and began franchising in 1995. Today, the typical Curves, which is strictly for women, is in a strip mall and offers no showers, lockers, massages, or refreshment bars. The eight to twelve machines on which members work out are arranged in a circle. Every 30 seconds, the women exercising are told to move to the next station, which is either another machine that works different muscle groups or is a space between two machines where exercisers run or walk in place.

A typical Curves workout regimen is 30 minutes a day, three times a week—a schedule working women and mothers find relatively easy to meet. "The most frequent reason cited by people who don't exercise is lack of time," says Cedric Bryant, chief exercise physiologist at the San Diego–based American Council on Exercise, who adds that although some Curves members will eventually seek a more strenuous workout, the 30-minute resistance workout is enough to keep most members fit.[2] Memberships cost less than $50 a month and a franchise costs around $25,000, which includes eight exercise machines.

As Barbara Mikkelson notes on Snopes.com, "Because the equipment is hydraulic, it adapts to each user's level of fitness, making these workouts suitable for anyone regardless of physical conditioning. Women like the Curves program for its '30 minutes and you're on your way' aspect, but also for the camaraderie that comes from exercising with others, which appears to be spurred on by the arrangement of the workout stations in a circle. Friendships form. Encouragement is given. A sense of 'We're all in this together' pervades."[3]

So, with the marketing orientation, a new target, a real positioning, and products and services addressed to the customer's needs, how well has Curves performed? Curves International, which is privately held, has more than 9,300 clubs and serves an estimated four million members in 50 states and 31 countries.[4]

The Appeal of Gut-Driven "Thinking without Thinking"

The decision-making-from-the-gut school of marketing received a major boost a few years ago when Malcolm Gladwell published *Blink: The Power of Thinking without Thinking*. Gladwell, a staff writer for *The New Yorker* magazine, earned his marketing chops with an earlier book, *The Tipping Point*, which pointed out that small changes can have big effects; when small numbers of people start behaving differently, that behavior can ripple outward until a critical mass or tipping point is reached, changing the world. Marketers have long known that if we can get the so-called thought leaders, innovators, or early adopters to try our product and talk it up, word spreads and sales will build. Who would deny it?

Blink advances an even more appealing idea: Our snap judgments and first impressions are often better than decisions made after hours of research and deliberation. The book begins with the story of a purported Greek statue dating from the sixth century B.C. The J. Paul Getty Museum was thinking of buying it and spent 14 months in research and due diligence confirming its age and authenticity. Two other experts, however, after just glancing at the statue concluded that something was not right. The Getty ignored them and bought the statue. And guess what? The statue was a fake. The intuitive judgments of the experts were better than the 14 months of research.

Obviously, these ideas—first impressions are good (except when they're not), snap judgments are often more correct than carefully considered decisions, and analysis sometimes provides less information than more—are popular. There are 1.3 million copies of *Blink* in print (and we know from personal experience that publishers do not print books unless they expect them to sell). Organizations pay Gladwell something like $40,000 per lecture, and he's spoken at West Point, the National Institutes of Health, Google, Microsoft, and Hewlett-Packard, among other companies.[5]

Larry Kubal, a partner at Labrador Ventures, writing in *Venture Capital Journal* asks, "Can we listen to a pitch and know minutes into the PowerPoint—perhaps minutes after shaking an entrepreneur's hand—whether a deal 'feels' like something we should take a deeper look at? We at Labrador think that the answer is yes, that we can 'blink' and know whether a deal feels right or wrong."[6]

On the other hand, Felix Dennis, chairman of Dennis Publishing, says about *Blink*, "It takes about 280 pages of claptrap, psychobabble and snappy subheadings . . . for Malcolm Gladwell to reach an astonishing conclusion. This is that certain people have an apparent innate ability to make faultless snap decisions while others do not."[7]

In our experience, too many marketing executives believe they have an innate ability to make faultless snap decisions. They manage to retain this belief even as the projects on which they have made decisions—to introduce this product with this feature, to run this commercial, to choose this medium for the advertising, to adopt this positioning—routinely crash and burn. Chief marketing officers who embrace the idea of "thinking without thinking" may help explain

marketing programs in the middle of our bell curve—it's a failure—
and why the average CMO tenure is only 23 months.

To buttress our experience, we included questions about marketing decision-making in our summer 2006 study. The majority
of the 256 marketing executive respondents agreed with the statements, "I feel very confident making marketing decisions based on
my own sense of what our customers will respond to" (66 percent);
"Generally speaking, I tend to make decisions quickly based on my
judgment and experience" (62 percent); and "I agree with Malcolm
Gladwell in his book *Blink* when he argues that senior marketing
managers should rely more on intuition and judgment in making
major decisions and avoid becoming mired in data" (53 percent).

Four out of 10 marketing executives openly admitted that
"With the right people in place, companies can liberate themselves
from their obsession with data-driven decisions" and "I rely more
heavily on intuition and judgment than science in making marketing decisions."

One-third were skeptical toward fact-based decision-making.
They said, "Research people are often interested in research for its
own sake—they're like frustrated PhDs" and "Much of the research
done in our organization becomes a paperweight—it just sits on a
shelf—and has little impact on our business."

We were surprised to find so many executives believing that
"Making marketing decisions based only on a very few focus
groups tends to lead to very poor decision-making" (57 percent)
and "For every major marketing decision that needs to be made,
there are tens, sometimes thousands, of alternatives. Hard data—
not intuition—is required to identify the ones forecast to be the
most profitable" (39 percent).

Despite these few suggestions of fact-based decision-making,
our data suggest that intuition-based decision-making is rampant
in marketing and sales organizations. Gladwell's book has only
reinforced a long-standing approach to how marketing decisions
get made.

Yet Gladwell's own illustration of the difference between intuitive thinking and articulate (deliberate, analytic) thinking is flawed.

As federal judge and author Richard Posner pointed out in a crushing book review, Gladwell's Greek statue case does not illustrate the difference between intuitive and articulate thinking, "but different articulate methods of determining the authenticity of a work of art. One method is to trace the chain of title, ideally back to the artist himself (impossible in this case); another is to perform chemical tests on the material of the work; and a third is to compare the appearance of the work to that of works of art known to be authentic.

"The fact that the first two methods happened to take longer in the particular case of the Getty statue is happenstance. Had the seller produced a bill of sale from Phidias to Cleopatra, or the chemist noticed that the statue was made out of plastic rather than marble, the fake would have been detected in the blink of an eye. Conversely, had the statue looked more like authentic statues of its type, the art historians might have had to conduct a painstakingly detailed comparison of each feature of the work with the corresponding features of authentic works. Thus the speed with which the historians spotted this particular fake is irrelevant to Gladwell's thesis. Practice may not make perfect, but it enables an experienced person to arrive at conclusions more quickly than a neophyte. The expert's snap judgment is the result of a deliberative process made unconscious through habituation."[8]

Decisions made in a blink may be based on experiences inappropriate for the situation. Example: A friend rented a moped to tool around Bermuda. He had no trouble driving on the left, English style, as long as he thought about what he was doing. Coming up a narrow road, however, he met a truck coming down, and in a blink swerved to the right to get out of the truck's way and straight into the truck's path. Fortunately, the truck driver was more experienced with American tourists than our friend was with Bermuda's roads and stopped long enough for my friend to recover.

We are *not* saying that judgment and experience have no place in marketing decision-making. Judgment and experience coupled with careful analysis of unimpeachable data is an unbeatable combination. Judgment and experience allow you to see what should be present but is not. Of course, this assumes you *have* unimpeachable data, and that raises another issue: What *are* the hot and exciting research techniques that are capturing the imagination of marketers around the world?

"We Can Always Use the Paranormal"

Well, one option is "Imara," a so-called business intuitive with a master of business administration (MBA) who attracted entrepreneurs and venture capitalists seeking her investment and business-development advice that she acquires by extrasensory perception. Her web site reports, "Imara has over 25 years of business experience and over 12 years working independently with executives and business owners as their secret asset. Imara has built reputations in both the business and paranormal worlds for her skill and expertise. Accurate and incisive about your career or company issues, opportunities, and needed priorities, she is no ordinary MBA."[9] An Imara associate told *U.S. News & World Report*, "In these troubled times, people are looking for a different insight that gives them a competitive edge." Imara herself said, "Companies don't have time to do market research studies, which can take months. I can give them feedback in an hour."[10]

As we have written elsewhere, too many companies look for instant feedback, often on the cheap because they say they haven't the time or the money to really nail the decision. We ask: How is it you don't have the time or the money to do it right the first time, but do have the time and money to do it over and over again? Why, except to be quick and cheap, would you ever use the Three Apple Technique?

In the Three Apple Technique, marketing executives are told they have three apples representing three new product concepts. The task is to choose one to take into test market. "Now, close your eyes and concentrate on the three apples floating in space about eighteen inches beyond your nose. Think of Apple A as new product A; Apple B is new product B, and Apple C is new product C. Keep staring mentally at those apples. One of them is going to become redder, riper than the others, and when it does, tell me which one." That's the new product concept you should go with.

Or you can try focus groups conducted under hypnosis. As Salon.com reported, Sixtus Oeschle, Shell Oil's manager of corporate advertising, hired Hal Goldberg, an Irvine, California–based consumer researcher. "I've got to tell you, it was fascinating, fascinating stuff," said Oeschle. After dimming the lights, Goldberg asked respondents to fix their eyes on a green spot on the wall. Then he took them back . . . back . . . back . . . back to the last time they purchased gasoline. "What were you doing?" asked Goldberg. "What were you thinking?" Goldberg didn't stop, Oeschle recalls, until the participants had regressed to a state of mewling infancy. "He just kept taking them back and back," he says. "Until 40 minutes later, he's saying, 'Tell me about your first experience in a gas station.' And people were actually having memory flashbacks. I mean, they were going there. They were saying, 'I was three-and-a-half years old. I was in the back of my dad's brand new Chevy.' It was like it was yesterday to them. I was stunned.

"It dawned on us, as a result of this process, that we'd better figure out how to favorably impact people from an early age," said Oeschle. Shell apparently had gone wrong in reasoning that, because people don't start buying gas until at least age 16, there was no need to target children. "They weren't even on Shell's radar."[11] Not only is this crazy, marketing gasoline to children exposes Shell to all kinds of criticism from groups trying to protect young people from the worst effects of marketing.

Other companies are giving up on focus groups entirely. "My research department doesn't know it, but I'm killing all our focus groups," said Cammie Dunaway, chief marketing officer at Yahoo!, Inc. She told a Silicon Valley conference that Yahoo has been getting little useful information from such groups. "She prefers 'immersion groups'—four or five people with whom Yahoo's product developers talk informally, without a professional moderator typical of focus groups."[12]

We say there is nothing wrong with focus groups, immersion groups, even the selective use of hypnosis *in their place*. They can provide you with insights into how people feel about a new product, what a print ad communicated, what language consumers would use to describe a new service, or how people behave at the moment of truth when they're buying a product or how they use it at home or in the workplace. Focus groups can be a helpful first step in a serious research process, and we do a lot of them.

But when this first step is the only step, the research is in trouble. Because participants cannot represent a given universe, corporations are basing multimillion-dollar marketing decisions on the offhand opinions of small groups of people who are willing to give up a couple hours for $50 and free donuts. If the focus group company recruits participants on a different afternoon or in a different mall, the results might be completely different—unless, of course, the moderator leads the group into a foregone conclusion, which is another danger.

Dozens of irrational dynamics skew what group participants say. One man likes the sound of his voice and pontificates. A woman wonders whether she's giving the "right" answer. Another is uncomfortable confessing her true feelings or lack of knowledge in front of strangers. Still another has no opinion about a subject but feels obligated to contribute something. These factors mean that the information the group leader draws from the participants may have little real value. America Online found that men in focus groups were reluctant to admit they did not fully understand their laptops and ways to block spam.

Focus group research should have a clear point of view on a particular topic so the conversation does not wander off into irrelevancies. But sometimes the moderator and the analysis tend to emphasize that point of view no matter what the product category. We had an experience in which the moderator shaped the questions and the discussion so that every group had a similar perspective, no matter what the subject, the people in the group, or the client.

There is, of course, no way to turn qualitative (exploratory) research into quantitative findings that can be projected to a market as a whole. Some clients and agencies claim they have held so many focus groups that by now the results must be quantitative, that it is possible to project the findings. This is not the case. There are no facts in focus groups, only verbatim opinions.

Many executives think they understand focus group results. They prompt real opinions from real people. Even though these managers may know little about marketing—or little about market research—they feel they can sit behind a one-way mirror and draw conclusions. They need not know about statistics, about sampling, or about models. They are willing to bet the brand (or the company) on the half-baked opinions of six or a dozen average people.

But because word is getting out—the chief marketing officer of Yahoo!, Inc. has doubtless explained focus group limitations to her research department—companies are casting about for alternatives.

Freud Has Overstepped His Bounds

One of the alternatives grows out of Sigmund Freud's writings. At one point, the most famous explorer of the unconscious mind wrote, "The mind is an iceberg; it floats with one-seventh of its bulk above water."

Freud developed psychoanalysis as a means to explore repressed or unconscious feelings and issues and coined terms such as *anal retentive*, *oral fixation*, and *Oedipal complex*, which have become part of our everyday lexicon. Originally developed to treat mental disorders and neuroses, psychoanalysis didn't stay within the confines of the medical community for long. In post–World War II United States, it caught the attention of marketers who were increasingly interested not so much in anticipating demand for their products and services as in stimulating it. "More and more advertising and marketing strategists are adapting their sales campaigns to the psychologists' findings," observed *The Wall Street Journal* in 1954.

Fast-forward fifty-plus years. Psychoanalysis as it applies to treating mental disorders has been largely sidelined, replaced by medication and behavior therapy. Thankfully for underemployed psychoanalysts, marketing remains appreciative. Otherwise rational, experienced, and intelligent executives will turn to us in a meeting and wax poetic about the "incredible insights" and "invaluable information" buyer research grounded in psychoanalytic methodology has revealed to them about the unconscious motivations of their customers and prospects.

"Even as Freudianism is increasingly viewed as suspect in society at large," writes reporter Ruth Shalit on Salon.com, "it has been worshipfully embraced by no-nonsense, jut-jawed captains of industry."[13] Today, the number of companies applying research methods guided by the teachings of Freud, Jung, and others is getting more attention (and more funding) than ever.

In 1939, an enterprising young psychoanalyst from Vienna named Ernest Dichter wrote to six U.S. corporate giants, saying he had "some interesting new ideas which can help you be more successful, effective, sell more and communicate better with your potential clients." He believed the assumption that all buyers made purchase decisions based purely on rational reasoning, the questionnaire-based approach to collecting data about consumer preferences, and statistical number crunching were fundamentally flawed. As he once explained, "people were being asked through questionnaires why they were buying milk. . . . It was almost comparable to asking people why they thought they were neurotic or to a physician asking a patient whatever disease he thought he had. . . . The last thing I should do is let the person who behaves in one form or another interpret his or her behavior . . . because you cannot get reliable answers that way. You get rationalized answers."

Instead, Dichter recommended the Depth Interview in which the interviewee could talk in a free-associative way about his or her preferences and proclivities and then Dichter would analyze the conversation to understand unconscious motivations. He also encouraged the use of the so-called psychodrama to "penetrate just a few pegs deeper than the depth interview." He asked interviewees to essentially act out a product: "You are a car. How old are you? What color? Are you manly? Are you womanly?" Dichter dubbed his approach Motivational Research and, with the help of Freud's daughter Anna, founded the Institute for Motivational Research to promote this approach to corporate clients.

Dichter and his conclusions grabbed more than their fair share of attention. As a guest on *The David Frost Show*, he demonstrated the psychodrama technique to millions of TV viewers. A two-column article in *Time* magazine under the headline "Viennese Psychologist Discovers Gold Mine for Chrysler Corporation," proclaimed he was "the first to apply to advertising the really scientific psychology" that tapped "hidden desires and urges." By the late 1950s, business was totally enraptured by motivational research and its psychoanalytic underpinnings. The Advertising Research Foundation (ARF) had 82 organizations listed as offering motivational research, and Dichter's group had grown from 6 to 60 employees with offices in 11 countries.

When Kevin Clancy was research director at ad agency BBDO and Pepsi was an agency client, Clancy invited Dichter to meet the agency creative people and review a reel of Pepsi commercials. Dichter ended the review when, after the third commercial, he announced in his heavily accented English, "Kevin, stop! You are showing Pepsi in all these commercials with ice . . . served with ice . . . cans *encased* in ice! You must not do this! Ice is the symbol of *death*. You are associating your client with death!"

Dichter's pronouncement killed any interest in the research. One creative group head exclaimed, "This is too nutty for us and for the client. Can't we do something else?" (As another example, Dichter once explained that sex was responsible for the half-billion-dollar blunder with the Ford Edsel: "Some designer who knew little about human motivations castrated the car. It has a gaping hole at the front end.")

The love affair between marketing and psychoanalysis grew somewhat strained as critical voices grew both within and outside the business community. At the same time, marketing researchers developed ways to tap into buyer motivations—both rational and irrational—quantitatively, providing more reliable, concrete, and (let's be honest) far less nutty results and conclusions than those Dichter and his followers offered.

Once the darling of the psychiatric community, psychoanalysis fell out of favor as its scientific merits came under increasing fire. One of the central sticking points among critics is whether psychoanalysis is just not a science or is simply a really bad one.

On the not-a-science side stands Karl Popper, who maintains that psychoanalysis cannot be a science because it is not falsifiable, its "so-called predictions are not predictions of overt behavior but of hidden psychological states. This is why they are so untestable." Scientific theories, says Popper, can be falsified by empirical data. Freud's writings cite only clinical evidence—one case in full and oblique, incomplete references to others—and there is no empirical data. There is no test, says Popper, that can confirm or disprove Freud's assumption that, for instance, everyone suffered a repressed trauma at some point in their lifetimes.

Other not-a-science critics also point out there are no codified rules, regulations, or standards for interpreting observations. One analyst might draw one conclusion, whereas a second analyst would come up with something completely different based on the same information. Critics are also bothered by psychoanalysis's lack of predictive capabilities. If a particular childhood trauma leads to a specific set of personality traits, it would follow that adults who display certain of these characteristics experienced this particular childhood trauma. Yet no one can make these predictions with any degree of accuracy. As Harvard psychologist Dr. Susan Ketelhohn has noted, "Freud was a philosopher, not a scientist."

In the bad-science camp stands Adolf Grünbaum. He argued that the reasoning on which Freud based his entire psychoanalytic theory was "fundamentally flawed, even if the validity of his clinical evidence were not in question" because "the clinical data are themselves suspect; more often than not, they may be the patient's responses to the suggestions and expectations of the analyst." To validate Freud's theories, says Grünbaum, requires data collection outside the clinical setting between analyst and analysand.

To sum it all up, there's no empirical evidence to date that validates psychoanalytic theories; predictive capabilities are nonexistent; and observations are open to interpretation. Freudian Ernest Dichter saw death fears and sexual desires, whereas Clothaire Rapaille, a Jungian psychoanalytic researcher today, sees reptilian drives for freedom and cleanliness. Moreover, personal bias renders observations unreliable. Two different analysts or observers hearing or seeing the same phenomena will report it differently.

The Search for the Buyer's Unconscious

If these criticisms sound familiar, look no further than your last focus group, the source of many a failed product, service, and ad campaign. As we've just seen, more astute marketing organizations are simply dumping focus groups. So why, if psychoanalytic theory has been discounted by the academic community as false and bad science, is marketing enraptured again?

A variety of psychoanalysis-based techniques supposedly enable firms to tap into the unconscious minds of buyers. Some involve lying on mats in quiet rooms, some involve pasting together collages and individual interviews, and others involve hypnosis. By all accounts, these techniques have generated some very creative ideas that companies hadn't thought of before. Nothing wrong with generating creative ideas.

But the unconscious mind offers little in the way of information about profitability of different sets of buyers in a market or the media channels they use. Nor does it assist in identifying the most profitable configuration of product or service attributes. Great brand positioning is a combination of buyer motivations, perceptions of the brand relative to competitors, and the company's ability to deliver on a particular positioning at a profit. Although psychoanalysis might help with the motivations part, it offers little in terms of competitive perceptions and feasibility.

Remember, too, that these are qualitative research methods, which come with distinct limitations. Researchers may say they purposely choose folks for sessions who are different from each other to "reflect the culture" or they bring in only women in a particular age group and income level, but they simply cannot select participants scientifically to represent the population or the target market.

Scientific selection—using a specific process that objectively chooses the final sample components (gender, age, income, education, etc.) versus the personal opinions and beliefs of the researcher—makes it possible to assess the information's reliability or how well it represents the universe. If you don't have a gauge of reliability, you can't tell how precise the information you've collected is or whether it really represents the thinking of the population to which you're planning to market.

What's more, most of these methods appear to involve a small number of participants. For instance, ZMET typically involves twelve to thirty people, according to the company web site.[14] This is a very small number on which to base a multimillion-dollar marketing program. "So much of what drives our behavior happens without our awareness, how can business learn what people don't know?" asked Gerald Zaltman, inventor of the ZMET Method, which, according to *Fast Company*, "combines neurobiology, psychoanalysis, linguistics, and art theory to try to uncover the mental models that guide consumer behavior."[15] We agree that you can't expect to find out what's motivating a buyer's purchase or what's important to them by asking them flat out. Dichter was right; you do get rational and socially acceptable answers.

And we certainly recognize the need for companies to move way beyond standard product category attributes and benefits and come up with completely off-the-wall, even nutty ideas for new products and services, brand positionings, messaging, and media options. So we also agree with Zaltman when he says that this is where tools like ZMET, archetype research, and other psycho-analysis-driven techniques fit in. *If* he means tools for generating hypotheses about what might lead to a successful products and marketing programs. But we need to emphasize *hypotheses* and *might*.

As intriguing as personality may be and as much as the language of psychoanalysis has become part of our culture, there is nothing scientifically validated, replicable, or projectable about psychoanalysis or the research methods derived from it. The so-called insights and information gleaned from these methods are interesting, colorful, and creative, but they need quantitative, scientific—not pseudoscientific—research to demonstrate their validity, reliability, and projectability.

Bring in the Anthropologists

Perhaps the hottest research technique in major corporations today is the use of ethnography to help make more informed business decisions. Ethnography has been around for more than seventy-five years. It is an approach to research favored by anthropologists and based on the notion that to understand behavior you need to observe it. Popularized by Margaret Mead back in the 1930s, it became an indispensable tool to anthropologists, sociologists, and political scientists in the 1960s and 1970s. Like many research approaches born and nourished in the social sciences, it was adopted by marketers in the 1990s and has become in this new century a much-valued approach by large companies. Today General Electric, Marriott Hotels, Intel, Sirius Satellite Radio, and others are all using ethnography.

As *Business Week* reports in its June 5, 2006, issue, a portable satellite radio, Hipper, more user-friendly hotel lobbies, and cheap PCs designed to run in rural Indian villages all "happened with the guidance of ethnographers, a species of anthropologist who can, among other things, identify what's missing in people's lives—the perfect cell phone, home appliance, or piece of furniture—and work with designers and engineers to help dream up products and services to help fill those needs."[16]

Our own experience with ethnographic research covers product categories as diverse as house paints, banking, beer, credit cards, drugstores, and supermarkets. In each case, the application of the tool began with much excitement on the client's part and ended with disappointment that we did not learn more, given the relatively high price of the research. In the never-to-be-forgotten drugstore study, for example, in which the objective was to gather some insights into how to make the stores more efficient to shop and how to make the typical shopper buy more, the major learning was about shoplifting, which, although illuminating, took us far afield.

The results, moreover, like the results of focus groups, are unstable because they're based on small, nonprojectable samples of consumers and industrial buyers and the skills and biases brought to the task by the social scientists hired to do the work. Just as different psychologists will see different things in a Rorschach Test and in a focus group, different observers see and report different things observing behavior. Our advice to clients looking to undertake some new and different work should regard ethnographic research as another useful tool in their shed that would precede any quantitative study in the product category.

We can't end this chapter without commenting on a research tool that was born in the United States in the mid-1960s, died by the late 1970s, and has been resurrected in the past decade. Milton Rokeach, a brainy social psychologist at Michigan State University, published a few books in the 1960s in which he argued that 18 values (self-respect, achievement, security, etc.) underlie all human behavior. His ideas and similar theories, tested in the decades that followed, proved wanting. The general conclusion of the academic literature is that values and personality are useful tools to help profile consumers in any product category, but they are relatively undistinguished predictors of future behavior.

Recently, we sat in on a presentation made by a prominent and successful European firm. The executives argued that 98 percent of human choice behavior (e.g., brand choice) can be explained only at the unconscious level. A few slides later, we learned—without attribution—that 12 of Rokeach's values explain not only what we buy but also the media we watch, read, and listen to.

Clever and proven qualitative research techniques that enable marketers to get at what's truly motivating to customers—whether it be rational or irrational, conscious or unconscious—have existed for decades. Psychoanalytic techniques do not have a corner on the market on understanding real customer motivations. Making major marketing decisions based on focus groups, psychological, or anthropological research is the same as flipping a coin; it's completely random and is as likely to get you closer to the wrong answer as it is to the right answer.

A Quick Look at Research that *Does* Work

If this is kooky research, what techniques *do* work? In the chapters ahead, we'll talk in detail about research techniques you can use to identify a profitable target market, develop a profitable positioning, generate a profitable product or service offer, improve the return on your advertising investment, and more. (Note the emphasis on *profitable* as opposed to *creative* or *original* or *inspired*.) But generally, the principles for any valid, replicable, projectable research study are the same.

- Survey a population that represents the total universe as defined by the company. Whether your market is women who might be interested in a new health club, food-store decision makers responsible for shopping carts, or homemakers who buy ground coffee, ensure that your sample represents the population. For example, an Internet survey that is not weighted to control for bias is not representative of any population other than people willing to participate in Internet surveys. It understates the proportion of the market who are not connected (i.e., minorities) and people who have neither the time nor the interest in cooperating with survey researchers (i.e., busy executives, hassled moms, professionals in general). In such cases, you must take care to recruit these underrepresented groups into the study and to weight different types of buyers into their correct proportions in the population.
- Sample enough people within this universe so that their responses are reasonably stable. Interview 500, for example, and any percentage that you get is stable plus or minus about 5 percent. Interview only 50 people, and the wobble in your data increases to a point at which it is relatively unusable. This is particularly important when you are looking to break down your total sample into subgroups such as users versus nonusers, men versus women, high income versus low, and the like.
- Test the questionnaire to ensure that respondents understand what is being asked and are not being prompted to

answer one way or another. This is called pretesting and is something that is becoming more and more rare in marketing research studies.

- Conduct experiments within your survey wherever it makes sense. Expose half the sample to one new product concept, the other half to another. Show respondents three different price levels. Expose people to four different positionings.
- Analyze the responses in a way that makes logical sense. Don't confuse correlation with causation; just because one thing is related to another does not necessarily mean that the first caused the second.

Just as senior managers need not be accountants to understand the principles and lessons of the profit-and-loss statement, balance sheet, and cash-flow budget, neither do they need to be statisticians to understand the principles and lessons of fact-based market research. With a firm grasp of the difference between qualitative and quantitative research and the value of each, they have a competitive advantage over their less knowledgeable competitors.

The first task in a fact-based marketing program is to evaluate the product/brand/company's current situation, as we discuss in the next chapter.

3

How to Give Your Marketing a "Performance Review"

Recently the head of strategic planning and the vice president of research for a major transportation company visited our offices to discuss a potential project. Among their questions: "How much should we spend on an advertising campaign, and which media should we use?" We asked about the information the company had available in its files. What do consumers think of the brand? Where does the brand exist relative to competitors? What are the company's strengths and weaknesses?

Given the corporation's size and long history, we were surprised to discover—and our guests were chagrined to admit—they had virtually no information about their brand. They said they could show us historic and current sales information by territory, but they did not know the sales of their competitors. They did not know their share of the market. They did not know what levels of awareness or familiarity they enjoyed among prospective customers for their business. They had no information on brand image on themselves compared to any other company, no brand equity data, no market structure insights, no intelligence on customer decisions—nothing. Without this information, it is nearly impossible to tell where the company's marketing budget should go and totally impossible to know whether the current marketing efforts are making any difference.

Although we often find that companies do not have the information they need to make informed plans, most large corporations have *something*, even if it is fragmentary and out of date. The transportation company's admission was unusual because such giants usually collect some kind of data. But if you don't know where you are, it's difficult to discover just how to get to where you want to go.

First See Where You Are

Every marketing plan or marketing strategy begins by developing an understanding of what is taking place in the marketplace today. Smart companies do three things. The first is a marketing performance audit. The second is a best-practices bench marketing audit. The third is a marketing competency audit. All of these, whatever you call them, are looking in the rearview mirror to see where you are.

The marketing performance audit is to the marketing department what a financial audit is to the accounting department: a comprehensive review of a company's marketing environment, objectives, strategies, and activities. The performance audit identifies operational strengths and weaknesses and recommends changes to the company's marketing plans and programs. Here's our top 10 list of what a marketing performance audit should assess:

1. The key so-called climate changes taking place in the business (economic, demographic, competitive, marketing, technological, environmental) that impacted the business (for good or for bad) during the past year. It includes an evaluation of marketing surprises—the unanticipated competitive

actions or changes in the marketing climate that affected the performance of the marketing programs.

2. How each decision in the marketing mix—targeting, positioning, pricing, advertising, and the like—was made after evaluating many alternatives in terms of profit-related criteria.

3. What kind of research was undertaken to support all of the key marketing decisions? Was a large-scale market segmentation and targeting study done in the past three years? What kind of work was undertaken to help the sales force develop a script to approach key targets?

4. How the marketing plans were developed. Did management use knowledge of the historical relationship between marketing investments—the sales force, advertising, direct mail, sponsorships, and more—and revenues to firm up the strategy and tactics recommended?

5. The extent to which the marketing program was marketed internally and bought into by top management and non-marketing executives.

6. What programs were instituted to monitor and manage the plan's implementation?

7. The current performance of the company or brand in terms of key indicators of success in the marketplace such as brand awareness, brand perception on different dimensions, predisposition to act, and customer satisfaction among buyers, distributors, and vendors. This performance analysis must take into account the effects of different components of the marketing mix in driving brand equity, sales, profits, and ultimately return on investment (ROI).

8. Whether the marketing plan achieved its stated financial and nonfinancial goals and objectives.

9. Which aspects of the plan failed to meet objectives and specific recommendations for improving next year's performance.

10. The current value of brand and customer equity for each brand in the product portfolio.

What You Need to Evaluate

Even small companies can establish where a product, service, or brand is at a moment in time using the ten metrics in Table 3.1. This intelligence would have helped immeasurably the transportation company and other firms small and large discussed in this book as they started to think about next year's marketing programs.

The place to start is with customer awareness of the industry, the product, the company, and the brand. For example, you ask a representative sample of customers and prospective customers whether they have ever heard of _____ (your brand, be it Kia, Sage Software, Movielink, Network Solutions, Residence Inn, Patagonia, or Texas Instruments DLP).

Obviously, if a new company offers a brand-new, never-been-seen-in-the-world-before product or service, there is no customer awareness. That situation is rare, however. Consumers had never heard of Vonage in 2000 (the company was founded in January 2001), but some people *had* heard of voice-over-Internet-protocol telephony (VoIP)—the service that Vonage markets—so Vonage could have established the awareness of VoIP, and having established it, begun its marketing planning from there.

Table 3.1   Metrics in a Marketing Performance Audit

1. Total awareness (unaided and aided).
2. Familiarity with the product or service.
3. Favorable impressions of the product.
4. Predisposition to act.
5. Ever purchased or used the product or service.
6. Bought or used the product the last time the customer made a purchase decision.
7. Customer delight/annoyance; switching behavior.
8. Satisfaction with the brand; would recommend to others.
9. Intent to reorder or buy again.
10. Brand and customer equity.

So you first want to establish customer awareness of the industry. Do you know you can make long-distance telephone calls over the Internet? Do you know you can buy designer checks from a source other than your bank? Do you know you can order your groceries online and have them delivered?

Customer response to the industry question would have told a marketer like Vonage that it needed to promote the industry as much as—or more than—its service. There is little point (although companies routinely do it) in promoting the brand to prospective customers who do not know the industry exists.

Among those consumers who are familiar with the industry, how many are familiar with the company's product or service? For a mature product with high household penetration—a soft drink, an automobile, a television set—the goal is to discover consumer awareness of the company or the brand. Are you familiar with Jones Soda? Hyundai cars? Samsung televisions?

This research, of course, is not limited to major corporations and national brands. It is equally valid for local or regional businesses. The difference is only that the marketer surveys consumers in the local or regional trading area. Are you familiar with Bruegger's Bagels? Wegmans Food Markets? Pacific Pavingstone?

Nor should this research be limited only to consumer products and services; it is equally important for business-to-business products and services. How familiar are you with Xerox and Kyocera printers and copiers? Amica and FirstComp workers' compensation insurance? Intel and eSilicon microchips?

Learn why Customers Buy and Prospects Don't

Once you've established consumer familiarity with the company, product, or brand (or all three), you want to know the impressions customers and prospects have of the brand. Why do they buy? Why don't they buy?

For example, for the business Christmas card division of a greeting card company, we found the top reasons for buying the firm's products were: "It is less expensive" (79 percent), "I can choose from many designs" (73 percent), and "It is easier/more convenient to order direct" (33 percent). What about the people who buy pre-printed Christmas cards but did not buy from our client? They told us: "It is more convenient to order from my office supply store or copy center" (59 percent), "I don't see any real benefit to ordering directly from a greeting card company" (35 percent), "I can get my cards faster from my office supply store or copy center" (28 percent).

These answers already start to offer some marketing guidance. Because convenience is a major issue for both buyers and nonbuyers, this company can increase sales by improving the convenience element and by promoting convenience as a major benefit.

Begin to Define the Market Potential

In addition to establishing a predisposition to act, you should know whether the consumer has bought the product or brand in the past year or in the past month (depending, of course, on the category). This will begin to define the current market potential, and it may help you see whether the market itself is growing or shrinking.

You want to know whether your customers are loyal. What is the likelihood of the customer switching from another brand to your brand or vice versa? How strongly do existing customers feel about your brand? If a store is temporarily out of stock, will your customer go to another store rather than buy a substitute?

When customers *do* switch, what drives their decision? Are they unhappy with your quality, service, convenience, price? For example, Christmas card customers who reported using multiple suppliers during the past three years gave as their reasons discounts/promotions (76 percent), better designs (51 percent), saw an advertisement (44 percent), and lost reorder information (11 percent). (The percentages add to more than 100 because respondents could give more than one answer.)

Here's an example of looking in the rearview mirror to help your marketing. Regina Lewis, director of the Consumer/Brand Insight Group at Dunkin' Brands, and Rebecca Mardula, the group's manager, told an American Marketing Association conference that with

Dunkin' Donuts store development heavily concentrated in the Northeast, the company wanted to know if the concept would work across the United States. Would the corporation need to make any changes to ensure success nationally?

Lewis said that the first step was to understand internal ideas, motivations, wants, fears, opinions, and more. Simultaneously, Dunkin' Donuts obtained a broad understanding of the external trends, consumer opinions, and surveyed consumer needs and opinions of the brand. Once management understood what consumers thought/felt about the brand, it was possible to establish the best route to reach the corporate goals (a process we'll describe in Chapter 6).[1]

A key factor in brand loyalty (or inoculation to switching) is, not surprisingly, satisfaction with the company, brand, or product. The more satisfied a customer, the less likely she is to switch. For instance, among those customers who remembered which Christmas card supplier they used, we found universally high satisfaction with all suppliers. Purchase intent, however, was much lower than what one might expect given the high satisfaction scores.

We researched satisfaction and purchase intent on a 0 percent to 100 percent scale. Our client's customer satisfaction score was 92 percent, which was high relative to the scores of its two largest competitors, which were 81 percent and 79 percent, and much higher than a national average of 74 percent, which we talked about earlier. Our client's purchase intent score on the other hand was less than 50 percent. With high satisfaction scores and relatively low purchase intent scores, the company had a clear opportunity to improve sales.

Finally, you want to know your current share of the market, in both units and dollars, and the market's trend. If the market is growing, say, 7 percent a year and your unit sales are growing 5 percent, you are not doing well. If the market is shrinking 7 percent a year and your sales are growing 5 percent, you are doing all right for now, but if the trends continue long enough, eventually you will have 100 percent of nothing.

Share-of-market figures lend themselves to managerial self-delusion. How one defines the market determines share, and it is possible to define most markets in a way that makes the company look particularly good (or bad). What you want, of course, is to define it in a way that reflects the reality of the arena in which the company operates.

Measure against Marketing's Best Practices

For over a decade, we have been gathering information on the best practices in marketing to help companies understand what goes into exceptional marketing decisions and as an aid to conducting a so-called performance review for the marketing department. What characterizes the best marketing climate analysis? The best targeting decision? The best distribution/channel management?

We have broken all marketing decision areas into 26 specific marketing management functions, everything from objectives and strategies to the marketing organization. We further divided these 26 marketing management functions into 96 benchmark areas. For example, under new product development, one can look at the new product planning and development process, new product idea generation and screening, new product development and evaluation, and new product testing and commercialization.

In total, we can look at more than 800 marketing activities, analyses, and decision processes and score each. For example, under target selection: How many potential targets did the company evaluate? One? Two to five? Six to ten? Eleven to twenty? Thirty or more? Best practice companies evaluate thirty or more potential targets.

Another example: How different is the company's target from the competitor's? Very similar to competitor's? More similar than different? More different than similar? Very different in attitude, behavior, demographics? It does not take a Ph.D. in marketing to realize that it is better to have a target very different from the competition's.

Answers to these 800-plus questions show where a company's marketing is relatively strong and where it is relatively weak. On a scale of 0 percent to 100 percent, the average marketing Best Practices Score for North American companies is 51 percent in

2006. This is like buying a new car with a promised top speed of 120 miles per hour only to discover that you can barely break 60 on the highway.

Although we have found companies that are strong in one or more of the 26 marketing management functions, we have yet to analyze any company that earns an overall score greater than 80 percent. With such poor marketing practices common in even forward-looking companies (management has to be somewhat forward-looking to submit to a best practices analysis in the first place), is it any surprise that we see so many marketing programs are failures?

Measure the Ability of the Marketing Staff

Without an experienced and knowledgeable staff, it is difficult to improve the firm's marketing efforts. Coca-Cola CEO E. Neville Isdell originally thought the corporation would be able to build sales relatively quickly. When it didn't, he said there just weren't the marketing people available within Coke to do so.

As anyone who watches football knows, if you don't have a back-field that can run the ball and catch a pass, you can't win a game. Senior management must know the strengths and limitations of marketing management, how the firm's talent pool compares to marketing best practices, and how the firm's talent pool compares to that of key competitors. Depending on the time and money available, it is possible to do an in-depth evaluation program that forms a foundation for a long-term marketing improvement program and a streamlined evaluation that makes results available quickly and provides a snapshot of today's situation.

An in-depth evaluation reviews all documents that relate to marketing competencies. These include the factors listed in Table 3.2. The evaluation continues with five to ten interviews with senior marketing managers to gather the managers' perspectives on the overall quality of their marketing processes, their view of marketing competencies required for the future, and specific ratings of their own marketing managers' talent with respect to critical competencies.

Table 3.2 Document Review of Marketing Competencies

Resumes (marketing education and experience).

Position descriptions (current responsibilities/accountabilities).

Marketing aptitude and achievement (based on standardized testing).

Marketing work product/output/analyses.

  Marketing plans.

  Marketing programs.

  Performance against the plans.

  Performance of the programs.

Formal and informal assessments of the manager's performance in terms of planning and implementation of marketing programs.

These interviews provide significant directional guidance and a qualitative feel for the state of marketing management processes. This is followed by a relatively short half-hour Intranet-based interview between everyone in the company involved in the marketing function. In a large corporation, this will involve several hundred midlevel marketing managers.

The measuring instrument should cover all of the fundamental topics in marketing—the same subjects included in the best practices audit—except that here you are asking managers to report on their own beliefs and practices rather than those of the department, division, or company they work for. The idea is to score every manager in terms of overall competency and competency within different functional areas. This kind of analysis provides companies with clear insights into what kinds of training programs need to be instituted to close the gap between what people should be doing and what they are doing.

The analysis also looks for enablers and disablers within the organization. Common marketing enablers are an organizational focus on critical variables and appropriate levels of senior management attention. Common marketing disablers are marketing/sales silos (we'll discuss the sales reps in Chapter 10), inadequate systems, competing views on the business model, inside-out thinking, and a bias for award-winning creative advertising rather than advertising that actually sells the product (Chapter 8).

In such an analysis of enablers/disablers, senior managers should be asking questions like:

- Did all functional areas in the company that might be impacted (e.g., brand management, advertising, pricing, sales, PR, etc.) participate in the development of the marketing strategy and plan?
- Is there enthusiastic commitment to the marketing program throughout the entire organization?
- Has the organization allocated adequate resources to ensure the objectives can actually be met?
- Does the organization work to clarify roles and responsibilities?
- Has the organization developed and tracked the proper metrics to support the strategy? (Business cliché no. 708: You can't manage what you don't measure.)
- Does the organization have an inside-out bias rather than a customer-in bias?
- What is the organizational mechanism that keeps tactics and execution consistent with the strategy?

At the end of such an effort, management will have a profile of individual marketing talent relative to best practices. Management also will understand the strengths and limitations of the marketing talent pool, identify and characterize developmental issues, and identify organization enablers/disablers.

Every organization is unique, and although we will throughout this book explore certainly broadly applicable principles, you ought to apply them sensibly to your individual situation rather than accepting them on faith. That, in turn, presumes you understand your individual company's situation clearly. To help you, we will provide a series of questions at the end of each chapter that, we are convinced, can illuminate the key marketing issues we've discussed in the chapter. For example, when you want to give your marketing a performance review (before beginning a fact-based marketing program), here are factors to investigate:

- How are the needs, problems, values, and behavior patterns of our customers and prospective customers changing?
- How will these changes affect consumer or business customers' decision-making?
- What do these changes mean for the way we do business?
- What are the key marketing decisions that need to be made and were they made after evaluating many alternatives in terms of estimated profitability?
- What kind of research was taken to support all key marketing decisions?
- Did management use knowledge of the historical relationship between marketing investments and revenues to firm up the strategy and tactics recommended?
- Very importantly, what has been the performance of the company or brands over time and relative to competitors in terms of the 10 key metrics discussed in this chapter? Everything from awareness and familiarity to market share, brand equity, and customer equity?

With this as a foundation for making fact-based marketing decisions, let's talk about targeting.

SECTION II

Six Easy Steps (and One Hard One) to Better Marketing

4

So Many Targets . . . So Which Are Worth Targeting?

When it comes to targeting, your brain definitely knows more than your gut. Consider our meeting with the senior management of one of the largest financial service companies in the United States. The meeting included the chief executive officer (CEO), the chief marketing officer (CMO), and several marketing managers. The CMO told us that the company was going to expand beyond its traditional marketing efforts (a large network of distributors: brokers, agents, and the like) to focus company resources against individual consumers, a strategy akin to what pharmaceutical companies are doing in their direct-to-consumer marketing efforts. Indeed, the CMO told us that they were inspired by all the pharmaceutical advertising that they see on television. "If a drug company can get patients to talk to their doctors about a drug, why can't we get consumers to contact a broker about our products and services?"

The company is famous for its investment and insurance products, which they sell exclusively to pension funds, large companies, and the distributor network. But now they wanted to direct their efforts toward individuals, and the budget for the effort would not be insubstantial—perhaps $100 million in the first year alone.

We began our inquiry into their situation by asking, as we always do, "Who is the target for this effort, and how did you arrive at that decision?" The response did not surprise us: "We haven't spent that much time on the targeting issue because we're really in a rush to get the program into the marketplace. The advertising agency is planning to launch a campaign in four months."

We wouldn't let it go at that, and responded with, "Yes, but, as Phil Kotler says, all marketing starts with targeting and positioning. Who is your target? And how did you make that decision? Whether you start the campaign in four months or eight months from now, you still have to have a target. You have to have a target just to buy the media."

The CMO said, "Well, we've been thinking about that for a while. In fact, we started thinking about that issue before we even hired the ad agency, and we're reasonably comfortable with what we've got." After a moment of reflection, he added, "These are mutual funds and insurance products any household could buy. Our intention is to target the upper half of all households in America in terms of income. We are going to go after adults in homes with incomes above $45,000."

We said, "Okay, that's interesting. You know that's a profitable target to go after?" The CMO answered, "We know they account for the lion's share of all the mutual funds and insurance purchased in America." We followed up: "Do you know the other players in the category? Players like Charles Schwab, Merrill Lynch, Edward Jones, Fidelity, and others are also chasing them?" The CMO looked uncomfortable. "Well, I guess you could say that. But it's still a very big target, and it's who we plan to go after."

At the end of two hours, we understood that this company was making a major foray into a totally different line of business with generic, plain vanilla, me-too products, and they were doing so without any insight into whether their market target would be good (responsive, profitable, growing) for the business. We could almost guarantee it wouldn't be, but these executives did not want to hear that view.

Finding a Profitable Target

The targeting issue is one we often confront. We have a client in the direct marketing industry, that, for the purpose of this chapter, we'll say sells collectable porcelain figures. Although they've enjoyed a successful business for more than a decade, it is slowing. Both sales and market share are declining. In an early meeting, we asked about the advertising budget and were astonished to find out that it was $44 million. We asked what on earth the company spent it on because we had never seen an ad for any of their products. "Sunday supplements," the CMO said. "We're in Sunday supplements all over the country all the time." So, we asked, who is your market target? She said, "Well, I guess our market target is everyone." But then thinking about it for a moment, she said, "It's everybody who gets a Sunday paper and who reads the Sunday supplement section in it."

(As an aside, we suggested the company do a marketing audit to learn, among other things, its awareness among consumers. The awareness turned out to be reasonably high among people who get the supplements and who read them, but almost nonexistent among people who do not take a Sunday paper.)

This is an example of a company that said, "Our target is the world," but the media plan narrowed that world down to, at best, about 19 percent of the population (total Sunday newspaper circulation divided by total U.S. population). That 19 percent is not projectable to any group other than those who like to cut out coupons and save money, and that could be an adequate target for this company. It certainly can't be the most profitable target. Our audit also revealed that less than 30 percent of the population who read Sunday supplements has any interest in porcelain collectables. Thus the real target in this case is no larger than 30 percent of the 19 percent, or about 6 percent of the population.

Yet the business remains profitable. A profitable business that is slowly dying because fewer and fewer people are buying newspapers.

When we questioned the long-term strategy, the CMO asked if we could make a business case for why they should take another approach. The CMO provided us with historical data that showed the relationship between investments made in Sunday supplements in 2006 and response rates in terms of products ordered.

We analyzed the data and reported: "You are not getting anything for the last 10 percent, the last $4 million of your investment. This happens in virtually every product category, and there's no reason why it shouldn't be happening in yours. If you put $3.5 million of that money in the bank and spent the rest on a consulting engagement that would give you a strong targeting, positioning, advertising, and media strategy, you could improve your marketing—and profitability—dramatically."

The company wasn't interested because it would have to do things differently. If it picked a different target, it would have to use media vehicles with which it had no experience. It would also have to change the advertising copy and, in fact, change everything. End of target market conversation.

The Two Types of Targets

Marketers face two different types of decisions in targeting. Sometimes they have a target—a fixed target—and they're interested in crafting a new product or service to meet the needs/wants/desires of that target. Other times they have developed a product or service and they are trying to find the customers for it.

When Gary and Diane Heavin were thinking about a new health club, they thought about the needs/wants/desires of women who would work out at such a club if it met their needs. Curves was the result. When Procter & Gamble decided to address the household cleaning problems of middle-class, stay-at-home moms, Swiffer was the result. When Monsanto focused its research and development on the needs of farmers for superior corn products, Monsanto corn seed was the result. When Scott's decided to pay attention to its Miracle-Gro users' complaints about the messiness of mixing the product with water, Liquid Miracle-Gro was the result.

Grace, Kennedy, one of the Caribbean's largest and most dynamic food conglomerates, decided to focus its new product development on current users of single-serve juice products. At the time, V8 Splash, owned by Campbell Soup, dominated the Caribbean juice drink market but did not own the single-serve juice market.

As Grace, Kennedy searched for new product ideas to boost the profitability of its ailing foods division, management realized that the single-serve juice category had potential. Not only was it viable in the target Caribbean market, it had great potential worldwide, driven by growing consumer demand for convenience and more healthful juice drinks.

Consumers were open to considering other brands, particularly from companies they trusted, that offered healthful options with quality ingredients (best/natural ingredients, a high percentage of real fruit juice), or both. Grace already had entries in the ready-to-drink juice category—Grace Juices—in family-size bottles and cans, so it had juice category experience, brand credibility, the capability, and the infrastructure to enter the single-serve juice market. All it needed was the right product.

Grace decided to target current users of single-serve juices and tested Grace Juice in single-serve containers, but with new, exotic, and tropical flavors. Particularly among key target market segments, trial scores were significantly higher than the average new product. Based on the positive reactions to the concept by the target market, Grace created a new product, Tropical Rhythms, to address needs that customers expressed for a single-serve juice: healthful, thirst-quenching, and with genuine fruit taste.

Launched in November 2001, Tropical Rhythms exceeded "even our most optimistic projections," according to Grace. It quickly became the Caribbean market leader with a 50 percent share—cutting V8 Splash's share in half—and helped propel the Grace, Kennedy Foods Division out of the red and into the black.

The sales momentum continued after launch, boosting international sales dramatically.

Different Approaches to Targeting

More common than creating a product or service from scratch, of course, is the situation in which a company has an existing product and would like to identify (or refine) a target market. Management knows it cannot—indeed should not—appeal to everyone because that would be expensive and wasteful. Therefore, executives use their gut, picking a target that makes intuitive sense. These are target markets like "heavy users," "category users," "15- to 22-year-olds," "18- to 34-year-old women," or "nonbuyers/nonusers." Maybe these targets *seem* appropriate, but here again, the brain is smarter.

What's wrong is that management has no knowledge that these are the most profitable targets to pursue. Indeed, in our experience a company could evaluate 2,000 or more different targets in every product category, consumer, and business-to-business, and the result is usually that conventional targets such as heavy users and 25- to 49-year-old women are in the bottom 20 percent in terms of profitability.

These markets, popular with "gut" marketers, are not great targets to go after. Take, for example, the heavy users. These are the buyers in every product category who buy more, use more, and spend more than anyone else. Marketers are often elated to be able to say, "I found the 23 percent of the population that accounts for 82 percent of the volume in the category." Superficially, heavy users seem like a great target, but they're not.

Heavy users are often price-conscious and deal-prone, and therefore not loyal to any brand. Others are committed to the brand they've been using and cannot be induced to switch by advertising, salesmanship, free samples, or rebates. As a group, they are usually far more heterogeneous than homogeneous, so it is difficult to reach them efficiently with media. And most problematic of all, every marketer in the category is chasing them, which means that your dollars have to compete with the marketing investments of an entire category. No wonder profitability analyses almost always find heavy users near the bottom of the list in terms of potentially profitable targets.

Another group too heterogeneous to target efficiently is that of category users. Think of categories like cereal, soft drinks, cold remedies, salty snacks, lipstick, computers, hotels, theme parks, vacuum cleaners, vitamins . . . the list is endless. Different people take different vitamins (to use just one example) for different reasons. Category users do actually buy the product, but that is usually the only thing that distinguishes them.

At least once a year, we do a segmentation study that deals with women versus men. Virtually every marketer's gut instinct is that female consumers are different from men. And they are different in certain categories—automobiles, cosmetics, baby food—but not in every category. If you screen for business travelers who stay in hotels, there is almost no difference in terms of what women and men want. Women are perhaps marginally more concerned about security, but they both are business travelers. And they essentially want the same things from a hotel.

What about 15- to 22-year-olds or 18- to 34-year-old women or 25- to 54-year-old women, all favorites among consumer package goods companies? Like heavy users, these targets are too heterogeneous to reach efficiently. Are we talking about college students? Working singles? Young mothers? Working mothers? Professional? Blue collar? Your optimal target market may be *among* 18- to 34-year-old women, but without some careful research, you waste time and money reaching far too many nonbuyers/nonusers.

Nonbuyers/nonusers themselves may seem appealing because there are usually so many of them. These are the people who have never gone on a cruise, never bought flavored rum, never driven a pickup truck . . . another endless list. What a wealth of prospective customers for cruise lines, rum distillers, truck manufacturers! In fact, it is almost axiomatic that when we present the results of a segmentation study that clearly and unequivocally demonstrates that nonbuyers/nonusers have zero value and represent zero return on investment, some seemingly serious marketer in the room will say, "I think you're misreading the data. There are just so many of these people they represent a giant opportunity that we can't ignore."

Unfortunately, there's usually a reason they are nonbuyers, a good reason that neither an outstanding product nor spectacular marketing can overcome. The husband gets seasick, the couple does not drink strong waters, the family won't fit in a truck's cab. Unless a product category is brand new (the Apple iPod is a recent example), and there *are* no buyers or users yet, it is usually a massive waste of marketing resources to target nonbuyers/nonusers.

Table 4.1 shows some of the most common ways that people segment markets. In each case, the pros and the cons of a particular mode of market segmentation are listed.

The principle remains: The better you can identify the profitable target market, the more efficient your marketing will be.

The Problem with Target Segmentation

Yet it is clear that senior management is not happy with studies that identify presumably profitable market targets. A recent Marakon Associates and Economist Intelligence Unit survey of 200 senior executives of large companies reported that, though 59 percent had conducted a major market segmentation exercise within the past two years, only 14 percent said they derived any real value from it.[1] Many companies say that market segmentation reports make excellent doorstops because they are thick, often a couple hundred pages or more, and put in hard binders.

We recently met with top management of a popular cable TV channel. The company was interested in an audience segmentation study to see what they could do to expand their viewership. While having the conversation, we noticed a thick binder of what appeared to be a segmentation report by a well-known consulting firm on the bookshelf right behind the CEO's head. At an appropriate point we said, "Have you ever done one of these before? There appears to be a strategy study right behind you."

"Yes, we did it, but it wasn't helpful." Why wasn't it helpful? "We didn't know what to do with it. It wasn't actionable."

Table 4.1   Five Segmentation Approaches: Pros and Cons

Need/Benefit Segmentation

Pros

- So-called natural segmentations because buyer needs seem so simple, so basic.
- Easy to do.
- Intellectually interesting.
- People love to name the groups.
- Good for new product ideas.
- Some insights for advertising copy

Cons

- Needs (i.e., importance ratings) should not be mistaken for problems.
- Different techniques for measuring needs yield different outcomes.
- Common approaches understate the true importance of intangible, emotional attributes and benefits.
- Generally, the segments have similar brand preferences, consumption patterns, demographics, and media exposure patterns.
- Segments can't be found in databases.

Behavioral Segmentation

Pros

- Easy to find a small group of consumers who account for the lion's share of category volume.
- Managers love to talk about the 20/80 rule.
- Very easy to do.
- Simple and capable of being understood by everyone in the organization.
- Because it's based on only one or two questions, the segmentation can be found in other databases.

Cons

- Heavy buyers are often price conscious and psychologically locked into whatever brands are available on sale.
- Product usage is often not correlated with any variable other than family size.
- Generally, the segments have similar brand preferences, consumption patterns, demographics, and media exposure patterns.

(continued)

Table 4.1 *(Continued)*

- Little understanding of the differential needs of the target. Compared to other targets, they are more similar than different.

Psychographic Segmentation

Pros

- Like need/benefit segmentation, attitudes and personality characteristics are interesting and fun to work with.
- People love to name the groups.
- Simple and capable of being understood by everyone in the organization.
- Offer some insights for advertising copy.

Cons

- Attitudes are often weak predictors of buyer behavior and brand choice.
- As a result, the segments have similar brand preferences, consumption patterns, demographics, and media exposure patterns.
- Segments can't be found in databases.
- Little understanding of the different needs of the segments. Compared to other targets, they are more similar than different.

Demographic Segmentation

Pros

- Simple and easily understood by everyone in the organization.
- Describes people you're familiar with: spouse, daughter, next-door neighbor.
- Media services and agencies find demographics easy to work with.
- Because it's based on only one to three standard demographic questions, the segments can be found in other databases.
- Groups are often differentially reachable with media.

Cons

- Demographics rarely predict buyer behavior.
- Little understanding of the differential needs of the segments. Compared to other targets, they are more similar than different.

Table 4.1 *(Continued)*

- Generally the segments have similar brand preferences, consumption patterns, demographics, and media exposure patterns.
- Not being different, the targets represent an inefficient media buy.

Job Segmentation

Pros

- Currently popular among top management; recently featured in *The Harvard Business Review.*
- So commonsensical, it's a wonder marketers haven't discovered it before.
- Simple and capable of being understood by everyone in the organization.
- Appeals to rational decision makers.

Cons

- It's a 30-year-old approach masquerading as something new.
- Emphasis is on rational drivers of brand choice. Ignores the role of emotional triggers.
- Overlaps with occasion-based and needs-based segmentation. Hard to tell where one ends and other starts.
- Segments have similar needs, brand preferences, consumption patterns, demographics, and media exposure patterns.
- Segments can't be found in databases.

This is a common response. Why don't marketing executives know what to do with segmentation information? Most say they don't know how to find the people identified in the segments. Or the people in the segments weren't different in terms of anything other than the variables that created the segmentation itself. If you do a demographic segmentation, the segments differ demographically but are the same in attitudes and behavior. If you do a behavioral segmentation, they are different behaviorally, but the attitudes, values, and the media profiles are all the same. Essentially, the people identified are not different enough that marketers can find them in databases such as the U.S. census or in syndicated databases such as Prism, MRI, or Simmons.

Perhaps a high level of interest/low level of satisfaction with target market segmentation was the impetus behind recent *Harvard*

Business Review articles on this relatively neglected—though key—marketing decision area. Daniel Yankelovich and David Meer, a partner at Marakon Associates, offer their perspectives on why market segmentation has failed to deliver and some recommendations for how to derive value from it.[2]

They complain that market segmentation today has become "the marketing equivalent of central casting," a guide to the kind of characters that should populate commercials. Indeed, we've come across many recent examples of firms creating so-called personas to help marketers and their advertising agencies "empathize with their customers and to understand what moves and motivates them," to quote *The Wall Street Journal*. Chrysler has actually gone so far as to build different "persona rooms" complete with a color scheme, furniture, knickknacks, bric-a-brac, and other items that reflect the unique tastes, personalities, attitudes, and lifestyles of consumers in different segments.[3] If only Chrysler marketers—and Chrysler is by no means alone—spent as much time on making their targeting decision as they do constructing rooms and fake personal histories, their marketing would be much more effective. As Yankelovich and Meer rightly point out, "segmentation can do vastly more than serve as a source of human types."

The authors tell companies to consider first the level of importance that people generally attach to a purchase decision: "Some decisions people make, such as trying a new brand of toilet paper or applying for a credit card, are relatively inconsequential. . . . But decisions such as buying a home or choosing a cancer treatment have momentous significance." The end of what they call the "gravity of decision spectrum" on which the category falls dictates the types of issues business should address, what the buyer's concerns will be, and the criteria on which to base the segmentation. For example, they say that in low-importance categories, the segmentation should consider buying and usage behavior, price sensitivity, and degree of loyalty to a brand.

Go Beyond Conventional Wisdom

In contrast, we have found the importance placed on a purchase decision—what we call *involvement*—is a characteristic of an individual buyer, not of the product or service. Some consumers will spend almost as much time weighing the merits of different toilet paper brands as others do in choosing a new car. To assume that all buyers in a category will feel the same way about a purchase decision is simply incorrect. Based on our work in hundreds of different categories, we've discovered that actual individual buyer involvement varies considerably for every product and service, as Table 4.2 shows.

As the table suggests, conventional wisdom is wrong. In categories in which involvement is allegedly high, there are actually more average- and low-involvement buyers (58 percent) than high-involvement buyers. In categories with the highest/deepest level of involvement, almost half the buyers (45 percent) are low or average in involvement. In supposedly low-involvement categories, average- or high-involvement buyers represent 36 percent of the market—hardly an insignificant number.

It's important for marketers to know the relative distribution of low-, average-, and high-involvement buyers in a product category because each type requires a different marketing strategy. Involvement could be an important criterion on which to base a segmentation—it could predict buying behavior and indicate potential profitability—but it should never be used as *the* deciding factor on what types of questions, buyer concerns, and segmentation criteria companies should use.

Table 4.2 Conventional-Wisdom-Dictated Product Category Involvement

Actual Individual Buyer Involvement	Low/ Shallowest Decisions (i.e., Toilet Paper)	Average/ Middle of the Spectrum (i.e., New Suit, HDTV)	High/Deep Decisions (i.e., Automobile)	Highest/ Deepest Decisions (i.e., Retirement Planning)
Low	64%	34%	21%	13%
Average	23%	45%	37%	32%
High	13%	21%	42%	55%

This brings us to our next point about trusting the brain rather than the gut. No one can know a priori the best way to segment a market. Yankelovich and Meer say—and we agree—that, to be valid, "a segmentation must identify groups that matter to a company's financial performance." However, there's just no way to know what factors will predict behavior and profitability before one morsel of data has been collected or ounce of analysis run. Marketers should consider hundreds of ways to divide the market—not some preprescribed list—to create detail-rich, proprietary segments that competitors don't even know exist. This is how a market segmentation study can become a valuable strategic asset instead of a shelf decoration.

Targeting is the single most important element in the marketing plan. "To win a war you need to know where to attack," Dwight Eisenhower might have said to an audience of business managers. "We wouldn't have brought the Nazis to their knees if we had landed the Allied forces at Calais instead of the beaches of Normandy." A segmentation exercise should enable a company to identify which group (or groups) of buyers represents the best opportunity to grow sales and profits over time—in other words, to make the targeting decision.

Such an exercise should tell company management what the different segments are worth; what message the company needs to communicate to them; what their profile is attitudinally, demographically, sociographically, so the advertising casts the right people in the ads and captures the right tonality. And it should say, "Here are the television shows, the radio programs, the newspapers, the magazines, and the nontraditional media that will impact a disproportionate number of these folks efficiently."

For a business-to-business product or service, where there isn't the same kind of consumer syndicated data available, marketers can use data on organization size, growth, and decision-makers in some categories. It is possible to segment in terms of standard industrial classification (SIC) code, faculty rooftop size, dollar sales, and number of employees. Market segmentation doesn't just "reflect the company's strategy," as Yankelovich and Meer maintain, it *drives* the strategy.

How to Identify a Profitable Target Market

So how do you find the segment of the total market that will be the most responsive and profitable? Before you even begin, you need to understand exactly who in the company plans to use the study results and how they plan (or hope) to use them. This knowledge will have direct bearing on two research issues.

First, what are the number and the nature of the variables to be used in the ultimate segmentation scheme? Will you use numerous variables (20 to 30) in a complex algorithm or a handful (5 to 10) to construct a fairly simple scoring scheme? And can it include database variables—customer account data, third-party data, or block-level census data (or all three)?

Second, what does management want this segmentation to predict? How does management want the segmentation to be used? What is the research trying to explain (brand preference, openness to switching accounts, vulnerability to leaving the customer base)? Does management want to understand high versus low consumption of the product/service category or which types of consumers are going to the different distribution channels? And perhaps the most important question smart management would want answered: Which customers and which segments of customers will be the most profitable for the firm to pursue for the long haul? With these decisions settled, the useful segmentation study to identify a profitable target takes different steps and creates the wide range of possible segmentation variables to be studied.

Start by creating the variables to be considered. We have found that we might easily have 150 or more independent variables from a typical, in-depth interview with a consumer. These consist of 15 to 20 demographics, 40 to 50 attitudes, 20 to 40 behaviors, 30 to 50 motivations to buy in the category and the brand, 20 to 30 media habits, and numerous database variables.

Some of these are relatively simple variables, like gender, age, marital status, and purchasing behavior. Others are more complicated variables such as relative income, which is the subject's income relative to people in the same ZIP code or even block. Sometimes, very complex variables are created such as household income per capita compared to that of close friends and relatives. Factor analysis can reduce the large number of these variables; it will take the 150 variables and identify the things they have in common to reduce the list to perhaps 30 or 40 variables overall. Now test all these variables to see which are related to profitability, not just market behaviors.

Establish Responsiveness to Your Brand

One of the hottest areas in marketing today is the idea of responsiveness to your brand. There are folks who, if they are not using your brand already, are willing to consider it. They are willing to try it. If they are already using it, they will try a line extension. They know your brand exists and have positive feelings about it. If someone hates your brand or has no interest in it, she or he is unlikely to ever move in your direction, no matter what you do. They will not even take the free sample you hand out on the street. They are unresponsive.

The marketing challenge is to scale every potential person in the target market from 0 to 100 and calculate the probability that individuals could be moved by your marketing efforts. At one extreme, nothing you do will make much difference; at the other, your enthusiastic fans and word of mouth will do your work for you. So one dimension you should measure is responsiveness (and not use your gut to estimate responsiveness) to your brand.

The other dimension is opinion leadership. Again, we find a continuum (almost nothing in marketing is clearly black or white.) At one extreme are the people who are so disengaged in the product category or who have such a small network of friends and acquaintances, they don't exercise any more influence on behavior other than what they themselves buy and use.

At the other extreme, you have raging fans, people who not only buy and use the product and service, they are knowledgeable, have a wide circle of friends, and are both consulted for and volunteer their expertise. For instance, these are the car enthusiasts who just love cars, read everything about cars, and have a large network of acquaintances. Computer enthusiasts with many acquaintances affect many more sales than their own. They have value far in excess of what they buy themselves.

Customer price sensitivity is another critical targeting issue. As products drift more and more toward commodities, price becomes more and more important. And everybody in marketing and sales is focused on price. Salespeople say price is the only thing that matters; can we drop the price? Distributors say the same thing. Brand managers assume that price is the most important element and therefore they are playing with what can they do beyond price to move the brand.

We say that in almost every product category there are many people—as many as two-thirds, in fact—who are relatively price-insensitive. We do not say you can double the price, but in most cases you can increase price by 10 percent or 15 percent. You are not going to lose your loyal customers—the people you want.

Now test all these possible variables to see which are related to profitability or proxies for profitability. Chief among these is brand preference or, more to the point, an openness to the firm's brand (see Table 4.3 for a dozen proxies that we often include in consumer and business-to-business targeting engagements). Among these are sales potential, growth potential, decision-making power, and retention potential. You don't want to predict who has bought the brand in the past, you want to see who might buy it in the future. (More on responsiveness in a moment.)

Next, identify the key variables about people (or firms for a business-to-business product) that best predict what they are doing or will do (or both) in the market place. In business-to-business marketing, you typically are looking for fewer predictors (5 to 10) because the ultimate use of the segmentation will be fairly straightforward, such as by salespeople or searching business databases. In consumer research, in which large companies will use sophisticated media plans or database modeling, a company can afford to entertain a larger number of variables.

Table 4.3   Profitable Target Market Characteristics

Decision-making power—The more responsibility a target group has for making sales decisions, the more valuable it is.

Category involvement—The more involved a target group is in the product category, the more valuable it is.

Growth potential—The more a target group is growing in size over time, the more valuable it is.

Personal influence—The more personal influence a target group has in the product category, the more valuable it is.

Responsiveness—The more a target group responds to a company's marketing efforts, the more valuable it is.

Common motivations—The more homogeneous and preemptible a target's needs are, the more valuable it is.

Problem potential—The bigger the problem the target has that the marketer can solve, the more valuable it is.

Retention potential—The more likely it is that a target can be economically sustained and therefore retained over time, the more valuable it is.

Lifetime value—The more a product is expected to buy over its lifetime, the more valuable it is.

Profit potential—The more a target group buys, the more it buys in high-margin channels, and the more price insensitive it is, the more valuable it is.

Findability—The more easily a target can be identified in databases, the more valuable it is.

Media exposure costs—The easier and less expensive it is to reach a target, the more valuable it is.

At this point, you can group consumers into segments based on their answers to these 5 to 25 variables. The company can use different methods here, such as cluster analyses, latent class analysis, neural networks, and the like.

Finally, test again, looking at numerous segmentation schemes. Apply the same managerial, statistical, and financial criteria you used earlier. Do you see different brand preferences? Different consumption levels? Different channels? Different media profiles? And very important, different levels of future profitability?

When to Use Targeting by Occasion

The usage or buying occasion has a major effect on purchase of certain products. If you manage a fast-food restaurant chain, you should know that research can identify at least ten distinct occasions: giving the kids a treat, ordering for a family night in, taking a night off from cooking, staying home alone, a weekend together, a social evening out, working take-out, a change of taste, a quick pit stop, and a casual lunch. Research has also established that these different occasions involve different venues (dine-in or take-out), different moods, different times of day, and typically involve different food: burgers for the kids' treat, home alone, working take-out, and pit stop; pizza for family night in, night off, weekend together, and social evening out; a sandwich for weekend together and change of taste; Mexican for night off and change of taste; chicken for night off and social evening out.

If you are a business-to-business marketer selling personal computers, you will find at least four different purchase-related occasions: installing totally new systems or solutions or both, adding significant capacity or utility to core systems, PC/work station purchases in batches, and individual/ad hoc information technology purchasing.

Very little has been written about occasion segmentation, yet it can be significant for many products and services. Here's how such an effort could work for, as an example, Blue Hen vodka.

Let's say we have interviewed 1,000 people and identified five different types of vodka drinkers. The aficionados represent 16 percent of the population and account for 52.6 percent of profit potential for Blue Hen with an estimated ROI of 323. This clearly is the most profitable target for our brand. But what are the occasions for which vodka is purchased by this target? Here's how we learn. In the same survey, we say to the respondents, "Let's talk about the last three times that you bought vodka. Do you remember the last time you bought vodka?" The respondent (in this example) says, yes, he was having a party. We ask: "Let's talk about what brand you bought for that occasion. What size was the bottle? Did you buy more than one bottle or one bottle? What size was that bottle?"

We next ask about some of the same attributes and benefits they had gone through earlier in the overall study. (They cannot go through the whole list again because it's too time-consuming, so they go through a list of, say, a dozen attributes and benefits.) We ask the respondents what they were looking for when they bought on the occasion and their perceptions of different brands on the occasion. Then we move to the next occasion and do the same thing. "What was the purpose of the purchase, for home consumption or as a gift, and so on?" At the end of this process, the research has 3,000 occasions (1,000 respondents, three occasions each).

In the original segmentation analysis, a statistical algorithm evaluates the key profit drivers to reveal three, four, five, or as many as seven different targets. This was the analysis that turned up the 16 percent of the population accounting for 53 percent of profit potential. The analysis now takes the data on the 3,000 occasions and runs the cluster analysis as if it were 3,000 people—no profitability drivers. The computer finds homogeneous groups, and a cluster analysis (or whatever pattern recognition tool you use) tells us that there are basically four different occasions when people buy vodka.

One occasion is buying it for personal consumption at home; it can be cheaper, doesn't have to be one of the major brands, and it is a larger-than-average size bottle. Another is buying it for a gift; here consumers want to spend more money. A third occasion is to serve to guests, where the consumer does not want to be perceived as cheap. The fourth occasion is consumption outside the home. The attributes and benefits of the vodka that consumers look for on these four different occasions are somewhat different.

But now you can do some clever things with the data. For example, you can assess the profitability of each occasion. You can then connect the people segments to the occasion segments to learn, say, that party animals spend 50 percent of their vodka budget on party occasions outside the home, 25 percent on vodka for the house, 15 percent on vodka for parties at home, and 10 percent for gifts. In theory, one could position Blue Hen for a given occasion. Your gut couldn't do this kind of sophisticated analysis.

Table 4.4 shows the average dollars spent on vodka for each market segment. The group identified as "Aficionados" spends the most on in-home consumption; "Aficionados" love a martini or Cosmo before dinner. "Party Animals" spend the most while prowling, looking for a good time; "Fine Diners," like "Party Animals," do the bulk of the drinking outside the home, but it's in white-tablecloth restaurants, not bars and clubs. "Price Sensitive" and "Infrequent Drinkers" are relatively poor targets for Blue Hen with ROIs under 100. They are targets to be ignored, not pursued.

Before the segmentation research even begins, you should learn if this is a product or service in which occasion has any real impact. If occasion has little impact on customer buying decisions, that's fine. The original people segmentation will suffice. But if occasion has a major impact, the marketer should know it. Is the consumer looking for a car as transportation back and forth to the train station, versus a car for a lot of long-distance driving, versus a car that is going

Table 4.4   Self-Reported Annual Dollars Spent on Vodka

	Consumer Segments				
	Aficionados	Party Animals	Fine Diners	Price Sensitive	Infrequent Drinkers
Personal consumption at home	$293.20	$68.65	$9.06	$14.40	$8.69
Gifts for someone else	$140.65	$35.14	$3.42	$18.14	$7.50
Serve to guests	$106.13	$44.77	$28.59	$16.85	$11.19
Consumption outside the home	$88.87	$141.11	$63.91	$17.37	$14.10
% of category profitability	52.6%	24.5%	12.7%	6.9%	3.3%
Return on Investment	323	165	101	83	48

to impress the neighbors? These are all different situations that can affect the company's marketing efforts, and they certainly affect the way the company positions its product.

To ensure that the company's targeting efforts remain current and—you'll excuse the expression—on target, top management and chief marketing officers ought to ask several questions such as the following:

- Have we segmented each market in which we operate to identify and describe the most profitable market targets to pursue?
- Are we able to find the targets in media, (e.g., MRI) or other commercially available databases? Can we find the segments in our company-owned database of customers and prospects?
- Have our targets changed in the last few years? Are we seeking the same targets we always went after?
- What was our rationale for selecting these targets? What process did we use to find them?
- Can we prove our targets are profitable? Can we show that they have made money for us in the past or will make money in the future?
- For each of our core businesses or brands, how do we describe—in detail—the market target? How does the target market compare to nontargets in terms of attitudes, behavior, values, motivations, perceptions of our brand versus competitors, media exposure patterns, demographics, psychographics, and sociographics? Business-to-business marketers need to describe their targets in terms of industry characteristics such as SIC codes, corporate traits, company size, and the characteristics of the decision-maker such as title, years of experience, and decision-making power.
- Is there some other target or targets that might be more profitable?

The managers who ask these questions and receive good answers have a major competitive advantage over most managers, not to mention a lead over business competitors. Of course, once you have a profitable target, the next challenge is to position the product or service in the minds of those target customers—using your brain, not your gut.

5

Positioning: The Battle for the Mind Is Lost before the First Shot Is Fired

Positioning is the mental image or impression consumers (or, in the case of business-to-business marketing, customers) have of your product or service or brand, the idea that sets it apart from competing products and brands. What do consumers think when they hear about or see your brand? Here is another decision in which you should trust your brain, not your gut.

We recently asked beer drinkers age 21 to 65 what Bud and Miller stand for; how were they different from other brands; what messages are communicated about how they are different? The answer, not surprisingly, is "Not much." Fewer than 10 percent of beer drinkers associate the brands with anything one could begin to call positioning. Compare that to a time not all that long ago when most red-blooded American men thought of Budweiser as the "King of Beers," Miller as the "Champagne of Bottled Beers," when

"Weekends Were Made for Michelob," and Schaefer was "The One Beer to Have When You Are Having More than One." Today they stand for nothing.

It's not surprising given all the years that Budweiser was running its frogs and lizards advertising. One of the creative directors at the agency told us that a couple of guys had come up with the notion of croaking frogs for a campaign—any campaign—and they shopped it around the agency trying to get a brand group to pick up the idea as an execution vehicle for a brand—any brand. The Bud account group thought it was appealing, and before long they were running it.

Now, what message does croaking frogs communicate about a brand? When the frogs were able to pronounce "Bud . . . weiser," one could say it enhanced awareness. But awareness of Budweiser is in the 90s and doesn't need to be improved. What Budweiser needs is a message that motivates more people to buy. Budweiser advertising— with the exception of occasional spots featuring August Busch and its history and tradition of advertising—has communicated nothing.

Or worse, the industry has managed to position beer products as the drink of—and for—rowdy fraternity boys. Think of the Miller commercials in which two women have a mud fight. Or the Bud Light spots featuring flatulent horses and a dog attacking a man's crotch. Or the twins in bikinis for Coors Light. These are designed for 21- to 27-year-old men, the beer industry's prime market target, but even young men may be having second thoughts about beer as the drink of choice.

Beer's share of the overall U.S. alcoholic-beverage market peaked in 1995 at about 61 percent, falling to under 57 percent by 2006, according to *The Wall Street Journal*.[1] In the same period, wine and spirits' share of the market has climbed from just less than 39 percent to more than 42 percent.

"Is it just a coincidence that while the beer industry has been hitting these [frat party] advertising themes, three important groups have begun to turn away from beer in favor of wine and mixed drinks?" asked the *Journal*. "Baby boomers increasingly are drinking wine, young women now often find it more fashionable to drink a low-carb cocktail than a brew, and older members of the so-called echo-boom, the children of baby boomers born from the late 1970s through the early 1990s, also seem drawn to cocktails, in large part because of the more-sophisticated image the spirits industry has created for its products."

Some in the beer industry recognize the positioning problem: "People will tell you that beer is not sophisticated enough, or stylish enough, to compete with wine and spirits," says Tom Long, the chief marketing officer of SAB Miller PLC. "Why do they think that? Well, I believe it's because we told them to." Long also notes, "We've marketed our way into this problem, and we can market ourselves out of it."

As of this writing, it remains very much to be seen whether the beer industry will be able to reposition its product—to market its way back to market share growth—but there is no question that positioning is a key to marketing success. We offer our experience with Skol brand beer in Brazil as evidence.

Repositioning Skol Beer

Brazil is the third largest beer market in the world, with more than one hundred brands competing for share. Most of these brands are undifferentiated, and, as in the United States, the category was becoming a commodity market, where brand name means little to consumers and they base their purchase decisions largely on price. Skol, with a 15 percent share of the Brazilian beer market, was the fourth largest brand, trailing far behind power beer brands Brahma and Antarctica, which together commanded more than 60 percent of the total category. The Skol brand lacked a clear and differentiating market target and positioning. The brand was lifeless and boring.

Although Brahma and Antarctica enjoyed 90 percent distribution through all on- and off-premise channels, Skol had only 50 percent distribution; it was sold mostly through supermarkets and grocery stores. Skol's distribution was particularly weak in bars, the primary channel for on-premise beer sales.

To identify their strategic options, Skol's management commissioned us to field a large study among 1,300 beer drinkers in 26 large and small Brazilian cities. The study assessed the needs, problems, and motivations of beer drinkers as well as their perceptions of different brands. We identified the most profitable customers and the occasions when they bought and consumed beer, the most compelling positioning, and an effective and efficient media strategy. Skol followed this with a program of copytesting that evaluated many creative executions of the winning positioning to select an advertising campaign to communicate the positioning and to stimulate buying behavior.

Once it had all this information, Skol's management considered several strategic options: Skol could be phased out of the market, freeing up marketing dollars for other brands; Skol could continue to focus distribution on the supermarket and simply maintain current market share; Skol could make a play for market share by dropping prices; or Skol could be repositioned as a lighter, smoother beer supported by a substantial marketing budget.

Skol's management wanted the brand to be more than a weak fourth, so it decided to build a strategy based on the attribute (or benefit) that key targets indicated was most motivating and on which Skol could deliver: smooth flavor. "It goes down smooth" became the central message of the advertising and marketing communications campaign (and one particularly effective in Portuguese). Skol increased its communications spending significantly to reflect brand-building objectives. We developed a marketing mix model for the Brazilian beer market that allowed Skol to test the effect of marketing plan inputs (including strategic elements such as targeting and positioning and tactical elements such as prime-time gross rating points) on outputs (market share and brand equity). Moreover, the marketing mix model fostered a better understanding among the sales force of key distribution channels and helped set specific and realistic distribution targets for the next 24 months. The sales force redirected efforts to include broader distribution to get the product to the target beer drinkers, with a heavy emphasis on on-premise sales.

In four years, Skol rocketed from fourth to first position in its home market. Its market share doubled to 31 percent. Skol's distribution reached 93 percent, surpassing Brahma and Antarctica, the leading beers in South America. When Skol launched the "smooth" strategy internationally, the brand achieved unprecedented sales, becoming the third largest beer brand in the world in 2005 without a single drop sold in North America. The brand manager on Skol became CEO of Inbev, the world's largest brewer in 2005.

No Clear Positioning Can Mean Failure

After two decades of testing and research into marketing failures, we've established that the absence of a clear, definable positioning for the brand is one of the most frequent reasons for failure. In parallel research into positioning strengths and failures, we asked buyers to tell us about brand positioning strategies. What do the five leading brands in a wide variety of categories stand for? What do they communicate about themselves that makes them different from other brands? Fewer than 8 percent of respondents were able to associate *anything* with the brands that indicated recognizable "positioning" in any way.

When we told respondents in our summer 2006 survey among more than 1,100 people the brand's positioning or slogan or both (for example, "Have you ever heard Coke use the slogan, 'It's the real thing!'"), we found that the average, fully prompted, completely clued positioning awareness score for the top two brands in most categories was just less than 30 percent. These scores, we should add, have been adjusted for false claims or dissimulation, and some of them are shown in Table 5.1.

Note that State Farm, Wal-Mart, Master Card, Burger King, Nike, and McDonald's are among the top performers with scores of 60 percent or more, whereas Adidas, Ameritrade, Shell, Lincoln, and Revlon are among the worst performers with scores of less than 10 percent. In comparison, three fake slogans—for Honda, Amazon.com, and Microsoft—performed between 23 and 49 percent, thus suggesting how important it is to correct false reporting, which we did, when undertaking surveys like this.

Table 5.1 "True" Advertising Penetration

State Farm—"Like a good neighbor"	71%
Wal-Mart—"Always low prices"	68%
Maxwell House—"Good to the last drop"	67%
Burger King—"Have it your way"	66%
MasterCard—"There are some things that money can't buy. For everything else there's MasterCard"	66%
Nike—"Just do it"	62%
McDonald's—"I'm lovin' it"	61%
UPS—"See what brown can do for you"	61%
Chevrolet—"An American revolution"	52%
L'Oréal—"Because I'm worth it"	49%
GE—"Imagination at work"	48%
Gillette—"The best a man can get"	43%
Visa—"Life takes Visa"	41%
American Express—"My life. My card."	39%
Schick—"The Power of 4"	37%
Charles Schwab—"Talk to Chuck"	36%
Bank of America—"Higher Standards"	31%
Garnier—"Get longer, stronger hair"	23%
Ford—"Bold Moves"	22%
Nissan—"Shift"	22%
American Airlines—"We know why you fly"	17%
Purina—"Your pet. Our passion"	14%
Wachovia—"Uncommon wisdom"	12%
Pepsi—"It's the cola"	12%
Miller—"Beer. Grown Up"	10%
Coke—"The Coke Side of Life"	9%
Adidas—"Impossible is nothing"	9%
Ameritrade—"Welcome to the 21st Century. Now trade like it"	9%
Shell—"Go well. Go Shell"	7%
Lincoln—"Reach higher"	6%
Revlon—"Stay busy. Stay beautiful. No sweat."	5%
Fake Slogans	
Honda—"Drivers Wanted"	49%
Amazon.com—"Want it? We got it"	29%
Microsoft—"Life. Evolved."	23%

Of course, when the consumer pushes her cart down a supermarket aisle and when a small businessman walks through Staples, they are not seeing advertising. They are not being asked, "Do you remember the ad that does such and such?" If there is any stimulus at all, the stimulus comes from the package itself, shelf talkers, or end-aisle displays. Often, the advertising message is not replicated in any of these forms, which is a separate issue. In fact, many ads never show the package, so consumers have a hard time making a visual connection between the two anyway.

On the other hand, some brands make this connection extremely well. For example, during the 2005–2006 football season, we saw a great deal of advertising for the new chili variety of Campbell's Chunky Soup, for which the message, the brand, and the packaging are one and the same—it's chunky. But that is unusual. Usually, there is a disconnect between what people see in a real shopping environment and what some researchers are asking about in measuring advertising recall.

What a Positioning Is . . . and Does for You

Marketers and advertisers define positioning in a number of ways. To paraphrase the classic work on the subject by Al Ries and Jack Trout,[2] it's the unique perceptual image that consumers carry in their minds about your brand that sets it beneficially apart from competing products and brands.

Or it is: "The story you want to plant in people's minds about your product and why it's better (than competitors and alternatives)."

Or it is: "The bundle of attributes and benefits you want to tell people about, or simply, your unique selling proposition—the reason why people should buy your product rather than someone else's."

In plain English, it's the sales message, the elevator pitch designed to motivate someone to buy your brand. At the most fundamental, it's the brand's essence, its raison d'être, its reason to be. Common to all definitions, however, is the idea that brands truly achieve positioning when the benefit-providing solutions and promises meet the category preferences, needs, and expectations of the target consumer in a way that makes the brand appear compellingly unique among alternatives. In an advertising context, positioning is a motivating, persuasively communicated message that gives prospective customers a positive reason why they should think of and remember the product as having a unique-among-alternatives capacity to deliver benefits that satisfy their needs and desires.

Unfortunately, through a customer's bad experience, negative word of mouth, or inattention, you may also be positioned negatively: the brand is too expensive, too cheap, too complicated, shoddy, tasteless, unsophisticated, ugly, gets poor gas mileage, difficult to use, to find, to repair. The list of reasons *not* to buy a product or service is endless.

A positioning must be a few words, phrases, or sentences about your brand that you want to fix in the minds of your target prospects. Our longest positioning was for Green Mountain Energy: "Clean, green power made from the raging rivers of North America, the prevailing winds, and the sun." The shortest was for Universal theme parks: "Escape."

The statement should be so clear, so succinct, and so powerful that once launched, it leads to a powerful brand. Examples include 3M, "Innovation"; Coke, "Authentic, Real, Original"; General Electric, "Imagination at Work"; Mobil, "Fast, Friendly Service"; Federal Express, "Overnight Delivery"; BMW, "German Engineering"; Wal-Mart, "Low Prices Everyday"; Target, "Style and Quality at Reasonable Prices"; Disney, "Wholesome Family Entertainment"; and Visa, "Accepted Everywhere."

When the product and communications do not address a serious consumer problem—which, sadly, covers 95 percent of all brands—they have no impact on brand equity, modest effects on sales, and a negligible return on the investment. There is no impact beyond the present.

Many marketers today argue that a strong product-based positioning strategy is a thing of the past. It worked, they say, back in the 1950s and 1960s when marketing and advertising were new, brands were relatively few, and positioning possibilities were unlimited. As

Table 5.2 Positioning Strategies (1950–2010)

Time Period	Dominant Positioning	Advertising ROI	Positioning Today
1950s–1960s	Mostly tangible, product-based	10%–15%	5%
1970s–1980s	Mix of tangible and ethereal	5%–9%	35%
1990s–2010s	Mostly ethereal, image-based	1%–4%	60%

Table 5.2 suggests, the view seems to be that image-based positionings were born out of necessity in the 1990s and that they can be as effective as the traditional "product difference/reason why" approach popular decades ago.

To this we usually say "perhaps" or "maybe," but we're tempted to say "nonsense." True, competition is tougher today, but for many brands in many product categories there are still important differences the marketer can communicate. Moreover, on average, these strategies are stronger—work better—than their modern image-oriented counterparts.

The table suggests that only about 1 in 20 companies/services/products/brands employs a clear, powerful, preemptive product-based positioning strategy and that most—perhaps 6 out of 10—represent ethereal fun. This in our view is highly ineffective advertising that diverts scarce resources the company could use to better advantage elsewhere. Nevertheless, if you're inclined to believe that an image campaign may work in your category, the research approach we describe later in this chapter will help you evaluate product (tangible) versus image (intangible) positionings long before you've invested the total advertising budget in another image campaign.

When business-to-business or business-to-consumer product and communications *are* designed to address a serious consumer problem—the other 5 percent of companies and brands—they can have a dramatic impact on brand equity, a substantial effect on sales and profitability (a return on investment, or ROI, of 25 percent or more), and the word is spread by trendsetters. All this, of course, affects the quality of life of consumers and business decision-makers, positively impacts corporate reputation and equity, has strong word-of-mouth effects, and has carryover effects for a generation.

Unfortunately, as with the beer industry, too many companies promote the wrong positioning or advertise a weak or confusing positioning. Three years ago, we undertook a research and development study for which we hired Dr. David Lloyd, a content analyst, to examine more than 400 different prime-time television commercials that we taped off air and provided to Lloyd to study.

He found that only 7 percent of these commercials communicate a clear and compelling selling message, which is why so few consumers can say anything about the two leading brands in the 50 largest product categories that one could begin to call positioning. As Philip Kotler points out, "One of the tragic flaws in General Motors' car lineup is that it designs cars without distinctive positionings. After the car is made, GM struggles to decide how to position it."[3]

If advertisers are not communicating a clear positioning, either by accident or on purpose, is it any wonder that brand equity scores in most product categories are declining the way we outlined in Chapter 1? We're continually surprised when a corporation like Coke, which has not communicated a clear positioning for its brand in a quarter century, seems surprised when both brand equity and sales have been flagging for years. We are always asking CMOs why they would expect sales or equity to be growing when they are not giving consumers a clear reason to buy the brand.

Some marketers respond by saying that positioning is an outmoded concept: "It's not relevant any more." Larry Light, CMO of McDonald's argues that so-called brand journalism has replaced brand positioning. By brand journalism, Light means that you don't need a single positioning strategy; you need a different story to communicate with different targets. McDonald's, for example, has five main market targets. Light could be correct about positioning in the rarified world of companies that spend $200 million-plus on communications in the United States. If you have a giant budget, perhaps you can afford to target different groups with different messages. Perhaps. Our own sense, however, is that McDonald's would be more successful and its equity would be improving if it could only figure out what it wants to be and imprint that in the heads of every American.

Over the years, any number of marketers have said, "We have to educate consumers on our positioning." For twenty years, the motor oil industry has tried to educate consumers that synthetic is good and actually makes for better oil. It produces a higher quality; it produces purity, more consistency, and better protection. All these are benefits.

But they keep using the word *synthetic*, which means nothing to most people and is negative to the rest. For ten years we've been saying that nobody understands that synthetic is good, our evidence being the unremarkable sales of synthetic motor oil. Call the stuff "HyperSlick," or come up with a name that people understand. The marketers say they want to call it synthetic, and they will just have to educate consumers what it means. But consumers generally don't want to be educated.

In contrast, we worked with a bottled water company and suggested it position its product as "Purified." Absolutely not. The marketer was convinced that *purified* was a bad idea. Their gut told them people didn't like that word on their bottled water. What was their evidence? Other water brands: Evian, Natural Spring, Poland Spring, Mountain Spring, and the like. We did some work and found that people loved the idea of *purified*. This brand was the only one that was in fact purified, and the word gave them a major competitive positioning advantage. After three or four years, Aquafina adopted the positioning and the brand's sales accelerated.

To those who say that positioning is dead, we say look around. Remember that advertising has a negative ROI. Brand equity is in a broad decline. New product failure is at record levels. Marketers who think brands don't need a strong positioning sales message are reasoning from their guts, not from their brains. So how do you develop strong, positive positioning?

How to Develop an Effective Positioning

Whether you are a small business or a major corporation, start with a clear understanding of the needs, problems, and pains (the motivations) of your prime target customers. It is a marketing axiom that the bigger the problem you can solve for buyers, the bigger the market response. But be careful when you do this research. The all-time most popular form of quantitative research for uncovering needs, problems, and motivations can lead you seriously astray (and possibly out of a job when the consequences come back to bite you).

In such a study, researchers create a list of 25 to 100 different product attributes and benefits and ask prospective customers to rate the importance of each on a five-point scale, in which 5 is "extremely important," 4 is "very important," and so forth. For example, customers might rate "Secure," "Reliable," and "Easy to manage" as the three most important characteristics of a new data storage system yet rate "Uses new X-1 process," "Makes you look smart," and "Lowest price" as the least important.

The flaw in such research is that it mistakes importance ratings for real problems, and marketing is about solving customer problems. People will rate the most generic, rational, and tangible characteristics in a category as the most important: 200 gig for data storage, has four wheels for a car, tastes great for a beer. Given that all data storage systems offer lots of capacity, all cars have four wheels, and most cold beers on a hot day taste good, these are not problems a marketer should address.

Further, people will say something is unimportant if they don't know anything about it (what is the X-1 process?). Most people hesitate to say anything that makes them seem superficial. (I want to drive a car that makes me look sexy, but I'm not going to tell you *that*.) And many people do not want to admit they are price sensitive. In other words, the leading questioning method for measuring motivations is seriously compromised.

The way we've found to uncover customer problems is to interview 100 or more customer and prospective customers to create a list of 50 or more "problems" in the category in which your product or service is designed (or will be designed) to perform, the more problems the better. For example, if Gary and Diane Heavins had done this kind of formal research, they might have learned that for many women, traditional full-service health clubs have the following problems (all problems they had identified through personal experience):

- Workout takes too much time.
- More facilities than I can use.
- Not comfortable exercising with men.
- Demands too much commitment.
- Don't like showering with other women.

If Interstate Bakeries, which clearly did not do this kind of research, had done so, they might have learned that among their target customers, white bread's problems included:

- Isn't "natural."
- Is tasteless, overprocessed.
- Does not have whole grains.
- Has a spongy texture.
- Does not stay fresh for very long.

Because this process is appropriate for all kinds of businesses, large and small, a child-care center might learn that parents in their target market see the following as problems:

- Too much teacher turnover.
- Teachers don't receive ongoing training.
- Difficult to extend care hours.
- No weekly reports on our child's development.
- Inconvenient hours.

Once you have identified as many problems as possible, ask customers and prospects to rate each problem on a five-point scale on four dimensions. If you are a relatively small business, 100 customers and prospects may be plenty. If you are a national corporation—Interstate Bakeries, Procter & Gamble, Pepsi—you need 500 or more and, depending on the market, may need ethnic (Hispanic, Asian, African American) or regional segments.

The dimensions to ask about each one of the 100 or more problems are:

(a) **Severity.** The answers range from 1, "Doesn't bother me at all," to 5, "Makes me furious."

(b) **Frequency.** From 1, "Never happens," to 5, "Happens all the time."

(c) **Brand perception.** From 1, "My regular brand takes care of this problem," to 5, "My brand doesn't solve this problem at all."

(d) **Quality of life improvement if this problem were solved.** Rated on a scale from 1, "Not at all," to 5, "A great deal."

Multiply (a) by (b) by (c) by (d) to obtain a "Quality of life improvement potential score" for each person you ask. Next, calculate the average for each attribute and benefit for the total sample and rank each problem from the most to the least important. This works best if you are able to focus the research on the most profitable target, the one we described in Chapter 4.

For example, the child-care center might learn that consumers consider the worst problem is that "Teachers are not well-qualified. They're glorified babysitters, not real teachers." Knowing what consumers consider the worst problems, the child-care center can develop a potential positioning like: "Best teachers. We pay our teachers above industry standards and offer ongoing training and career development opportunities to ensure our best asset—our teachers—are there for your kids day after day, week after week, year after year." This is a problem-detection approach to positioning and is one any marketer, small are large, can use.

Developing a Positioning for an Intangible

In some product categories, such as cosmetics, automobiles, and beverages, emotional triggers of brand or category are just as important—and sometimes even more important—than rational triggers. For example, the new Axe deodorant became a sensation among teenage boys when the advertising depicted the sexual attraction that even mannequins had for young men who used Axe.

A sophisticated approach to measuring what motivates consumers is a three-dimensional model that a large corporation could use. This is particularly useful in product categories driven by a combination of rational/tangible and intangible/irrational product attributes and benefits and features. The three dimensions involve dream detection, problem detection, and brand preference detection. Psychologists and human behaviorists have argued for decades that all human attitudes are formulated through these three components. Marketing science uses the three-component theory of attitude as a starting point.

Dream detection, the affective component of motivating power, assesses the interest level of each attribute and benefit. What do consumers truly want in the category, no matter how unrealistic or preposterous? Example: "It's very desirable to have a car that makes me more attractive to the opposite sex."

We use a desirability scale rather than an importance measure because people tend to report intangible attributes and benefits as being more appealing when they answer on a desirability scale. Ask "How important is it that the next automobile you buy impress your brother-in-law?" and people tend to say it's not very important. Ask "How desirable is it that the next automobile you buy impress your brother-in-law?" and people (some people, anyway) will say it's "somewhat desirable."

Importance implies rational decision-making. People want to give a response they think will make them look good in the interviewer's eyes. *Desirability* is less loaded. R&D reveals that people are more likely to rate intangible attributes and benefits as desirable than rate them as important.

Problem detection, the difference between dream and reality, is the cognitive component. This is the factor we discussed in the child-care center example. Interestingly, this measure is at the heart of what marketing as a discipline is all about, and yet marketing research studies rarely use it. Many would agree with Procter & Gamble: Marketing is the discipline concerned with solving people's problems with products and services for a profit. The definition, however, assumes you know the problem, and you do not learn that by asking people what is important. How important is it that your next car have four wheels? Extremely important. But all new cars have four wheels so it's not a problem.

Brand preference detection, the behavior component, determines which attribute ratings are correlated with, or predict, purchase behavior. In a typical study, we ask respondents to rate each of the leading brands in terms of each of the 50+ attributes and benefits being studied. Later in the interview, we also ask questions concerning purchase probabilities for each of these brands.

Sometimes we use a constant-sum tool, particularly for packaged goods: "Out of the next ten times you make a purchase in this product category, how many times are you likely to purchase these different brands?" The brands we ask about are the same brands we've asked the respondent to rate a few minutes earlier. It's then a simple matter of a correlation/regression analysis to predict the overall rating. This analysis, however, must be done for each individual respondent separately, not the aggregate.

For example, characteristics having to do with automotive performance are highly correlated with overall preference for BMW. Characteristics having to do with youthfulness are highly correlated with preference for Pepsi. Characteristics having to do with being good for children, fun for children, a place that children like are highly correlated with preference for McDonald's. In contrast, "old-fashioned" and "stodginess" are negatively related to a choice of a BMW. "Authenticity" and "nineteenth-century Americana" are inversely related to preference for Pepsi. And table service is negatively related to the choice of McDonald's.

The next step is to rescale all three of these dimensions *for each respondent* from −100 (overwhelmingly demotivating) to +100 (overwhelmingly motivating). Then take a weighted average of the three components to establish the motivating power of each attribute. Remember: Motivating power is not just about consumer dreams, problems, and behavior but is a composite of all three.

Marketing executives sometimes want to limit the study to identifying characteristics that predict category behavior (for example, the higher a brand's perceived reliability, the more ready a consumer is to purchase the brand). Why would a company want anything else? If a company knows what predicts behavior, it's done.

Not so fast. Although certain characteristics can be critical to consumers, they may not drive behavior because everyone offers the benefit (four wheels, brakes) or no one does. For example, ten years ago, you could have found that people liked and wanted a car that gave directions as they drove. Of course, they couldn't get this feature. Thus, the "electronic mapping" attribute could not have predicted purchase behavior because at the time no company offered it.

Because an attribute can be strong in one component but weak in others, it's important to evaluate it on each of the three dimensions to avoid overlooking potential strengths. Ideally, you'd like positioning items to excel on all three components: People say they want really it, don't get it with the products they currently use, and would buy a product with it if they could.

One simple way to do this is to weight each dimension equally for each respondent and average them. Long experience has shown, however, that for *new* products the desirability component should be ratcheted up and the leverage estimate ratcheted down, whereas for *established* products and services the problem scores are more important.

Motivations Are Not Enough

You cannot predict consumer reaction to positioning strategies based only on the motivations in the category. You also have to know how buyers perceive your product and competitive products. That knowledge leads to the brand strategy matrix, illustrated in Table 5.3.

To the extent that consumers are increasingly unable to differentiate competing brands in the same category by their function and imagery, companies have a positioning problem. The beer industry is unusual in positioning its products as unappealing to responsible adults. The more common difficulty today is that more and more brands are communicating the same positioning as their competitors; it is just hard to separate them. If we took a Chevrolet Tahoe SUV ad and slapped Ford Explorer on it, how many people would know the difference?

Worse are brands that, in an effort to differentiate themselves, move away from the core, essential positionings that made them great originally and begin to work on secondary or even tertiary claims. Here's an example: Instead of the "frozen lasagna based on Mama Italiana's family recipe," it's the "frozen lasagna that has the special probe that tells you when the product is cooked." People are much more interested in the recipe, but we're talking about peripheral things like the packaging.

Because positioning involves the packaging, distribution, pricing, advertising, point-of-purchase material—everything about the product—the basic issue is: What does a company want to communicate about its product to its prospective audiences? These are not only the ultimate consumers but also the distributors who stock the product, the retailers who sell it, and the people who buy it. When marketing executives think of positioning, they generally think in terms only of advertising, but that's much too narrow.

At the end of a positioning study, a company would like to have the sort of blueprint for action illustrated in Table 5.3. The motivating power extends from high to low (the rows), and the company versus the competition extends from superior to inferior (the columns). This hypothetical example compares IBM with EMC.

It is possible to rank-order each cell in the brand strategy matrix in terms of how much positioning potential that cell has as the basis for a powerful positioning strategy. If you find attributes that are highly motivating and your brand also enjoys advantages relative to the major competitor, then you have the basis for a strong positioning strategy. In this hypothetical case, IBM's "broad but nimble technology expertise" is both highly motivating and superior to EMC. Conversely, you may find attributes high in motivating power

Table 5.3 A Hypothetical Brand Strategy Matrix: IBM vs. EMC

		IBM Superior	Both the Same			EMC Superior
			Excellent: Could Not Be Better	Acceptable But Could Be Better	Unacceptable	
Motivating Power of Attribute/Benefit	High	Broad but nimble technology expertise	Extremely secure	Highly reliable	Self-healing	Data storage specialists
	Mod	Flexible	Can process huge volumes of data	24/7 tech support	Self-optimizing	Experienced data Storage engineers
	Low	Bundled with services	Handles multiple data formats	Multiple contract options	On-site training	Preferred by the financial services industry

in which your brand is inferior; this gives your product development people something to do.

Recent research reveals that if you know how motivating a dimension is to the target market and where your brand stands today—or could stand tomorrow relative to competition on the same dimension—you can predict the likelihood of market share improvements.

After you know what motivates consumers and how your brand performs on each dimension, you can rank-order your final list of category characteristics or potential positioning themes. Now the task is creative: putting together your strengths and weaknesses and developing a message strategy that puts your brand in the most favorable light, which is where the advertising/marketing communications people go to work. Although there is no fixed rule for how to write positioning/message concepts, one common approach is to couple a brand promise (often the key benefit) with its support and promise (that is, a product attribute). "IBM's Data Storage System is better in terms of _____ because _____."

We suggest that you write and test positioning concepts among 150 or more respondents. Companies often evaluate three to seven different positioning strategies in terms of three major criteria: purchase interest, uniqueness, and product/brand superiority. The company incorporates the winning strategy in all the advertising it develops. Better yet, the positioning becomes the underlying strategy for the brand in everything it does: point of sale, packaging, public relations, sales pieces, the web site, everything. It becomes the simple declarative statements that are essential to marketing success for any brand, product, or service. Other firms decide that, for their product or service, the positioning strategy is inseparable from the advertising execution and hence, rather than taking this intermediate positioning testing step, go on to create rough commercials and test them in a simulated setting. We'll talk more about this in Chapter 8.

We want to emphasize that without a strategic positioning analysis, a company or brand is just one more indistinguishable drop in a sea of products; with it, a company can identify innovative and preemptive positioning opportunities that set the brand apart in a positive way from all others.

Many Opportunities for Strong Positionings

In most companies, if products and services and brands are positioned at all, it appears to be in the minds of the marketing managers—not consumers. (Which makes sense; the marketing manager lives with the brand 24 hours a day. Most consumers have only a fleeting association—all the more reason to improve the positioning.) This is unfortunate because virtually every product has a wealth of positioning opportunities, characteristics to which consumers will respond. The list in Table 5.4 may provoke some ideas as a starting point for your company.

Table 5.4   Potential Positioning Opportunities

Attributes—A patch versus a pill in a pharmaceutical, a new ingredient in a toothpaste, longer life in a battery.

Benefits—Clears up your skin, stops joint damage, you can send pictures with your cell phone.

Target market characteristics—Would-be athletes, working moms, style-conscious teenagers.

Occasions or situations in which the product is valuable—Weddings, business meetings, social gatherings.

Celebrity endorsements—George Clooney, Tom Brady, Bode Miller.

Sports teams connections—Red Sox, New York Knicks, Pittsburgh Steelers.

Affinity groups—U.S. Marine Corps, Notre Dame, Shriners Hospitals.

Qualifications—Most rigorously tested, associated with UCLA Medical Center, top rated by J. D. Power.

Social responsibility—20% of all profits to go World Health Organization immunization programs, we support Breast Cancer Awareness.

Intangibles—Makes you glad to be alive, more patient with your kids, you feel more secure behind the wheel.

To ensure that the company's positioning efforts are effective, top management and senior marketing executives ought to be asking numerous questions:

- Do we have a clear, powerful, preemptive positioning strategy for our company and our brands?
- Describe our positioning(s) in words.
- Did we develop and formally evaluate a broad spectrum of possible positionings for each?
- Does our positioning tap into what we have determined to be the business's key motivators?
- Is this positioning based on something our company or brand can deliver?
- How well have we imprinted this positioning in the minds of our key targets?
- Do half or more of our key target markets recognize this positioning?

As Philip Kotler suggested in his remark about General Motors, the time to identify a strong positioning is *before* you develop and offer the product or service. Rather than design a solution and then try to find a problem, it's usually better to find the problem first. That puts you a long way toward finding your target market (the people with the problem) and your positioning (how you solve it). So we ought to spend some time talking about the issues in designing a profitable—keyword—solution to customer problems.

6

Generate Two Billion Product Ideas and Choose the Best One

Many managers use their gut when they think about offering new products or services. We once worked with the CMO of a national convenience store chain who wanted to redesign all the stores. He was looking for a consulting partner to help implement his ideas, which included a much more upscale set of product offerings (fresh fruit, gourmet coffee, organic cereals, fresh pastry, and the like). When we pointed out that his own research showed that the stores' primary customers were young men who came in for a pack of cigarettes, a lottery ticket, a Coke or a beer, and that the average sales ticket was less than $10, he was untroubled. He insisted that a new concept for a new target would change the game. We worked with him and his agency on research, concept ideas, and creative executions to develop a new convenience store in which his friends would be pleased to shop. It was a fiasco. Forecast to generate revenues about 10 percent greater than current stores, the new stores would cost twice as much to operate. They never changed the game.

We had the same experience with a hotel chain known for its moderately priced lodgings. They had recently designed and were starting to build super luxury facilities. We asked the CEO why the chain was building these palaces. He told us, "Because this is where people want to be." We asked, "What people?" It came out that the people he had in mind were his circle of friends and acquaintances. He would go to cocktail parties, and his friends would talk about hotels in which they stayed, hotels like the Four Seasons, Jumeirah, Mandarin Oriental, and the Ritz-Carlton. He wanted to make hotels for his friends.

The issue was not that the company couldn't design and build three- or four-star hotels; it certainly had the financial resources to do so. The problem was one of operations; the company had no experience in delivering the services such hotels require. Luxury hotels moved them out of their comfort zone entirely and into a situation in which they were unlikely to succeed.

We find this assumption—that our customers are like my friends—is a common gut decision, often made in a blink. When you use your intuition about who is buying your product, you tend to think about your friends. This is fine if you and your friends are, in fact, in the target market. But it's not so fine if you are the multimillionaire CEO, your friends all make a million dollars a year or better, and your target market is moderate-income families.

Rather than using gut instinct, we recommend using a more reasoned, scientific (and reliable) approach to generating and choosing the new product ideas you take to market.

How to Develop New Products

New ideas come from everywhere. Senior executives wake up with them in the middle of the night or the company has an opportunity to license an idea from another country or the firm does some new product idea generation sessions and comes up with dozens of possibilities. Unfortunately, we know that—having done a lot of new product work that concludes with sales forecasts—nine times out of ten the idea is no good. The company may change the game, but consumers refuse to play. The sales forecast is much worse than the company expected, but nobody wants to hear it. They want this idea to be the one in ten in which the product looks like a solid winner. Sometime they shoot the messenger, ignore the forecast, and introduce the product anyway. It almost inevitably fails.

Before sophisticated marketers introduce a new product, they have done serious thinking or research. They generally go through a process that begins with understanding the marketplace as it exists, consumer trends and consumer problems in the marketplace—that is, gaps between what people are looking for and what they're getting right now—technological improvements, new materials, everything.

Following this, they often undertake qualitative research. They may hold six to eight or, as we've seen in one recent case, as many as forty focus group interviews as part of "skunk works" projects designed to generate some really new ideas. This work is often followed by daylong creativity sessions, in which key company people come together along with outside experts and sometimes consumers who are likely prospects for the new products.

Following the ideation session and based on the knowledge of the market, the company creates new product concepts. The more concepts that evolve from this work, we think, the better. Some companies tend to focus on one or two; others might go for fifteen or twenty different ideas. Sometimes, marketers do more qualitative research to flesh out those ideas. And then the companies move into a screening phase.

In a screening phase, marketers often undertake a survey among two hundred to six hundred buyers in the product category, whether the category is toothpaste or business software. Each of these buyers is exposed to five or more alternative concepts, generally unbranded (branding tends to diminish discrimination between the concepts), and measured in terms of purchase probability, uniqueness, whether the product represents a solution to their problems, fit with the company's image, fit with the corporate brand, and more. Figure 6.1 illustrates this process.

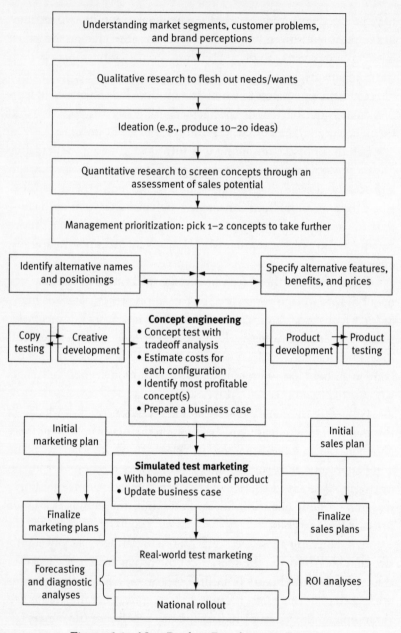

Figure 6.1 New Product Development Process.

Really sophisticated companies will take one or two of these concepts into concept optimization work, using a hybrid variant of choice modeling technology (also known as concept engineering) to evaluate more than a million different configurations for new product and service ideas. We'll show this process in a minute with Dunkin' Donuts. They test these among large, representative groups of customers and prospects; they employ modeling to create a demand function for each configuration; they then couple these sales forecasts with net cost estimates for each. The net effect is the financially optimal concepts.

These are turned over to specialists who are charged with creating the actual product or service. At the same time, the advertising agency is developing and testing alternative ad executions. The company then tests the products and later, using simulation technology, evaluates their likely effect on incremental revenue and profit before it spends any money in the real world. Finally after all this work—work that might have taken a year and a half or two (although the process can be accelerated)—management decides to take the product or service into test markets or, as is sometimes the case, a regional or national introduction.

The Concept Test—and Why It's Not Effective

New products and services, line extensions, and repositioning efforts regularly fail because many—perhaps most—fail to ignite consumer interest. New concepts excite brand managers (they should), but they bore most prospects. Nevertheless, companies spend hundreds of thousands of dollars every year on concept tests. Take the new product idea, describe it in one or two paragraphs, put a price on it, and show it to a hundred or more buyers in a product category. They select the winning products/packages/sizes for market introduction, then stand back to watch as the products fail to live up to expectations. Two years and untold dollars later, the product is gone, another example of poor marketing. What's wrong? Often, it's the testing.

Concept testing is plagued with problems. Almost every marketer/ researcher has done one (if not hundreds) of these tests, yet such tests often raise as many questions as they answer. We hear marketing executives ask questions like, "Is 19 percent in the top box ['Definitely Will Buy'] a good score?" Or they say, "We studied three pricing variations. How could they *all* get 19 percent in the top box? Is there a *fourth* variation we should offer?" Or, "If we changed the price [or the formulation or the packaging], how much will trial increase? Would it go to 30 percent?"

An enthusiastic marketing manager triggers the traditional concept test when she asks, "What's the potential for this big new idea?" The idea might be a new coffee-flavored ice cream or a new palm-size PC or, we'll say for the sake of this example, a line of bread mixes.

The marketing manager notes that the new line could be positioned two different ways: the mix for serious bread bakers or the mix for people who don't bake at all. Each of these two positions could emphasize one of three different benefits: The bread is nutritious, it's convenient, or it's fresh. The marketing manager has now described six different concepts. But she immediately points out that each positioning/benefit option could be based on one of four different product attributes, or reason-why stories: the yeast (yeast included/ add yeast), the mix type, the vitamin content, or the whole-grain Italian recipe. Now we're up to 24 different concepts. Moreover, price remains problematic. The company's experience suggests five different price points, so the concept has five prices for the serious baker and five prices for the nonbaker. In a 10-minute conversation, the manager has transformed one idea into 120 different concepts, a process that takes place all the time.

Worse, most companies are too enthusiastic to stop at 120 different combinations ("We'll offer multigrain! And sourdough! And rye! And French!"), and every new variable multiplies the number of possibilities. Sometimes, researchers who are supposed to test the concepts leave a meeting bewildered by the number of possibilities; thousands, hundreds of thousands, millions of concepts could be tested. But what company would pay for such tests? Even if a company were willing to test an enormous number, traditional concept testing has serious limitations. These include:

Sample limitations. Research companies generally employ small (75 to 200), nonprojectable groups of men and women wandering through shopping malls and willing to answer questions for the research or a larger sample (200 to 400) willing to answer questions on an Internet panel.

Measurement problems. Researchers often use purchase intention and other rating scale measures with unknown reliability and validity. The scales miscarry because researchers don't know if they repeated the study they would obtain the same results or if the results actually reflect what they want to learn.

Alternative possibilities. Few researchers ask what-if questions concerning variations in concept features and benefits efficiently. What if the package is red? Green? Teal? What if the price is 98 cents? $1.98? $2.98?

Ignorance of costs. In our experience, marketing managers seldom know the fixed and variable manufacturing and marketing costs, and researchers never know them. But without knowing costs, a manager cannot estimate profitability.

Limited models. Finally, few researchers offer a valid model of the marketing mix into which to feed concept scores to predict sales and profitability. Researchers present concept scores to management as if they were discrete pieces of information in themselves: "This one got a 33 percent top two box score, beating the control concept by almost two to one." That's nice, but will it sell? And if it sells, will it be profitable? Blank looks from the researcher.

Ways to Reduce Testing Problems

It is possible to reduce these problems. Begin with a larger, more projectable sample of prospective buyers (300 to 500) in more locations than the ones traditionally used for such tests. These people should be serious respondents, people recruited via random digit dialing and then brought to a central location, not the first bodies willing to stand still in a shopping mall. If you use the Internet, work hard to ensure that a representative sample of buyers participates in the survey and weight the data to reflect some known characteristics of the population.

A client once asked us to learn what was wrong with their new product, a watch with a built-in pager. The marketer had introduced the product based on research a year earlier, but the watch wasn't selling as forecast. The study itself was fine, but we found the problem in the research firm's sampling technique. The researchers screened for people who were already interested in this concept. They asked people if they bought watches. When a prospective respondent said yes, they said, "We were thinking about a watch that has a pager in it. Would you be interested in talking more about that?" When a respondent again said yes, they went ahead with the survey questions.

As a result, the study was based on a self-selected sample, all people somewhat interested in the concept. The research firm did not record how many people said they did *not* buy watches, were *not* interested in a pager, or both. The research therefore discovered significant interest among people already selected to be interested. Something like 37 percent of the total survey sample said they were interested, but the marketer did not realize that the total sample was only a fraction of all adults.

Sampling often goes wrong as the researcher tries to find representative people to interview. A client will tell the research company something like, "We're targeting people who are interested in prestige and have a need to communicate with their friends." That target is not quantifiable, but the research company will screen for such people anyway and test among those they find. The results are inevitably misleading.

Once you have a sample that can be projected, expose the consumers to the big idea: a full description of the concept, complete with the name, positioning, packaging, features, and price (it's surprising how many concept tests ignore price). Present the concept in its competitive frame, that is, with competing products sold in the market at their actual prices. The more a test mirrors reality, the more accurate the forecast.

Have consumers rate the concept in terms of purchase probability using a scale that is superior to traditional three-, four-, or five-point purchase intention scales for predicting likely market response. We've discovered through extensive experimentation that an 11-point scale predicts real-world behavior more effectively than the alternatives.

Of course, like all self-reported measures of consumer buying, this scale overstates the actual purchasing that takes place. Researchers sometimes assume all prospective consumers will be aware of the product (which never happens) and all those aware of it will be able to buy it (which also never happens).

Moreover, people are more likely to say they "Definitely will buy" than in fact do buy. This is true in all product categories we have investigated. We have examined the relationship between people's intentions to buy and sales among people who were aware of the product and who could buy it for numerous products and services, including a new fast-food restaurant, a brokerage firm offering, a premium credit card, new car dealer visits, delivery services, personal computers, a premium engine lubricant, a new technology at the gas pump, and a branded electricity company.

Usually no more than 75 percent of those who claim they definitely will buy actually do buy. This figure declines as self-reported purchase probability declines, but the ratio is not constant. Indeed, the higher the level of self-reported behavior probability, the greater the ratio of reported-to-actual probability. Also, depending on the product category and the situation, virtually none of the people at the low end of the scale—those who say there is some possibility they will purchase—actually do buy. All purchase intent figures, therefore, must be adjusted downward.

Concept Tests Need Validated Sales Forecasts

Companies typically go to a research supplier who purports to know how to test concepts. The researcher comes back with a top box number of, say, 42 percent. Often, the research supplier writes in the report's conclusion section, "These are very promising results, and we believe you should move ahead." An opinion about moving ahead means the researcher has done no validated sales forecast. If the research includes a validated sales forecast—or a reasonable attempt at a forecast with some credibility—the research firm does not need to express an opinion; the numbers make their own case. An opinion means the researcher was not able to come up with a sales forecast on which the client could rely. If management goes ahead with a product introduction anyway, they usually wonder what went wrong. The product tested so well. The top box scores were extraordinary. And here's the product six months later, growing dusty on the shelves.

The marketer must decide whether the sales forecast justifies moving ahead or not. Kraft Foods may need to sell a bazillion boxes of reformulated Thick 'N Creamy Macaroni & Cheese to justify going into production, whereas Annie's Homegrown Shells & White Cheddar may be happy with a much smaller number. No research company can make this decision.

It is possible to produce a reasonably valid estimate of actual sales (i.e., the percentage of consumers who would buy the product at least once). However, forecasting errors (adjusting for consumer awareness and product distribution) average around 20 percent, which means that if a purchase intent study predicted that 30 percent of all consumers would try the product, the actual percentage could be as low as 24 percent or as high as 36 percent. Purchase intent, therefore, is an essential but insufficient predictor of market response.

To improve sales forecasts, we developed two additional measures: one to capture affective components, one to register the cognitive components of consumer attitudes. The affective components are the individual's emotional, or intangible, impressions of a product or service. The cognitive components are a person's intellectual impressions of the product. Table 6.1 shows these measures.

By comparing people's reactions to new products and services with their actual behavior, it is possible to develop a three-dimensional, six-factor behavior prediction battery. We've found this approach reduced forecasting error from 20 percent to about 14 percent. If a survey predicted 30 percent trial (always assuming

Table 6.1   Affective/Cognitive/Behavior Product Measures

Affective Measures	Cognitive Measures	Behavior Measures
• First impression	• Price	• 11-point purchase probability scale
• For people like me	• Value	
• For occasions I experience	• Clarity	
• Likeability	• Believability	
• Overall impression	• Uniqueness	
• Helpful at solving problem	• Superiority	

Note: [b1 (Factor 1) + b2 (Factor 2) + b3 (Factor 3) + etc.] + b13 (11-point scale) = Behavior.

consumer awareness and product distribution), the actual trial result might range from 26 percent to 34 percent. More than 100 validation studies that compared projected awareness-to-purchase conversion to actual sales suggest that the method is reasonably valid. Not perfect, but a major improvement over using your gut to introduce intuitively appealing approaches.

Often, as we just suggested, the marketing manager is not sure what concept to test or how to describe the product exactly, what features and benefits to stress, or what price to charge. The number of possible product configurations seems limitless. But because each test requires a sample of three hundred to five hundred people, we're talking real money to test them all. However, trade-off analysis in its two varieties—conjoint measurement and choice modeling—enables you to evaluate many, many different concepts at one time.

In trade-off analysis, the researcher designs an experiment to test multiple factors—name, positioning, key benefits, size, shape, color, price, and more—by showing different combinations to different people. By applying a multiple trade-off analysis, the researcher can capture the main effects of, say, seven factors by exposing respondents to a relatively small set of concepts (often 16 or fewer). In practice, this means the research can evaluate thousands of potential concepts at a price comparable to a traditional test of perhaps five concepts. The researcher's real hurdle to using these models often has been company managers who don't understand the procedures and sometimes don't want to understand. Also, trade-off and choice modeling studies have their own problems. They produce unreal measures of sales potential reflected in a spotty track record in predicting real-world sales.

Even worse, traditional trade-off and choice modeling studies tend to be misleading when they focus on the *most appealing* product. But neither top box scores on purchase probability scales nor trade-off/choice modeling utility or effect coefficients addresses the key question: Will the new product or service be *profitable?* What you *don't* want to do is introduce the most appealing new product.

The Most Appealing Is the Least Profitable

Most managers believe that the more a new product appeals to the target market, the more likely it will be successful. By "more appealing" we mean the research finds that many people say they would buy it. This is a common approach and a common fallacy. After twenty years' work and more computer simulation runs than we'd like to count, we've learned that the most appealing concept—the one offering the highest consumer trial figures—is the least profitable. This happens because, at the most simplistic level, the most appealing concept is a triple-shot espresso macchiato with soy milk for a quarter. The product may have enormous appeal, but if you sell much of it, it will put your coffee shop out of business.

That's an example all managers grasp immediately. They do not always understand that their new product is like that quarter coffee: It has consumer appeal but it loses money. Or—a more common situation—the new product will not actually lose money, but it will not make what it could. This problem would be of only academic concern if it were not for marketing's heavy focus on appeal scores. The product manager asks, "How did the concept perform in terms of top box purchase probability ratings?" The manager assumes that purchase interest and profitability move together and in the same direction. The higher the purchase probability score, the greater management's interest in offering the product, a temptation it should usually avoid. Purchase interest and profitability do not necessarily move in the same direction.

Service Ideas Can Be Hard to Research

A new service idea tends to be more difficult to research than a new product, and a truly new product tends to be more difficult to research than a new version of something that already exists. Among packaged goods, for example, people can easily identify with a product that has, say, lower salt. They can identify with a new vitamin that provides 100 percent minimum daily requirements. These concepts are easy to communicate; people understand them, and they can make a decision to buy or not. If the product does what it says it is going to do because the concept is easily communicated, the company can anticipate repeat purchase levels. If a new product promises to be less salty, and the product *is* less salty but still tasty, people will respond to it and behave in certain predictable ways.

A new service, however, is often difficult to communicate to a market. People often do not understand the concept clearly, and their decisions to buy or not in a research environment may not predict real-world behavior. Not until the company actually begins to deliver the service does it know whether it is acceptable. The connection between a service concept and the reality is more tenuous than between a tangible product concept and the reality.

Similarly with a truly new product, it is sometimes difficult to communicate effectively what the product is all about unless the prospect actually has one in hand. Again, this is not always true.

As a general rule, it is easy to communicate a new product or service concept when something similar exists or when consumers are predisposed to look for solutions to their problems. When a company wants to introduce a truly revolutionary new product for which nothing analogous exists or for which the consumer need is not clear (or both), the research becomes much more problematic.

Table 6.2 shows where different new products would fall based on ease of communication and consumer need. The DIVX limited-use DVD disk and player failed because not only was the consumer need low (it was competing with videocassette tapes, pay-per-view, and unlimited-play DVD disks) but also the communication challenge was insuperable; the company was unable to convince people the system was worth the money. Although there is no necessary connection between need, ease of communication, and sales, as a general rule, the greater the consumer need and the easier the communication, the greater the sales.

We have worked with two types of emerging product categories, which we've labeled as *evolutionary* growth and *revolutionary* growth products. Knowing into which column your new product falls can help clarify your thinking about market planning. Table 6.3 outlines the characteristics we've observed between these two kinds of products.

Table 6.2   New Product Need/Communication Matrix

| Consumer Need | Ease of Communication | | |
	Difficult	Moderate	Easy
Great	Medicare drug plans	Run-flat tires	Cell phones
Moderate	401(k) retirement plans	Multibenefit toothpaste	Personal finance software
Low	DIVX limited-use DVD	Videotape club	Prepared salsa

Table 6.3 Characteristics of Evolutionary versus Revolutionary Products

Evolutionary Growth	Revolutionary Growth
Category characteristics (type of growth)	
Tempered (10%–20% or less)	Explosive (30%–40% or more)
Clearly a new *subcategory*	Clearly a *new category*
Low ceiling on demand	High ceiling on demand (often 40% of population or more)
Multiple brands don't necessarily expand category size	Multiple brands generate "contagion effect," which expands the category
Product characteristics	
Address minor/moderate consumer problems	Address major/serious consumer problems
Entries are seen as substitutes for one another	Entries seen as complements to one another
Perceived as another new product/"commodity" orientation	Perceived as a breakthrough innovation
Consumer characteristics	
Low involvement	High involvement
Benefits sought are moderately motivating	Benefits sought are highly motivating
Weak brand loyalty/willingness to switch	Tendency to stay with first brand if it achieves customer satisfaction
Marketing characteristics	
Word-of-mouth and public relations almost nonexistent	Word-of-mouth and public relations accelerate demand
Advertising/promotion important to competing brands	Advertising/promotion less important as category seems to grow spontaneously
Difficult to communicate	Easy to communicate

The Problem with Line Extensions

There is another new product issue: a new shape/flavor/size/color may take sales away from the company's existing products. This is mainly a line extension problem, products designed to fill niches the company is not currently reaching.

Management usually wants to be sure that when it introduces a line extension its version does not cannibalize the current brand, but we regularly find that's exactly what happens. The line extension is projected to obtain, say, a 3 percent share of market, a share that would be a major accomplishment. When we analyze the forecast, however, we find that 2.5 of those percentage points come from the brand the extension was designed to flank and only 0.5 percent is truly incremental business. Given the line extension's production and marketing costs, it's just not worth the investment for that tiny piece of new business, to say nothing of the parent brand's lost sales.

True, some categories—soft drinks, cigarettes, and beer to name three—are so big and so profitable that one could argue that a company does not mind if it cannibalizes its current business; as long as it takes some share away from competitors—even a disproportionately low amount—it can still make money. Anheuser-Busch may not care if Bud Light and Bud Dry take share away from Budweiser as long as it also takes sales away from Coors, Miller, and Stroh.

Of course, there are situations in which, even if a line extension *does* cannibalize the existing brand, it may be a good move. The marketer of a well-known headache remedy introduced a line extension designed to relieve cold symptoms as well as headaches. The company expected the new formula to supplement its flagship product, but consumers saw it as a more powerful analgesic and bought it, abandoning the company's flagship product. Because the old product was slowly dying anyway, the new version, even as it took sales from the flagship product, turned out to be a brilliant strategic move that prolonged the brand's life.

When companies talk to us about introducing a line extension, they say something like, "We want to know whether this is a five million unit brand." That is not the real question, however. The real question is, "What are the incremental units or the incremental dollars this product will produce over the sales of our existing products?" And the supplement to the real question asks, "Are these incremental sales worth the additional costs?"

Harvard marketing professor Clayton Christensen writes when a brand is extended onto products that serve different purposes than the original, "it will lose its clear meaning as a purpose brand and develop a different character instead—an *endorser brand*. An endorser brand can impart a general sense of quality, and it thereby creates some value in the marketing equation." But if the parent—or endorser—brand becomes diluted because it has been extended to many different products, consumers become confused and disenchanted. Hence, says Christensen, "the value of an endorser brand will erode unless the company adds a second word to its brand architecture—a purpose brand alongside the endorser brand."[1]

Marriott International did that when it began extending its brand to other kinds of hotels. Marriott Hotels & Resorts are upscale, full-service facilities. Courtyard by Marriott is moderately priced for business travelers. Fairfield Inn by Marriott is moderately priced for families. Residence Inn by Marriott is designed as a home away from home. Four target markets, four different brands, all "endorsed" in Christensen's word by Marriott.

We routinely run across two other problems in new product development: the concept that just won't die and, far more common, the concept that needs help. In the first case, everybody wants a new product concept to do well. The company's health and, more importantly, the careers of the people involved depend on it. Once a new product idea is born, either it grows—the business feeds it with resources and money—or it dies. If it grows, it naturally gains momentum, and the momentum may overwhelm all symptoms of problems ahead. The more time and money a company has invested, the less management wants to hear that the product is, at best, marginal.

There's also the concept that can't get heard. This happens when a product manager or marketing executive comes up with a product improvement, a line extension, or brand-new product idea only to be told by management, "We're doing fine. If it ain't broke, don't fix it." As we've said, however, most brands *are* broke. Although most markets are growing only at the same rate as the population, companies continue to introduce new products that take business away from established brands. Today, most entrenched brands, from cars to breakfast cereals, are slowly eroding as new products come into the marketplace. Management should not be asking "Why tinker with success?" but "How can we stop the slide into oblivion?" The answer is change the formulation or introduce a new shape, a new package, a new color, a new size, a new function, or an entirely new item, one that is more appealing to consumers. (You don't slash costs like Interstate Bakeries unless the result is a better product at a lower price.)

Computer-Aided New Product Design

We believe that computer-aided product design—which tests hundreds, thousands, even millions of variations, used in conjunction with marketing mix models such as the one Dunkin' Donuts used—is better than either test marketing or concept tests. For one thing, the computer-aided product is virtually always more profitable than management's favorite concept. In our experience, management's favorite concept, the one their gut told them to take into a test market, tends to be average in consumer appeal and below average in profitability. The difference between the optimal concept and management's favorite can be substantial. In one study, we estimated the optimal concept to be more than ten times more profitable than management's—the difference between a major marketing success and a catastrophic failure.

Dunkin' Donuts used computer-aided design to map its strategic expansion. Regina Lewis, vice president of consumer brands and insights, and Rebecca Zogbi, manager, say that although Dunkin' Donuts has extremely high levels of brand recognition across the country, the stores are heavily concentrated in the Northeast. Management was looking at a major expansion and wanted to know if the Dunkin' concept would work across the United States or if the corporation needed to make changes to ensure national success.[2]

Managers and employees had no shortage of ideas about what the company *could* do: serve sandwiches, offer catering and delivery, offer cozier seating, be more sophisticated, and serve soup *and* sandwiches. But at the same time, Dunkin' Donut's management did not have much information about what the company *should* do. What do customers want/need? What will make us the most profitable? With those questions in mind, the corporation embarked on a massive study that will influence its product and service decisions for years.

Dunkin' first looked in its rearview mirror, asking questions like: Where are we now and where do we want to go? Management wanted to understand internal ideas, motivations, wants, fears, opinions, and the like. It also obtained a broad understanding of external trends and consumer opinions of coffee, doughnuts, and competitors. Finally, it looked at consumer needs and opinions of the Dunkin' Donuts brand.

Next, it employed retail concept engineering to map the best route to reach its goals. Without going into technical detail, retail concept engineering is a new tool designed to study millions of store ideas. It can help management understand how different characteristics— layout, color, lighting, location, and much more—affect store use and profitability. What trade-offs do customers make in deciding what and where to purchase? Ideally, a company conducts the research in a realistic context so that the findings can be projected to the overall marketplace. And such engineering has a strong focus on profitability to help build the business case for or against specific offerings.

The methodology has several advantages compared to typical concept testing and trade-off analysis. Respondents react to product/service/price configurations in a competitive context, one that more accurately reflects real-world decision-making than other techniques. Interest and trial are based on a battery of measures for a more accurate way to predict likely trial. Respondents react to full-profile descriptions of the service features, including the price, which obtains more accurate reactions than if respondents saw only partial concepts. Finally, the company tests concepts as a fit/replacement for actual recent visits.

This was a vast, collaborative effort from Dunkin' Donuts management and its partners to identify all possibilities to be tested—ultimately more than two billion. They developed a list of all the different ways they could change or configure their stores and combined them, everything from exterior store design, number of drive-through lanes, inside design, service offerings, menu choices, type of music (if any), and price. The company combined these factors into a constellation of alternative store scenarios, describing each on a concept card with a visual and written description. Three of the concepts were:

> *Current.* "A quick, convenient stop to get great coffee, donuts, and other baked treats. The shop is designed for maximum efficiency of the counter staff with tile floors, plastic laminate counters, and very bright overhead lighting. Donuts and other bakery items are displayed on the back wall and coffee grinding and brewing are not visible to the customer. Coolers hold bottled sodas, juice, and milk—much like in a convenience store."
>
> *Café.* "A calm, comfortable place to relax and savor the coffee. Soft, warm colors—a variety of furniture with some soft chairs, stone counter tops, and interesting pendant lighting hanging over café tables in the windows. Behind the counter you see big old-fashioned coffee grinders, coffee beans in burlap bags, and fresh coffee brewing in glass pots. Coffee is served in real coffee mugs. Everywhere you experience the sights, sounds, and smells of coffee. Coffee beans, brewers, cups, and espresso machines are for sale to bring home."
>
> *Bakery.* "The store feels and smells like a bakery. You see baked goods coming right from the ovens to the display shelves. The store smells of fresh bread, cookies. There are wooden butcher-block countertops. The staff wears bakers' aprons and hats. There is a glass display case with a variety of pastries and savories displayed at the front counter with specialty lighting highlighting the merchandise. In addition,

warm items fresh from the oven are sitting on a tray available for sampling."

The researchers interviewed approximately 1,000 people (customers and noncustomers, ages 18 to 55, a representative mix of the U.S. population), "If this restaurant had been available during your last trip, how likely is it that you would have gone to this restaurant instead of the one that you visited?" A follow-up question was, "Please tell me everything that you would have ordered at the restaurant if this were the menu this last trip."

With the survey data (eight concepts, two-day parts, 1,000 respondents, 16,000 data points), Dunkin' Donuts was able to identify the effect of each potential restaurant and menu change overall and for different types of customers. Take two hypothetical examples (Dunkin' Donut's exact results are proprietary): Typical fast-food uniforms or khakis and a white shirt had no effect on customer trips or profits; a retro Dunkin' uniform actually reduced trips and profits; black pants and a peach shirt improved trips and profits. Similarly, silence or pop music had no effect on trips or profits; soft music improved customer trips and store profits. "Once we knew the impact of each individual item, we 're-assembled' all possible restaurant and menu combinations to forecast visits and spending," said Lewis and Zogbi. "We overlayed the cost for each individual item and calculated the resulting profitability of various alternatives." Table 6.4 is a comparison of different store concepts using this process. Note that although the most appealing concept would bring in an additional four visits each month per customer on average, it would also reduce profits by $150,000 per store each year. The financially optimal concept—prices are slightly higher, fewer menu items, and a positive rather than superior service experience—brings in only three additional visits per month but increases profits $200,000 per year per store.

Dunkin' Donuts has begun opening shops based on this research. The second to open features a new logo, a heated bakery display and merchandiser, an espresso and self-service coffee station, and two drive-through windows. The store bakes items, and customers

Table 6.4 Hypothetical Comparison of Different Coffee Shop Concepts

Concept Configuration	Management's Favorite Concept	Most Appealing Concept	Financially Optimal Concept
Naming	European Café	Dunkin' Diner	Dunkin' Munchables
Price	Premium	Lower mid-tier	Upper mid-tier
Positioning	Sophisticated	Freshest Food and Beverages	Family-oriented
Interior design	Cozy, wood-paneling	Open, airy, white	Open, airy, white
Music	Jazz	Pop	News
Drive-through service	No	Yes	Yes
Menu items served	Focus on one item and its complements	Extensive choices	Limited choices
Snack items	Yes	Yes	Yes
Service experience	Exceptional	Exceptional	Positive
Forecasted Performance			
Incremental visits/month	1.1	4.6	3.3
Incremental profits	$100,000	−$150,000	$200,000

walking through the front door can see the baker. New menu items include warm baked goods—personal-size breakfast pizzas, muffins, Danish, croissants, cookies, and brownies—offered throughout the morning and afternoon. Other new items include bite-size snacks with a pulled-pork filling, mini kosher hot dogs, and three melt sandwiches (meatball, steak and cheese, and southwest chicken).[3]

In August 2006, more Dunkin' Donuts shops around the country began offering hot dogs wrapped in pasty, flatbread sandwiches, and other foods designed to draw more customers in the afternoon and evening.

"We do about 70 percent of our business between 6 A.M. and 11 A.M.," said John Motta, who owns 10 Dunkin' Donuts franchises in the Nashua, New Hampshire, area, including one store selected for a makeover to the new concept. "From 11 A.M. to the next morning, you do have customers but there's really not a lot of business."[4]

The computer-aided new product design that Dunkin' Donuts employed helps marketers design optimal products and services. The optimizer itself has several features: It predicts real-world behavior and sales, it covers millions of concepts, it identifies the most profitable concepts—the marketer can personally play out what-if scenarios—and it offers targeting and positioning guidance.

Why New Products Fail

Earlier, we talked about the high failure rate of new products and services: more than 90 percent across a broad range of industries. In our experience, new products fail for five reasons.

One common reason for failure is the choice of the wrong target. The insurance company discussed earlier, which has decided to launch a broad range of products and services, targeted to all Americans with annual incomes of over $45,000 is a representative example. With no data to guide their gut-based decision, the company aimed too broadly and therefore diffused its marketing efforts. Every brand, every new product deserves a clear and profitable target. To do otherwise invites failure.

Another major reason is a weak, poorly articulated positioning, which we discussed in the previous chapter. The product may be fine, superior in many ways to competitive products, but if it is not absolutely clear to prospects what sets it apart from every other similar product in the world, why should consumers buy it? They don't.

A third major reason is insufficient level of new product awareness (and, by extension, the product's reason for being). The product may be superior, you have positioned it well, but you do not (or cannot) spend enough money to tell the target market about it. Most successful new products succeed because the marketer invests in communications of different types (advertising, direct marketing, flyers, web site) and is able to spend enough to have an impact on the target market.

The fourth reason for failure is insufficient distribution. In our experience, companies—even large, sophisticated corporations—routinely overestimate their new product's distribution. Even with slotting fees that should guarantee shelf space, not every new product appears in every store, and if the prospect cannot find the product, she cannot buy it.

Not long ago, we met with a client who was concerned that his product, distributed exclusively through chain drugstores, was not doing well. He thought the problem was weak advertising and wanted to improve the product's image. However, only 20 percent of chain drugstores carried the product. That meant the company's total market share would be around 20 percent if the company were able to obtain *all* category sales in the stores that carried the product, which is impossible. The problem was not image, it was distribution.

Some managers are convinced that even if they have limited distribution, buyers will be so enthralled by the offering they will go out of their way to hunt it down. This is rarely true. It happens with a fad toy at Christmas, but most of the time it is far more likely that no one will look for your new product than anyone will go from store to store to find it.

Perhaps the most important reason for new product failure is product/service dissatisfaction: the failure to meet or exceed consumer expectations and competitive offerings. Customer dissatisfaction means poor repeat purchase rates and weak customer loyalty. The product itself is inadequate.

This, of course, is easy to establish. Whether you're marketing a loaf of bread, a health club, a redesigned shopping cart, or a hotel, it's not very difficult to determine what percentage of the target market loves it versus just likes it versus feels neutral or negatively about it. And current methods even enable you to forecast what the reaction will be before the product is built and introduced in the real world. Only those products and services that we expect will totally delight customers—products that are demonstrably superior to existing competitors—should be introduced.

The remaining failures are due to a variety of causes, a questionable pricing strategy, cannibalizing the parent brand, a public relations campaign that is not integrated with the advertising program, a web site that is all about the company and not about the new product, and many more.

When the product itself is not the reason for failure, there's a happy corollary: Many new products that fail upon introduction can be resuscitated. Often, it's a matter of fixing problems with the marketing plan, adjusting the targeting and positioning strategy, improving the advertising, or increasing the distribution and promotion. This is good news. It means that a seemingly dead product can be revived to go on to live a healthy and productive life.

The gut approach to new product and services is to take management's favorite concept—or worse, the most appealing concept—and introduce it as quickly as possible. To ensure that the company's new product development efforts are effective, top management and chief marketing officers ought to ask these questions:

- Are our products/services designed with the specific target and positioning in mind?
- Before introducing a new product, do we examine and test a constellation of alternatives in terms of sales potential?
- How do we estimate sales volume prior to making a serious product or pricing change?
- Does marketing take manufacturing costs into account to examine alternatives in light of their profitability?
- Do we select financially optimal product or service designs or are we pursuing maximally appealing offerings?

Once the company has an attractive new product or service offering, the next challenge is to get the word out to the target market.

7

Don't Slip in the Media Muddle

In summer 2006, we met with the CMO, the director of media, and the head of public relations for a major package goods company. They said they'd been observing the radical media changes Procter & Gamble (P&G) has been making.

Until recently, P&G spent 70 percent of its media budget in television, but it has been transferring dollars into other media vehicles, including sports marketing, brand experiences, simulated word-of-mouth buzz, outdoor, and more. The visitors wanted our help in making their own media decisions on the assumption that P&G knew something they didn't.

Our first reaction was that they ought to be talking to our parent company, Carat, because we are neither a media planning nor media buying company, and Carat is one of the largest media planning and buying companies in the world. But as we talked, it became evident that our guests did not want to talk to a media planning and buying company. So we began to discuss the relative impact of media vehicles other than the traditional newspapers, magazines, radio, and television. We told them there is very little information today about what you get for sports and event marketing, what you get for an electronic billboard in Times Square, or what you get for buzz marketing (shills talking about your product in supermarkets or riding elevators up and down extolling the brand's virtues).

"If you and the industry don't have much information on the effectiveness of these media," they said, "what's the basis for making a change?"

We said, "You got it. You don't think that television, print, and radio are working the way they ought to, and therefore you need to change to something else and you hope the something else you select is more engaging. But right now, there's no way to know."

Traditional Media Are in Disarray

These are uncertain days for advertisers and most traditional advertising media. Network television viewing has declined 50 percent in since 1996. NBC, CBS, and ABC are down a cumulative 13 percent in the key demographic: women aged 18 to 49. Men are watching 12 percent fewer prime-time shows than in 2005. Cable cumulatively has 52 percent of the prime-time TV audience, but no one cable channel has a mass audience.

Between 2000 and 2005, U.S. newspapers lost 4 percent of their circulation according to the World Association of Newspapers.

The Audit Bureau of Circulations (ABC) has been reporting declines in most consumer magazine circulations for five years, both at the newsstand and in subscriptions, a decline exacerbated recently when ABC auditors threw out thousands of subscribers who did not meet ABC standards to be counted.

The big television advertisers are aware of these statistics. American Express, which was spending 80 percent of its marketing dollars on network television advertising, is now spending about 35 percent. McDonald's cut its network TV spending from

75 percent of the budget to 34 percent. They are not spending less advertising money; they are spending it elsewhere. For example, nearly half of all major advertisers polled in 2005 said they planned to increase online advertising spending by 30 percent in 2006.

Management is now saying that all advertising efforts are "above the line." They used to say something like, "We put 80 percent of our money into above-the-line activities; 20 percent is below the line." This meant, in theory, they could measure the above-the-line activities' effects on consumer awareness, attitude, and propensity to try, whereas the below-the-line efforts were difficult or impossible to measure.

Table 7.1 illustrates the paradigm shifts that are affecting marketing and media. From a media planning concentration to a marketing communications orientation. From the idea that advertising creative is the most important element in marketing success to the knowledge that consumers rule. From trying to figure out what happened after the fact to watching events unfold and making changes in advertising, price, and distribution on the fly. And from brand equity to customer equity, which we'll talk about in detail in Chapter 13.

Table 7.1   A Paradigm Shift

The Traditional Model	The Emerging Model
• Media planning concentration	• Marketing communications orientation
• "Creative-dominant"	• "Consumers rule"
• Inadequate knowledge of below-the-line activities	• Deep knowledge of all activities and everything is above the line
• *Ex post facto* analytics	• Real-time analytics
• Brand equity	• Customer equity
• Targeting/positioning neglectful	• Targeting/positioning obsessed
• Zero sigma performance	• Six sigma dreams

Although marketers are trying to make sense of the media muddle and are experimenting with different vehicles (and we'll talk about some of them in a minute), we have yet to see any solid evidence of most alternative media's effectiveness, that is, its ability to affect sales and return on investment (ROI) positively.

A 2005 survey of marketing managers found that 15 percent had no formal objective for spending on nontraditional media; 35 percent said in effect, "We don't attempt to measure results . . . we trust our instincts"; and the rest do measure, but most of these measures are impressions they have made, not the effect on consumers. We suspect American Express has no more insight today into the ROI of these formerly below-the-line activities than it had a decade ago. They just seem to make sense.

On the other hand, according to a Credit Suisse First Boston report, advertisers plan to spend more on Internet advertising because they view online as being accountable. "The largest number of survey participants believe that Internet advertising methods have the highest perceived return on investment, significantly ahead of any other category."[1]

And as an indication of how significant the Internet is becoming, Ball State University's Center for Media Design tracked the media use of 350 people every 15 seconds and found that the Internet is the dominant at-work medium and is number two in the home. The subjects represented each gender about equally, across three age groups, 18 to 34, 35 to 49, and 50-plus. The people were monitored by another person for approximately 13 hours, or 80 percent of their waking day. "Someone actually came into their homes and workplaces and had a handheld computer, every 15 seconds registering their media consumption and life activities," said Pam Horan, president of the Online Publishers Association (OPA), which announced the study.[2]

According to the association, consumers often use the web consecutively or simultaneously with television, radio, and other media, allowing it to offer significant support. The research found that the web extends the reach of other media, specifically that the web increased the television's reach by 51 percent in the morning,

39 percent in the middle of the day, and 42 percent in the evening. With magazine advertising, the impact is even greater: The web more than doubles the reach of magazines.

Efforts to Improve TV Ad Effectiveness

Both TV advertisers and the television industry are doing their best to hold back this tidal change. One approach is to work with the technology and run commercials that reward the viewer who watches. For example, KFC produced a commercial that contained a secret word you could see only by recording it on your digital video recorder and watching the ad in slow motion. Once you learned the secret word, you could go to the KFC web site, type it in, and receive a $1 coupon for a Buffalo Snacker sandwich. Presumably, KFC has some idea of the promotion's impact through the number of redeemed coupons. Because the secret word was discussed exhaustively on the web, however, KFC may not be able to relate coupon redemptions to the commercial's effectiveness.

Another idea is to manufacture television sets and embed code in television broadcasts that disables the remote control during commercials: no more channel-surfing during commercial breaks. "If the viewer tried to circumvent the system by recording the program and skipping the ads during playback," wrote Randall Stross in *The New York Times*, "the new, improved recorder would detect when a commercial segment was being displayed and disable the fast-forward button for the duration."[3] If consumers wanted the freedom to surf or to zip past commercials, they would have to pay an extra fee.

Although Royal Philips Electronics has filed a patent on such a system, a company spokesman says Philips has no connection to any products under development. As Stross asked, "What consumer would voluntarily buy a television designed to charge fees for using it?" But television broadcasters are unhappy that more and more consumers are able to avoid the advertisements that pay the bills. "Four years ago," Stross wrote, "Jamie Kellner, then head of the Turner Broadcasting System, remarked in an interview in *CableWorld* that viewers who used DVRs to fast-forward past commercials were committing 'theft,' then a moment later described it as 'stealing the programming.' He did allow trips to the bathroom as a non-criminal exception."

TiVo has more than 4.4 million subscribers recording television shows, 70 percent of whom skip past commercials in the programs they've recorded. (Some 8 percent to 10 percent of all U.S. households have a digital recording device, a percentage that is growing rapidly as cable and satellite companies offer the machines.) As one response to viewers avoiding the commercials they don't want to see, TiVo is making it easier for them to find the commercials they do (or might) want to see. The company launched an advertising search product named TiVo Product Watch in May 2006. The service offers advertisers a way to reach TiVo subscribers who are actively looking for products with advertising content and information. Initially, TiVo Product Watch carried advertising content from more than seventy advertisers in five different product categories: automotive, entertainment, financial, lifestyles, and travel and leisure.

The idea is that TiVo subscribers are able to search and select ads, which range from 1 minute to 60 minutes, from any of the five different product categories and have them delivered directly to their Now Playing section of the TiVo service. TiVo Product Watch also offers subscribers the ability to create a search based on a brand, and they will be able to subscribe to a brand and opt in to routinely receive video content directly from that company.

TiVo says that Product Watch enhances viewing experience for its subscribers by providing searchable advertising and content in the five categories. For advertisers, it says the service will "deliver relevant, targeted product videos to TiVo's millions of subscribers and in particular 'In Market' consumers who are more likely to make purchasing decisions." Tom Rogers, president and CEO of TiVo, said in making the announcement, "TiVo Product Watch will, for the first time, enable TV viewers to get commercial information about a product they are interested [in], when they want it, rather than through traditional TV advertising, where a viewer has no control of what ad comes on when they are watching a program. TiVo is committed to creating advertising products that deliver real, relevant results for our advertising partners while at the same time enhancing the TV experience for subscribers."[4]

Although some of the initial ads on Product Watch will be nothing more than 30-second spots that have run elsewhere, Kraft and LendingTree appear to see the value of offering something more. For example, Kraft will offer 20 different cooking videos that show such things as how to grill its Tombstone pizza, potato salad basic, or how to create a cantaloupe and Jell-O dessert. LendingTree features personal finance expert Suze Orman giving step-by-step overviews of different types of loans.

So on the one hand, advertisers are working to make it as easy as possible for consumers to find the advertising in which they are interested, and on the other, media are working to reach only those consumers who are most likely to be in an advertiser's target market. For example, cable companies are developing software that sends different commercials to different viewers at the same time. Invidi Technologies, Inc. has developed a software system that targets individual households. According to Invidi, the system enables advertisers to target their audience on ad-supported cable regardless of programming. If a 50-year-old father and his 14-year-old son each watch a *Stargate* rerun on different TV sets, the system can send a different ad during the same commercial break, say a razor and an acne cream. By matching an advertiser's desired demographic target to audience profiles, Invidi claims that it pinpoints the placement of television advertising where it will be most effective, identifying the age, gender, and probably interests of people by analyzing what they watch.

That may be better than nothing, but it still assumes that once you identify consumers their demographics—age, gender, family status, household size, income, education, occupation, race, nationality, religion, and social class—you know what they will buy. Usually you don't.

The Call for Engaging Media

The current hot word in advertising is *engaging*. Wanda Harris Millard, Yahoo's chief revenue officer, has said, "In a world with so much consumer choice and with all the challenges they face, marketers need to make sure their advertising works. . . . The issue is how advertisers can connect with people. It is now about engagement."[5]

But what exactly is engagement? How do you know if your ad is engaging? It depends on to whom you talk. The Magazine Publishers Association, which sponsored and published an entire study on engagement, says, "Defining engagement can be a slippery endeavor. Is engagement what the consumer feels when he or she sees an ad? Is it degree of interest? Does it predict how a consumer will respond to advertising? Some would say that engagement is all of the above, plus many other qualities as well. . . . As with accountability, the creation of a 'one size fits all,' universal definition of engagement is unlikely, particularly across media."[6]

In other words, without general agreement on the definition, each medium is free to define this hot new concept in a way that most benefits itself. This also means that a marketer cannot compare media on the basis of how engaging they may be, unless the marketer is willing to use one medium's definition, which automatically skews the results. Here, we will use *engagement* loosely to mean advertising in whatever medium that viewers, readers, and listeners actually pay some attention to.

We see a continuum in marketing attitudes toward media. At one end of the spectrum, advertisers are dreaming up new ways to force people to watch or listen to ad messages whether they want to or not—the interruption model of advertising that depends on intrusiveness and attention-getting power. This is the dream of disabling the viewer's remote control. These are the commercials before movies, the health-related commercials in doctors' waiting rooms, and the food-related commercials on screens at supermarket checkouts. It includes posters above urinals. All those ads you avoid only by closing your eyes and ears.

At the other end of the advertising spectrum are those ads consumers find so informative or entertaining they go out of their way to seek them out—the engagement model of advertising that relies on inviting and rewards attention. These are the special-interest web sites that have links to companies and products.

Newspaper supplements that offer coupons. Print ads in special-interest magazines—golfing, sailing, computers, photography, cooking, gardening, quilting, the list goes on and on.

At both ends of the spectrum, of course, the advertising's content weighs heavily. If the commercials before movies are entertaining enough, they may engage (or, at least, not annoy) the patrons. If the food photography makes the product look unappetizing, putting the ad in a cooking magazine will not engage the readers. We'll talk about advertising content in the next chapter, but this is a key point: A strong advertisement in the wrong medium is ineffective; a weak advertisement in the right medium is still ineffective.

We have been looking at the trend toward cost per thousand consumers engaged (CPMEs). This contrasts with the traditional media decision, cost per thousand (CPM) viewers or readers or listeners potentially exposed to a given medium. At its most simple (and hypothetical), if two million people on average watch *Desperate Housewives*, and if a 30-second commercial costs $200,000, the CPM is $10.

In an earlier, simpler time, that was good enough. Now life is not so simple. How many of those two million viewers are actually watching the commercials? How many have gone to the toilet? Surfed to another channel during the commercials? Recorded the show and zipped past the commercials when they finally did watch? The issue is similar for print and direct mail: How many magazine or newspaper readers flipped past the ad and how many actually looked at it? How many recipients opened and read the mail solicitation? And the important questions: How many of those who actually saw the commercial or read the ad were actually engaged by it?

An ongoing debate within the marketing community has been the relationship between television involvement and advertising effectiveness. Some researchers, as an illustration, focus on the viewing environment: the real-world situation in which people watch a television program and the advertising. Some consumers watch programs by themselves without many interruptions and without switching channels. Others view programs with family members or friends, eating dinner, munching popcorn, taking telephone calls, and periodically surfing. The circumstances surrounding the viewing experience, with its interruptions and diversions, play a critical role in the nature and extent of the viewer's exposure to programs and to commercials.

Although we are intrigued by differences in the viewing environment, we've studied the phenomenon only indirectly. Viewer environment is not a variable over which the broadcast networks and cable channels and the advertisers have any control. So, although knowing more about the topic may help our understanding of the process, it's limited in terms of managerial implications. Rather, we were interested in the effects of viewer involvement in programs on their response to the advertising. Does an involving program suck the life out of the commercials it carries, perhaps because viewers resent the interruption? Or does an involving program actually help the commercials, perhaps because viewer involvement carries into the advertising?

We designed a series of experiments and found that, in fact, the more involved in the program viewers tend to be or the more involved readers are in a publication, the more involved they tend to be in the commercials or the ads. Common sense has told most advertisers that readers who consume, say, *Car and Driver* or *Road & Track* are interested in cars and, by extension, the advertising about cars in their pages. We've learned that reader involvement in less special-interest publications such as *The New Yorker* or *The New York Times* also carries into the advertising. This implies that if advertisers identify television programs that involve their target consumers, they will improve—sometimes dramatically—their advertising's effectiveness (assuming always that the advertising itself is involving).[7]

Billboards Help New Products

We recently did a study of outdoor billboards for Posterscope, a global outdoor advertising company. In the past, studies of billboard advertising relied on traffic counts: How many cars actually drove past a given billboard in a period? If the researchers were sophisticated, they had someone standing by the billboard counting the number of people in the cars. Unfortunately, that still did not tell you whether anybody in the passing cars actually saw or noticed the billboard.

For our study, we screened people on the Internet to learn whether they drove more than once a week and, if so, how frequently. We brought up a map on their screen that covered the geographic area where they lived and worked and queried them about the roads they travel on. Once respondents told us where they travel from and to, we knew what billboards they were exposed to along the way. Knowing exactly what billboards to which people were exposed meant we could ask about the advertising content.

We found that for established products—a retail store, or Budweiser beer, or Coca-Cola—for which awareness is already very high, billboard advertising did not do all that well. If the message for these high-awareness brands is new or different, the effectiveness needle jumps. However, given that advertisers have difficulty figuring out what message they want to communicate in their 30-second television commercials, the probability of their crafting a compelling message and putting it on billboards is slim. But for new products, the study found billboards exceptionally strong.

In fact, we believe that billboards could become the vehicle of choice for new products. They are dramatically cheaper than most television campaigns. And because driving behavior is reasonably habitual—people tend to follow the same route to and from work, five days a week—a good billboard attracts a lot of exposure in 30 days. A new billboard with a new message tends to stand out because something has changed in the landscape. A new commercial or magazine ad does not have the same impact because it doesn't stand out in the same way.

Decide on Advertising Vehicles

What all the media muddle means to marketing, of course, is that the task of selecting one or more advertising vehicles for a campaign has become both more complicated and—if done right—more efficient. With audiences fragmenting, it sometimes means that a smaller advertiser can afford to reach the fragment most likely to be responsive to the company's message.

The first step for advertisers large and small is to list all the different vehicles, traditional and nontraditional, they would consider using. Ideally, this list starts with the media consumption patterns of the target market and is available from the work you did in defining the target market as we discussed in Chapter 4. What television shows do they watch? What radio stations do they listen to? What newspapers and magazines do they read? What web sites do they visit? What video games do they play? Where do they shop? What are their hobbies, interests, diversions? The more you know about your target market and their media consumption patterns, the more likely you are to engage them.

The National Guard, for example, was hurting for recruitment with long deployments in Iraq and well-publicized casualties. To attract more recruits, the guard doubled the ad budget, increased enlistment and recruitment bonuses, and added thousands of recruiters across the country. But without a change in media, the increased spending would not have been effective and the new recruiters would not have had anyone to recruit.

The guard dramatically changed the media strategy. As *Newsweek* reported, "To appeal to 18- to 25-year-olds, the guard offered free iTunes downloads for surfers willing to scroll through a Web recruitment pitch. That gimmick drew 200,000 young people in under a year, 9,000 of whom went on and talked to a recruiter. Magazine ads gave way to promotions at NASCAR races and rodeos. At one point, their agency bought up 328,000 pizza boxes and had them printed with photos of handsome guard members and a slogan that highlights a key enlistment benefit: 'You've paid for the pizza, now how about your tuition?' The boxes were given to mom-and-pop pizzerias across the country at no charge." Between the advertising and bonuses, the guard's net gain was 6,174 recruits in the first five months of 2006.[8]

So, although pizza boxes can be one medium, here is a laundry list of other possibilities, none of which we are prepared to pass judgment on:

Custom publishing, a company's own magazine or newsletter, is growing as a way to stay connected with customers, bring them fresh information about your products or services or both, and maintain loyalty. It is not new, is generally not cheap (although prices are coming down), and requires a continuing commitment. But a cable television company, for example, could produce such a magazine to publicize a month's programs and increase viewership.

Product placement. Again, this is hardly new because marketers have been putting their products into movies and television shows for almost as long as they've existed. What's new is putting products and the advertising into video games and magazine editorials. A new food magazine, *Relish*, permits marketers to buy brand mentions in recipes prepared by the editorial staff and buy product placement among staff-recommended kitchen and home gadgets. Although this violates the spirit of American Society of Magazine Editor guidelines, a spokeswoman for *Relish* said, "As long as your magazine is about entertaining and lifestyle, I don't think we should be held to the same standard as *U.S. News & World Report.*"[9]

Direct-response TV (DRTV). With marketers concerned about ROI, direct response is attractive: "Call now! Operators are standing by!" With DRTV, an advertiser can track phone calls and web site hits generated by ads. DRTV ads are also cheaper to broadcast, usually 40 percent to 60 percent of the cost of traditional network ads. Also, marketers are increasingly finding ways to use DRTV to build brand awareness while simultaneously generating leads and sales. "It used to be you could have one or the other," says Susan Rowe, executive vice of integrated media at Carat. "The pure direct marketers would tell you they didn't care about their brand, they were just looking at leads and response. Now they realize that branding adds to the life of a product and provides better cost per lead and response rates. And the brand guys are saying, 'If I can engage someone with my brand by getting them to a Web site or an 800 number, that is important.' "[10]

Word-of-mouth marketing. "We know that the most powerful form of marketing is an advocacy message from a trusted friend," says Steve Knox, CEO of Vocalpoint, a Procter & Gamble (P&G) buzz-marketing unit that it launched nationally in 2006. By the end of April, it had 600,000 mom members, all screened for their propensity to spread the word to their friends. They give sales pitches, hand out samples and coupons, and express their own opinions about the products. Although Vocalpoint is a P&G unit and it has campaigned for P&G's Dawn Direct Foam dish detergent, Febreze Air Effect air freshener, and Millstone coffee, it also works for non–P&G products. And early reports suggest it does work: Unit sales of Dawn Direct Foam in markets where Vocalpoint was tested were double those in other markets.[11]

In pharmaceutical marketing, a specialized form of word of mouth is critically important. Pharmaceutical companies attempt to identify the key physician opinion leaders in their product categories. They make a strong attempt to persuade these doctors that their product is superior—using sales materials with lots of facts and figures—in the hope that these "advocates" will become heavy prescribers, talk about the value of the drug at professional meetings, and encourage fellow physicians to prescribe it.

One-second radio spots. Clear Channel Radio says that these, still in the concept stage at this writing, are designed to remind listeners of a brand: for example, a car horn and a man's voice saying "Mini" as an ad for BMW's MINI Cooper. "It's not building a brand; it's refreshing a brand," commented Jim Gaither, director of broadcast at Richards Group advertising.

"You can't use a one-second campaign for something that generally has not been advertised before."[12]

Once you have listed all the possible and realistic media, estimate the costs for each. For large firms, these estimates can be fairly solid. For smaller companies, the estimate may come from talking to the local newspaper or radio station. But both kinds of organizations should generate estimates for the people who would be exposed to each vehicle. Then put in estimates of the involvement level. Again, for a large corporation, these can be based on research. For a small company, the estimates will be all judgment, but judgment based on close, intimate knowledge of the market and the prospective customers. Finally, one can calculate a table on the cost per thousands engaged and start developing schedules based on the ones that delivered the best results.

Front-Loaded or Continuous Campaign?

It is possible to test your media schedule before putting it into the real world. Thirty years ago, it was common for P&G marketing executives to launch front-loaded campaigns for new and repositioned brands. By front-loaded, we mean that the bulk of the media buy would occur early, often within three months after launch so that the brand manager could be assured that brand awareness and trial (i.e., penetration) would peak within the first six months.

Word of the value of front-loaded campaigns spread from industry to industry like the plague. The result was the death of many advertising programs that might have survived with a different media schedule.

We have been using simulation technology for years to examine the relationship between type of media schedule (e.g., front-loaded, pulsed, or continuous), product (new or established), purchase cycle (once a week, once a month, six times a year, twice a year), and other factors. The results are fascinating. Front-loaded schedules always seem to work best for fast-turnover new products (one to four or more purchases per month). They fail for slow-turnover brands whether they are new or established (those brands purchased only twice a year or less frequently). The reason is simple: A front-loaded campaign will fire up awareness when people are not yet ready to buy. It's like firing the furnace on a July day. When people are ready to buy because they've used up their stock of whatever the new product is designed to replace (toothpaste, plastic wrap, toilet paper), they've already forgotten the new brand exists. When fall turns to winter, the fuel burned in summer does nothing to warm a cold house.

These, of course, are just a few examples. The facts are that media schedules are often built without much science and are based on hunch, tradition, mythology, and experience gained at roulette tables. Yet simulation technology can be employed to provide insights into what kind of media schedule is best for a particular product in a specific market.

As we'll discuss in Chapter 14, the days of investing $20 million in an advertising campaign and not tracking its performance are over. An increasing number of CEOs will demand accountability for this investment. A good evaluation study (and the key word here is *good*) can provide not only a scorecard on how the campaign is progressing but a blueprint for changes that management can use to improve the program. Increasingly, as we'll see, companies are able to tie ROI down to the level of specific traditional and nontraditional communications vehicles. When this becomes common practice in the industry, the glory days of gut decision-making in media will be over.

Smart advertisers intrigued by the rapidly changing media landscape are beginning to ask serious questions relevant to all advertisers:

- What are all the media vehicles, traditional and nontraditional, relevant for my brand and marketing program?
- What are the costs associated with each of these vehicles? Are some like prime-time television that are simply unaffordable?
- What do we know about the number of people in our target audience who are exposed to each vehicle?
- Have we done research on buyer involvement and engagement for different vehicles? Unless we have, any decision we make to move to a new vehicle will be a reflection of our gut rather than our head.

- Have we calculated costs per thousand target group members exposed and costs per thousand target group members involved/engaged for all candidate communication vehicles to help guide decision-making?
- Finally, have we undertaken ROI analyses to assess the effects of every media vehicle in our schedule on revenues and profitability? As a consequence, is the media plan we're running the best possible?

Of course, deciding on the best media vehicles only takes you halfway; the next question is to decide what to say in the advertising.

8

Why Your Advertising Is a Waste—and What to Do about It

We just talked about finding the right medium, but despite what many practitioners seem to be arguing today, the message is still important. Unfortunately, as we discussed in Chapter 1, advertising is underperforming in part because advertising creatives are more dedicated to their gut instincts than to any fact-based marketing information. Here are just two examples.

The product was motor oil. The advertising agency's storyboard commercial began with two bikini-clad girls standing beside a Scientific Researcher: beard, lab coat, clipboard, Einstein hair. He smears one girl with regular, average-grade motor oil. He smears the other with the client's superior product. The two women get in tanning beds. (Remember, this is for motor oil, the stuff you put in your car.) Two minutes later, the Scientific Researcher returns to see how they're doing. The one who was covered with the client's product is gorgeous, beautifully tanned and bronzed. Just fabulous. When the Scientific Researcher turns to the other tanning bed, he finds only a pile of cinders.

We thought it was a joke. The agency thought it was great. They thought marketing to guys—girls in bikinis (think garage calendars), sex, and cars—motor oil is a little like beer, liquid in a can. Their gut said this was a great commercial and we actually had to test it. No one understood what the client was selling, and the CMO killed the ad concept before the company actually ran it.

A second example: The product was a frozen pot roast. Our client had developed a process to precook and flash freeze beef so that the final product tasted really great. We were involved from the beginning, from the early segmentation work to finding the needs, to screening, to product development, to launch, and to tracking first-year sales. The product was a huge success, a multimillion dollar business in 18 months. (Incidentally, at every step along the way, someone either in the company or at the ad agency offered up an intuition-based approach to the next decision. And at every step we were able to do research that refuted the gut-based idea.)

The ad agency came up with the launch commercial. A Cub Scout, on the street, races home for this pot roast. That was the idea, but it wasn't perfectly clear what was going on, particularly as the kid runs for almost the entire 30 seconds. Rather than helping, he knocks an old lady flat on her face he's in such a hurry to get home to his pot roast. The ad was unclear and mean.

The agency people, as you would expect, thought it was a great commercial. They didn't want it tested; they felt no test could tell whether a commercial is really good or not. The client, however, had doubts. She told the agency she wanted to test it against another concept. A plain, romancing-the-product kind of commercial. A happy family around the table. Show the product. Show it's juicy. Show happy people eating the product.

The agency grudgingly said fine, and they made up a simple little commercial. We tested the two and the simple ad beat the Cub Scout on every measure of awareness (those measures are in Table 8.1). The client said she wanted to go with the romancing-the-product concept.

Table 8.1 Alternative Measures of Awareness

Awareness measure	Operational Definition for a Bookstore (Online and Traditional Category)
First brand	"When you think of places where you can buy books, what is the first name that comes to mind?"
Unaided brand	"What are all of the different booksellers and bookstores you can think of?"
Unaided advertising	"Which have you seen or heard advertised during the past 90 days?"
Proven recall	"What do you remember seeing or hearing in the advertising for this company?" (Proven recall if a person plays back something definitely or probably in the ad.)
Aided advertising	"Have you seen or heard any advertising for Amazon.com during the past 90 days?"
Partially aided advertising	"Which bookstore . . ." advertises 'All books, for all people, everywhere' [slogan example]? advertises 'Next day delivery' [message example]? uses Regis Philbin in their advertising [spokesperson or dominant visual example]?
Fully aided tracer penetration	"Have you seen or heard any advertising for Barnes & Noble, which uses the slogan . . . ?"
Aided brand	"I'm going to read you a list of booksellers. For each one I name, please tell me if you've ever heard of it."
Total brand	Unaided and aided brand awareness.
Campaign penetration	A weighted composite measure of all of the previous, scaled from 0% to 100%.

The agency said, "We refuse to make that commercial. It's just not us. It's not our agency," and they resigned the account. Which, as it turned out, did not hurt the client's business one bit.

Test before You Produce

In both of these cases, the company decided to test the commercial concepts before spending money on production and airtime. If that were always the case, it could save companies dollars (thousands for smaller companies, millions for major corporations). Unfortunately, marketers themselves are often making the gut decisions.

Take our experience with the founder of a Boston nonprofit that successfully provides emergency transportation to low-income families. Andrew, as we will call him, told us that his organization had been doing some good things, and he wanted to expand its mission. Would we meet with him? Two weeks later, we met with Andrew, his chief operating officer (COO), his chief financial officer, and the head of this new organization, which we will call The Poor Person's Pantry to protect the reputations of those involved.

Their opening question was, in essence, "How would you go about finding out whether the idea of offering reduced-cost groceries to low-income, working families would be appealing?" Their plan— which they'd already explored in two focus groups—was to develop a network of supermarkets and chain drugstores that would accept a card that gave low-income consumers a 30 percent discount on their grocery bill. Present the card at checkout and receive the benefit. The Poor Person's Pantry would pay the difference to the retailer in a deal to be negotiated. People who applied for the card would have to pay a monthly subscription fee, but that would be minimal and based on family income.

Andrew and his team wanted to offer The Poor Person's Pantry card to an a priori market target: people who met an income requirement (it would vary by family size and residence location) and who did not have food stamps. "We want to offer many, many more American families the opportunity to buy good, healthy food," said Andrew. "So what would you do?"

We proposed a study that would test the concept's different elements—the name, the price, the offer, the collateral material, virtually everything about the offering—to learn what turned people on and what turned them off. Most important, we could take the results of this study, add the marketing plan, and use a simulation model to provide a forecast. This forecast would give our clients insights into how the concept would perform long before money was invested in a real-world test market. As we described this, Andrew seemed to be less and less interested. For a moment, we thought he was going to fall asleep.

He told us once again he had a group of investors who wanted to do something about the nutritional needs of low-income Americans. Andrew said this group was very concerned about the risk of this new business. They were thinking of offering it not just in Hartford, but in many other parts of the country, particularly where a lot of the target market resides: inner cities, reservations, Appalachia, and the rural South.

As the meeting was winding down, they asked if we could write a proposal. We said we could and asked them to send us the concept they'd discussed in the focus groups. They sent it a few days later.

The three-page concept plus appendices read like a long entry in the *Federal Record*. It went on and on and on. And on. It was not clear who was eligible for the card, what you could actually use the card for (it excluded not only items like tobacco and alcoholic beverages but also soft drinks, processed cookies, frozen entrees—but not frozen bagged vegetables—"and certain other items at the retailer's discretion"), and what happened to your eligibility if your income rose above the maximum.

We called Andrew. "There's no analog to this concept in the real world. You're talking about using television. You've got 30 seconds to communicate a story. This is a 60-minute infomercial." He was not daunted.

We wrote a proposal based on the meeting, outlining exactly what we felt the organization needed. We felt a six-month study would remove virtually all the risk from marketing the idea. The results would tell them whether the concept would fly, what needed to be fixed to make it fly (we personally thought some prospects might have problems with the card's name), and where would it fly best.

Andrew's COO called back. "We've got to do this quickly. We need the results by middle of next month. No later than the end of the month." We said you can't get the results that quickly. You need to take the time to get it right rather than do it over and over. She said she'd get back to us.

A month later, Andrew's assistant called to say thanks so much for the help but they were going ahead and developing commercials. They were going to run the commercials in three different markets to see who saluted. We said, "Nobody's going to salute because you haven't figured out what the concept is, never mind how to communicate it efficiently. You don't have a positioning. You don't know how to describe the idea or what media to use. You don't know the right media budget. People aren't going to salute and you're going to walk away, concluding the idea is bad. The idea may be bad, or it may be good, but it's certainly bad marketing."

He said, "Well, that's what we want to do because Andrew just doesn't want to wait any longer."

The commercials ran, the organization wasted time and money, and the idea died, not to be revived.

Communicate Something Tangible

Many contemporary advertising campaigns do not communicate anything directly, perhaps because of legal constraints or because copywriters find literal communication boring. Suppose (as actually happened) we want the agency to communicate that our beer has all the flavor with half the calories. Our research shows this is what our target market wants in a beer. The agency told us, "You can't just say, 'Half the calories.' You can't just directly communicate that it has all the flavor." Calories are a tangible characteristic, and agency creative people find tangible characteristics banal. They want to communicate something more exciting, a brand personality. Chuck Porter, chairman of Crispin Porter + Bogusky, was quoted as saying,

"Given that there is not a lot of difference among products in any given category, advertising is the differentiator. We believe that making a brand a part of pop culture [is more effective]."[1]

Not long ago, we sat in a meeting with a client and the advertising agency to discuss a new sports drink. The product has a number of tangible benefits: It replaces vital electrolytes, it is all natural, and it does not have to be refrigerated. The agency wanted to ignore (or demote) these for something intangible. Drink our drink and when you play you'll feel like Derek Jeeter or Barry Bonds.

As a result, television is filled with commercials that do not communicate anything useful about the products. We routinely ask people, "What's the main point of this commercial?" Besides asking you to buy the product, what is the company trying to tell you? On average, we find 90 people in a 100 don't know the main point, or they say something like, "They want me to know there's a beach somewhere." How many advertisers think that's a great message?

As a specific example, Gillette spent around $100 million in the first half of 2006 to introduce and promote its new five-blade Fusion razor. Commercials talked about "fusion" for about 20 seconds of the 30-second commercials. However, after all that, only 31 percent of Americans understood what the word *fusion* was all about in the Gillette commercials.

Only about 10 people in a 100 who see a commercial can remember anything about it a day later, and that's with a lot of prompting. Of those who remember the advertising at all, only about one-quarter can play back a main point that suggests an advertising message, one that reflects a positioning statement. That is, fewer than 3 viewers in 100 can remember something about the advertiser's expensive message.

Poor targeting and positioning naturally affect advertising effectiveness. If you are a middle-aged man, you tend to ignore Clearasil, OXY, and Fostex ads. If your co-op does not permit washers, you tend to ignore Maytag, GE, and Whirlpool washer ads. If you're a young mother, you tend to ignore Depend ads. But as we've said, many advertisers select target markets without sufficient thought and give almost no thought to a positioning. People not in your target market tend to screen out ads not aimed at them, as they should.

At the same time, alas, having a clear and optimal target and powerful positioning does not guarantee great advertising. We have worked with clients who spent hundreds of thousands of dollars to identify financially optimal target groups and a powerful positioning strategy, only to have it all eviscerated by advertising that bore little relationship to the positioning, similar to the two examples at the beginning of this chapter. These are the obscure, creative, or me-too message strategies that fail to tap consumer needs and therefore fail to motivate consumers to buy. It's not unusual to see different brands in the same category using the same message strategy, and not a very good one at that. All new cars seem to be driven on empty, winding, rural western roads; all pickups bounce across the landscape.

Jim Farley, the new vice president for Toyota, appears to be aware of this issue. He told *The Wall Street Journal* about Toyota ads that turned consumers into props. The commercials showed people of different ethnicities standing between Toyota vehicles with everyone smiling, laughing, waving, and basically having way more fun than people usually have while standing beside parked cars. On a scale of 1 to 10 on representing the consumer, with 1 being the worst, Farley rated the ads a 2. "I'm not hearing the consumer," he said. "These ads are about the company's agenda. It's just not relevant to the customer."[2]

In summer 2006, we completed a study of brand commoditization. We wanted to see if U.S. consumers thought popular brands in 51 product categories were becoming more or less similar. We found that in 48 of the 51 categories, respondents felt the top two brands are becoming more similar. That is, Office Depot is becoming more like Staples; ExxonMobil like Shell; Home Depot like Lowe's; and Best Buy like Circuit City.

These respondents felt that in only three categories were the top two brands becoming more different: AOL is becoming less like PeoplePC; Wal-Mart than Target; Dunkin' Donuts than Starbucks.

Advertising is necessary to build a brand. Advertising is, in essence, communication, and marketers will always have to communicate with prospects and customers. The marketer's challenge is to produce memorable and effective communication and place it where it can have the greatest impact. How do you do that?

Give the Agency a Clear Brief

We've given considerable thought to what a marketer can do to improve advertising. It has to start with the targeting and the positioning strategy. Although we talked about this earlier, we cannot overstate their importance. As marketing authority Philip Kotler has written, "To get it right the first time, the most important steps are targeting and positioning. If you nail these two components of strategy, everything else follows." We need to know exactly who we are going after.

The target, as we've talked about, should be the most profitable, responsive group in the population. The marketer can then identify the media vehicles that are most efficient in communicating with that target. The positioning should be based on those motivations we discussed in Chapter 5. Which attributes and benefits, both tangible and intangible, rational and emotional, are the most motivating to consumers? Where does the brand have or could have an edge relative to competitors? That is number one.

Number two is what message is likely to move these target consumers in the direction of our brand? As Igor Stravinsky once said, "I cannot compose until I've decided what problem I must solve. . . . The more art is controlled, limited, worked over, the more it is free and the better it is." In too many cases, the advertiser does not give the agency a clear brief. The company does not say clearly, "These are the people we want to reach and this is what we want the campaign to communicate." Too often, the advertiser says to the agency, "You figure it out." Not that the agency minds. Advertising agency account executives do not routinely implore clients to give them guidance. They're cool; they're a strategic partner. They can come up with the positioning, the approach, the strategic direction. Although one cannot blame the advertising agencies for filling this vacuum, it is not a good situation.

Problems can arise even when the company actually *does* have a brief and wants to communicate it to the agency, which virtually always has two groups: the account management side and the creative. Sometimes the two don't talk to each other or don't like each other or both.

In one case in which we were actually acting as the client's marketing department, we presented findings from a strategic study. We had a clear targeting and positioning for the product. The advertising agency account executives attended the planning presentations, but the creative people did not. We said, "How about bringing the creative people along next time?" The account people nodded, but the creative people never came. Presumably, they were back in the office being creative.

Nevertheless, we gave a detailed brief to the account group. They said, "Don't worry, we'll tell the creative people." But this is cricketers trying to explain cricket to baseball fans; something gets lost in translation. We were not surprised, therefore, when a month later the account people were back with a creative idea that had nothing to do with what the campaign should have been about.

Table 8.2 has two reasonably strong briefs, one for a personal computer manufacture, one for an auto repair business. They contain a description of the target, the positioning strategy, a comment on the brand's personality, and the emotional benefit the brand offers. After a thorough discussion of these briefs, a professional advertising agency ought to able to create several alternative campaigns that are right on the money.

We regularly ask agencies, "Please come up with several ideas. You don't have to go very far with any of them. Just come up with 6 or 10, even 20, two-sentence ideas, three sentences, four sentences, just a nugget. Then let's talk." The goal is to have many ideas, not totally fleshed out, but a variety of creative approaches to consider.

The agency people look us in the eye and say, "Right! We'll be back in three weeks with bunches of ideas." A month later, they're back with one, fully developed approach. It's almost axiomatic. They have a storyboard, a location, a celebrity spokesperson (and have consulted with the spokesperson's manager), suggested background and music, and a $400,000 budget just to produce one 30-second spot. We ask about other ideas. They say, "This is such a dynamite approach, we didn't think they were necessary."

Sometimes the agency does come in with two ideas. If they've tried really hard, maybe three. But the prudent thing to do is send

Table 8.2 Advertising Creative Brief

. . . for a computer manufacturer

Our **primary target** is senior executives and managers/analysts in large companies ($500 million-plus annual sales). People faced with the challenge of helping grow their businesses while reducing costs and making those decisions today, not tomorrow.

Our **positioning** is that we are uniquely capable of quickly creating network solutions that address the specific, complex needs of businesses with many offices, customers, and suppliers around the world.

Our **products and services** can be installed faster than anything our competitors offer.

Our **personality** is serious about our work but fun and easy to work with. Our clients love the products and services but enjoy working with us to install them.

The **emotional benefit** we provide is psychological comfort; we can and will help our clients make better decisions quickly. They can count on it!

. . . for an auto repair business

Our **primary target** is middle- and upper-income individuals in Shaker Heights and the surrounding communities. This market looks for high quality and is willing to pay a premium to avoid the common inconveniences of having a vehicle tied up in a repair shop.

Our **positioning** is that we offer both auto services and parts at one convenient location for all makes and models of domestic and foreign vehicles, providing convenience, expedient auto repair services, and customer service excellence.

Our **products and services** are more comprehensive than any competitive business.

Our **personality** is professionalism and expertise. We love automobiles, and we want yours to run properly.

The **emotional benefit** we provide is psychological comfort; when we return your vehicle, you know that it has been inspected and repaired by professionals.

them back for five or more other ideas. Nothing elaborate, just a thumbnail sketch of a concept. But often at this point the client jumps in, "I've already bought air time. I have to get on the air." The company would rather take a chance on something feeble—and odds are that first concept *is* feeble—to fill the air. Often it's a better business decision to run nothing than to run something pathetic.

Even when the rare agency is actually willing to come up with 6 or 10 or a dozen approaches, the typical advertiser's reaction is that it's too expensive to develop several ideas, too expensive to test them.

There is no question that it is more expensive to develop four commercials than two. But consider the arithmetic: Although the average cost of production of a finished commercial is about $350,000, it costs about $25,000 apiece for the agency to take an idea to animatic or photomatic stage and $15,000 apiece for a research company to test it. Two commercials, $80,000 in creative and research; four commercials, $160,000. "Whoa!" says the client. "Too much money!! Too much time!!!"

This is foolish because one can easily demonstrate that for a major advertiser the more ideas tested the greater the probability of finding a blockbuster campaign. The cost of developing and testing many executions is modest compared to the payoff the company could achieve if it identifies a great execution. Consider Figure 8.1.

The chart at the top illustrates a typical performance of a 2,000 gross rating point (GRP) prime-time campaign over a six-month period for a new product or service. Awareness starts at zero and six months later ends up at a shade less than 50 percent. This performance is based on an average advertising campaign. But what would happen if a marketer chose an advertising campaign that was three standard deviations above average? In the latter case, the chart on the bottom, 825 GRPs produced the same effect of the average campaign with 2,000 GRPs behind it.

Now, considering the 2,000 GRP campaign today costs approximately $30 million and 825 GRPs costs approximately $12.5 million, this suggests a considerable savings—$17.5 million, or 59 percent of the original investment—by going with the more powerful advertising.

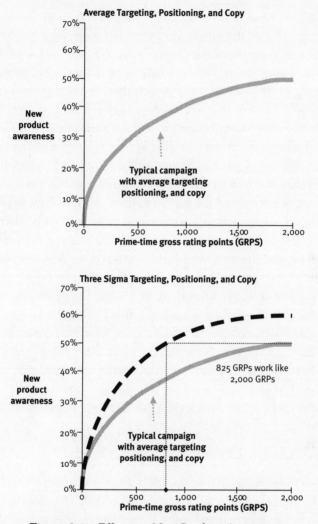

Figure 8.1 Effects on New Product Awareness.

Some marketers and agency executives argue that the reason they go with their gut is because advertising research is not a valid tool for selecting great advertising. Many point out that commercials are tested in rough form, often as animatics or photomatics, and therefore bear little resemblance to the finished product. Intuitively, this makes sense.

But 25 years of experience and research suggests that correlation between animatics and finished commercials is .87, which means that for all practical purposes, the inexpensive and the very expensive get the same scores (or, at the very least, turn in the same rank order performance). If you find an approach that, say, improves consumer awareness 20 percent over the average commercial, consider the impact on the advertising budget. If you are spending $20 million on media, the better commercial is like adding $4 million to the budget.

Actually, it's more than $4 million because there's a diminishing returns relationship between dollars invested and awareness. As a result, it might take an additional $6 million or $7 million to produce that 20 percent increase. Also, because sales tend to be correlated with awareness, the impact on sales of a 20 percent improvement in awareness is gigantic. Money for the creative development and research is well spent. But few managements will spend it.

Yet, because they do not, weak advertising provokes another crisis. Assume the company spends a third of the ad budget in the first quarter with no effect. That's money broadcast into the ozone with zero sales impact. Now management cries, "We've got to do better in the third quarter! Have the agency come up with another campaign." If the company had an effective commercial to begin with, it would not have to develop another one before year-end.

Devise Ads for Consumers, Not Awards

Why are so many commercials not doing their job properly? Aside from the reasons we've already touched on, we've come to believe that agencies design many ads to impress the client and the advertising community. The last thing many agencies worry about is whether it tests well against its target market. The first thing the agency worries about is how the work will go over with the client. To make the best possible impression, a commercial unveiling is highly dramatic, at the agency, in a conference room stocked with the drinks and munchies the client people especially like. A senior agency executive introduces the commercial with some earnest background: "We've thought long and hard about this product and its proper place in the market, and we pondered the brand's vision and personality, and that led us to think about the universe and the meaning of life." High drama. The lights go down, and the commercial comes up on a large-screen television set with the stereo volume cranked up to molar-rattling levels. Everybody thinks it's wonderful. They are knocked over by the impact, stunned by the color, the motion, the sound.

Then the research company puts the new spot in a reel with eight others, runs it in a TV program it shows to ordinary people on a Wednesday afternoon in a central testing location, and nobody even notices it. Or worse, the research company colludes with the ad agency to say everything's fine. We saw this happen with a client that marketed, we'll say, tires.

The company contracted with a world-famous director who had done some well-received animated movies. He spent a year and more than $1 million to make one 42-second commercial. And no, it couldn't be cut; cutting 12 seconds would spoil the whole impact. The ad conveyed the magical experience being a tire, zooming around mountain roads, up banked curves, and through tunnels, but the animation made you dizzy to watch it.

The company's gut told them this was so good. The best director, this amazing animation, the whole experience. Coincidentally, their Australian's subsidiary had made a commercial with a race-car driver, Peter Brock, who is well known in Australia and known nowhere else. He did a very nice 30-second spot in which he explained in his slight accent why the client's tires were really the best you could put on your car.

The client decided to test the two ads, and, as you might expect because of the way we're telling the story, Peter Brock crushed the animated spot on all the measures. But here's the twist. When the research company presented its findings, we happened to be in the audience. The research executive went through the numbers, and the numbers all showed Peter Brock was the better commercial. But in presenting the result, the researcher said, "But the animated thing, it really just feels better." Then he showed another chart in which the animated spot failed. His comment, "Oh, but the animated spot is right on your strategy." He did this three or four more times, going beyond the numbers to say how he felt the animated spot was the better commercial.

Finally, we put up our hand and said, "You have just shown six reasons why the animated spot sucks and Peter Brock is better, and you keep saying the animated is better. Are you going to use the numbers or are you going to use your feelings here?" No good answer.

As an epilogue, we came to realize that when this ad agency is forced to test, they strongly recommended this research company do all the testing. We concluded that even when a client is willing to test its commercials, don't let the ad agency pick the researcher. In this situation, it seemed that, in exchange for more testing business, the research company would say nice things about the agency's commercials.

How to Develop Strong Advertising

In theory, effective advertising is not that hard to produce. Take a motivating message, give it a memorable execution and proper exposure, and you have advertising that provides a healthy return on investment.

Because *message strategy* means different things to different managers, let's be sure we're talking about the same thing. The common theme is the notion, explicit or implicit, that the company wants to tell buyers something about its product, service, brand, or company. A message strategy is your basic selling proposition, the reason why consumers should buy your product rather than someone else's. What the company wants to communicate should positively differentiate its product or service from the competition's; it is your positioning. If the company differentiates itself well, it will ring up a sale. So how can the company develop a message strategy? We have put together a seven-step process that leads to powerful message strategies.

1. *Prepare a strong advertising brief.* We discussed this earlier, but it is important enough—and ignored so often—we should mention it again. A strong brief gets down on paper

the most profitable target; a compelling, unique, preemptive positioning strategy; the desired brand/product personality; and more. It forces client and agency strategic thinkers and researchers to comb through available research (and undertake quantitative marketing strategy research when what's available is inadequate) in order to rationally and carefully craft a powerful strategy. Supplementing this hard research with equal doses of experienced judgment and creativity should result in the transformational campaign we lobby for throughout this book.

2. *Evaluate attributes and benefits.* The next step is to evaluate in terms of motivating power and brand perceptions tangible and intangible attributes and benefits, usually expressed as a word, a phase, or no more than a sentence related to the advertising brief. These are things like "will help me live longer," "healthy tasting," "fresh tasting," "organically grown," "grown without hurting the environment," "no pesticides or preservatives," "good for you," and "very healthy."

3. *Tune up the messaging.* Convert the positioning statement into a single-minded, two- to four-sentence statement of what the brand stands for and how it's different from competitors. Some firms write these as two-part statements: a promise or claim supported by a "reason why." Also, some companies occasionally test the claim/promise to assist copywriters in evaluating alternative copy approaches. As an example: "The Good Earth food products taste great and are good for you because they are grown organically without chemicals and preservatives that mask flavors and harm the environment."

4. *Assess the advertising concepts.* Now skilled advertising copywriters enhance one or more alternative positioning concepts, bringing to life dry positioning statements. For example: "The Good Earth food products unleash the great taste of Mother Nature because they're grown and processed without chemicals. Equally important, because they're organic, they're good for you. As a result, The Good Earth

products will help you live a healthier, happier, and longer life."

5. *Pretest the advertising.* The advertising concept is taken to the next level in a rough commercial (often animatic or photomatic), print ad, or radio spot. Research shows that scores for these rough ads bear a strong correlation to finished ads.

6. *Test the advertising after it has run.* Companies sometimes do the same testing for a finished commercial after they introduce it and later on to measure possible wear-out.

7. *Track the campaign.* The company measures the entire advertising campaign (all media, all executions) over time to evaluate performance and determine what steps it might take to improve advertising return on investment.

People ask us all the time about advertising pretesting, which, as we've described previously, is an essential component in developing a powerful campaign. Ordinarily, we point out that there are a number of very fine firms in the copy-testing business—A.R.S., A.S.I., MSW, to name just three—that have decades of experience in helping separate the strong campaigns from the weak.

But we have uncovered two additional insights that we are happy to pass on to anyone who will listen. The first is that it *does* matter whether people like your ad or not. A seminal Advertising Research Foundation study found that the best predictors of sales effectiveness were attitudes toward the commercials; the more people like them, the better they work. But the same study also found that communicating new information about the product or service is equally important. Advertising today seems to obsess on the first dimension and ignore the second.

The second finding is that the type of environment in which respondents see your TV or print ad has dramatic effect on ad test scores. In one study we did, we designed an experiment in which people would watch a program and its commercials in either an "artificial forced-exposure viewing situation" (typical of ad testing) or a "simulated-natural environment situation" (typical of home viewing).[3]

Respondents assigned to the artificial, forced-exposure viewing environment sat in an undecorated room with folding chairs arranged in a semicircle in front of a video monitor. After completing a preexposure questionnaire, they were instructed to turn their attention to the monitor *only* and to refrain from talking with one another.

In the simulated-natural viewing condition, smaller groups watched in a room that simulated a living room atmosphere: carpet; comfortable chairs; sofas; a coffee table with newspapers, magazines, and snacks; and a buffet-style table with coffee and other beverages. From all seats in the room, respondents could watch a television set in one corner. After completing the preexposure questionnaire, respondents were told they could watch, read, eat, converse, write a letter, or do as they wished.

We found that simulated-natural testing provided higher levels of discrimination and validity in advertising test scores. By the nature of the viewing conditions, the simulated-natural test environment led to lower advertising response scores than the forced-exposure environment. At the same time, the simulated-natural environment resulted in more discrimination among commercials by respondents. Because respondent ability to discriminate between commercials is essential to separating effective from ineffective ads, the finding is key to better copy research.

To help senior executives determine whether the company's advertising produces the returns it should, they might ask the following questions:

- What financial return does our advertising investment produce?
- Are our advertising strategy and tactics clearly linked to the climate, the target, the positioning, the product, and the price?
- What have we done to ensure that the elements of our positioning strategy embedded in the advertising (also known as message strategy) are memorable and motivating?
- Do we evaluate many alternative ad executions using criteria that predict sales before going into the marketplace?

- Do we employ market response modeling approaches to help determine how much money to spend and when to spend it?
- Have we selected media vehicles based on their impact rather than the number of people they reach?
- Does our media schedule reflect knowledge of the relationship between type of product, frequency of product purchase, competitive effects, and other factors that interact to affect sales?
- Do we have a serious formal system to track advertising performance over time?

And, there's a question we hear more and more these days in planning meetings: Why don't we sponsor a NASCAR driver? Or a rock concert? Or become an official sponsor of the NBA? We'll tell you in the next chapter.

9

Sports Sponsorships Are Often a Mug's Game

Not long ago we went to a Red Sox game in Fenway Park with 10 executives, all marketing professionals, all friends and clients. At the ballpark, Clancy made a mental note of the sponsorships and signage, which ranged from Citizens Bank and Gillette to Volvo. During the seventh-inning stretch, he asked these 10 people to name as many sponsors as they could without looking around. How much of the advertising had actually registered?

Virtually none. Of the several dozen sponsors in Fenway Park that day, our group could name only a couple. By and large all of that advertising was wasted. And this was among people surrounded by the advertising messages.

As major advertisers have become disenchanted with broadcast television and other traditional media, sports and event sponsorships have benefited. "The sponsorship and events industry has evolved from the 1980s when we delivered signs and hospitality," says Mike Reisman, principal of Velocity Sports & Entertainment, a pioneering sponsorship marketing firm. "Today we are the funnel for reallocated marketing expenditures."[1]

According to SponsorClick, a sponsorship marketing consulting company, 54 percent of Fortune 500 companies reported that sponsorship is now "an integrated part of the marketing mix." Sports and event sponsorships are the fastest growing communications channel, with spending forecast to top $48 billion in 2006.[2] IEG, a sponsorship industry information resource, estimates that North American companies will increase spending by double digits—the first time since the go-go days of dot-coms—to $13.39 billion in 2006 alone.[3] A recent Intellitrends Survey from the Event Marketing Council reports that more than 22 percent of the total marketing budget is devoted to events, a number that is consistent across industries.[4]

This explosion in spending might lead one to conclude that these marketers have some significant, fact-based insights into the return on investment (ROI) and brand impact of sports and event sponsorships. They don't. Few marketers have a clue what sports and event sponsorships give them. In conversations we've had, in fact, marketers say they're not satisfied with their sponsorship ROI measurement capabilities, but at the same time they say they're going to increase their budgets.

The situation described in *The Wall Street Journal* article about tire manufacturers Michelin's and Bridgestone's Formula One sponsorship is not uncommon: Both companies say Formula One helps them sell more regular tires. But it is unclear whether either company is winning anything. Michelin spends about $70 million each year on Formula One, Bridgestone more than $100 million, people familiar with the numbers say. Neither company can point to hard evidence of a positive impact on sales and profits.[5]

We suspect there is none. Brahma beer in Brazil sponsored Formula One race cars for years. The relationship just felt right—young men and fast cars and beer all seemed to go together. But when we actually looked for the sponsorship's effect, we could not find one.

Brahma drinkers who knew the beer sponsored the cars were not influenced one way or another; the sponsorship affected neither their propensity to buy the beer nor their image of it. Non-Brahma beer drinkers who knew the corporation sponsored the cars were not inclined to try it because Brahma sponsored the cars. Brahma drinkers who didn't know the brand sponsored the cars showed essentially the same attitudes and behaviors as Brahma drinkers who knew about the sponsorship. The sports sponsorship did not help the brand, but it did not hurt it either (except to the extent that the budget could have been used more effectively on another activity).

All this may sound as if we are categorically against sports and event sponsorships. We're not. There is nothing wrong with sports events sponsorship as long as you know what you are doing. The problem we see is that many marketers are rushing into sponsorships without really understanding the issues and concerns.

The Argument for Sports Sponsorships

The New Century Marketing Concepts (NCMC) web site lays out the argument for sports and event sponsorship in a few paragraphs that mix the obvious with the questionable: "The essence of sport is passion. Sport is about athletes doing what they love and giving their sport the ultimate effort. As such, sport is a metaphor for life that brings to the fan an example of human accomplishment, struggle and effort, of seeing the best doing their best, of inspiring hope of success in life. Nothing is more important in life than having passion for what you do." Although one might debate the last sentence, let it go for now. Spectator sports, says NCMC, bring "the fan into the sport, giving him or her an experience they will never forget; an experience they can take into their daily living as an example of high courage and deep commitment."

Then getting down to business, NCMC says, "Sponsorship is a partnership between a corporate entity and a sports team whose goal is to leverage the power and the passion of sport in order to gain market share and new business for the sponsor. The tangible result of a sports partnership should be a return on investment for the sponsoring company of at least twice the value of the overall investment made in the sponsorship."[6]

The argument is that sports and event marketing enable you to build your brand around some kind of experience. You just don't go to a NASCAR race if you are a NASCAR enthusiast. You don't just watch it on television. You are really into the sport, and if a company can tie its brand in some fashion into the very fabric of the sport, it will do well. This, they say, is a lot better than just telling people about the brand. They can live the brand; they can experience the brand. We find this is a common story line without much solid evidence.

To have an effect, a company will run promotions, like free NASCAR tickets. It will bring NASCAR race cars to shopping malls around the country where people can actually get in one to see what it is like to grab the wheel. It will distribute free samples of its product and will try to get the drivers it sponsors to tell the story that without the sponsorship, there might not be any NASCAR.

This is similar to the priest on Sunday morning saying, "The contributions for the church are falling well below the budget, but I have great news. The local Dodge dealership, which is owned by Herb Sullivan—you all know Herb Sullivan—has decided to contribute two hundred thousand dollars this year to meet the shortfall. I am just suggesting to all you good people that if you are considering a new car, please go see Herb." Who wouldn't do that?

We are talking now about sponsorships that have high involvement with the audience. NASCAR is an example of that. It is not clear how many other sponsorships are like that. We were at a recent meeting of the sponsorship council of the Association of National Advertisers. We asked participants whether they had hard data on the effectiveness of what they were doing, and not a single person said yes.

True, it can have an effect. The Las Vegas–based Patrón Spirits Company, which manufactures premium tequila in Mexico, dipped its corporate toe into NASCAR sponsorship in 2005. "We try to stay limited in sports because of the responsibility you have as a spirits producer," says company president and CEO Ed Brown. "But if the competition is going to do it, it sort of forces your hand."

Rather than spending a ton of cash for the sponsorship, however, Patrón worked with a corporate trading company to exchange excess tequila-based coffee liqueur inventory for credits that it used to sponsor Kevin Lepage in the NASCAR Daytona 500. "NASCAR was not one hundred percent demographically a good fit for Patrón," says Brown, "but we wanted to see what kind of consumer we would pick up." Lepage came in ninth, and Patrón picked up 300 hits on the web site from consumers who said they noticed the company's sponsorship and had tried and enjoyed its tequila. This was enough encouragement for Brown to sponsor five more races. "I want to see how the next five races go, but it did seem to open up a whole other demographic that we didn't account for."[7]

We think that Brown is looking at Patrón's sports sponsorship correctly: as an experiment, not as a significant marketing plan element. If the company is satisfied with the responses the NASCAR sponsorship provokes, it should continue. If the responses level off or degrade, Patrón should probably revisit the question—regardless of what the competition is doing. The problem we see in many companies is that they don't know what their sponsorships are doing for them.

Another issue we see is that many companies are not spending enough to make the sales numbers pop out. If Green Mountain Power, for example, spends $90 million on marketing nationally, and it wanted to measure the effects of a James Taylor/Kenny Loggins concert in Philadelphia on overall sales, the numbers would be lost in the noise.

On the other hand, if a national advertiser such as Visa, spending more than $100 million a year on communication, spends 24 percent of the marketing budget on sports and event sponsorship today, an ROI analysis will be able to detect the effect. One could almost make a rule of thumb: If your marketing budget is sizable—say more than $25 million a year—and if you are investing a significant portion of that budget—say 20 percent or more—in some traditional or nontraditional media vehicle, then you can use econometric modeling to assess the effect of that investment on sales. If there is an effect, you'll see it. If there is no an effect, you can conclude it doesn't work.

If your total marketing budget is, say, $3 million and you put 2 percent into a particular sponsorship or event, you won't know whether it was effective or not, because the sales bump you get is so small it's lost. We believe you're far better off putting the money into marketing activities that are both effective and measurable.

The Problem with Head Counts

The majority of marketers today rely on head counts or "eyeballs exposed" to measure the return on sports and event sponsorships. According to *Promo Magazine*'s 2005 Event Marketing Survey, 51 percent of marketers measure return by head counts.[8] The problem is head counts are little better than the total audience reached for a TV buy or total circulation figures for a magazine or a newspaper. How many of that total actually registered the advertising? Head counts offer little if any information about the short- and long-term effects of a sponsorship and no insight into how it's working. Is awareness translating to brand preference, and if not, why not? (And what kind of awareness are we talking about anyway? See the discussion on awareness in Chapter 8.)

Following the NBA finals in 2006, we interviewed 1,133 adults and asked if they had watched the recently completed NBA finals and whether they considered themselves fans. Some 39 percent said they had seen at least some of the finals and about a third considered themselves fans.

We then asked those who had watched to name the official mobile/cell phone, automobile, fast-food restaurant, airline, and wireless phone service of the NBA without any clues. Even among fans, unaided awareness was extremely low. With the exception of McDonald's, which enjoyed a 34 percent level of awareness, all other official sponsor brands had awareness scores under 10 percent. Nokia had a 2 percent level of awareness, and Toyota a 5 percent. On an aided basis, the scores were higher: 12 percent for Toyota, 24 percent for Nokia, 27 percent for Southwest Airlines and T-Mobile, and 43 percent for McDonald's. Given that these scores were reported among NBA fans who watched one or more games, the findings have to be disappointing to these sponsors.

In some cases, far more fans believed that a competitor was the sponsor. For example, Toyota enjoyed a 12 percent level of sponsorship recognition, whereas Chevrolet, a nonsponsor, scored higher with 27 percent. Nokia did better with a 24 percent sponsorship recognition among fans; but Motorola, which had not sponsored the games, had a 30 percent. All in all, awareness of NBA sponsorship was not particularly strong, and viewers experienced massive confusion as to who was sponsoring what.

The results of New York research firm NOP World's Power of Olympics Advertising report are not an unusual finding. When asked if they could name *any* official Olympic sponsor, only 33 percent of U.S. consumers could name a single one on an unaided basis. McDonald's, a perennial sponsor, fared the best with a 10 percent recall. On an aided basis, 53 percent of consumers recalled Nike and Visa as sponsors.[9] Great news for Nike, which was not an Olympic sponsor, but not so great for Visa and the other 11 official sponsors that each paid upward of $50 million for the rights as well as significant dollars on advertising during the games to promote the sponsorship. Most sports and event sponsorships may prove to be just as disappointing in the ROI department as the traditional media they're supposed to replace, even when the value is puffed up by funny accounting.

Here's what we mean by that. Citibank feels it received $29.2 million in exposure by being a so-called presenting sponsor of the January 2006 Rose Bowl game. To come up with that figure, take the time that Citibank's logo "appeared clear and in-focus"—17 minutes, 46 seconds—and the number of times the announcers mentioned the company's name—15—and multiply all this by the cost of a 30-second commercial in the program. Using the same logic, FedEx was told it obtained $57.5 million in exposure out of 54 mentions and 30 minutes of footage when its logo was on the screen during the 2005 Orange Bowl game.[10] It is hard to believe that sophisticated marketing executives take these results seriously, but apparently they do.

Certainly you never expect 100 percent of the people who are exposed to be affected by these things, so the question is what percentage do you need? Not 100 percent, not even expect 50 percent.

But what percentage do you think should be affected by this event, this sponsorship?

When companies come to us, we explain how we can track the effectiveness and tell them we will come back with some numbers. But we always want them to say what numbers they would like to see before we do the research. This is not to give us a target to hit, but to give them a standard against which to measure the results. Does the CMO expect, as an example, the unaided awareness figure to be 9 percent, 18 percent, 36 percent as a result of the sponsorship?

Most marketing executives don't have that number in their heads. They do not institute these programs thinking, "Let's bring unaided awareness (or any other measure) from X to Y." They haven't thought about it, so they don't have a number when we ask the question. Ask what they hope or expect a sports or event sponsorship to accomplish, and they have to think about it for the first time. Then when we get a number, at least we can compare that number to what they thought, or hoped, they would get. Usually, the actual number is only about a third of what they thought they would get.

Though their current spending habits might seem to indicate otherwise, we doubt most marketers are completely confident or comfortable making decisions about sports and event sponsorships based on little more than the gut instinct that they will perform better than TV and other traditional media. We know CEOs and CFOs sure aren't. With little information about the performance of sports and event sponsorships, marketers have no guidance on steps they can take to fix problems and improve performance. That, however, is changing.

Converting Faith to Fact

As Mike Reisman at Velocity Sports & Entertainment put it, "Marketers have enjoyed a significant growth in sponsorship and event options to marry to the needs of their brands. However, this also puts a premium on the process of properly identifying investments for their event and sponsorship portfolios."[11] Clearly, marketers need and want to know what are we getting/will we get/did we get out of this sponsorship and how can we improve performance of our sponsorship and event marketing programs?

"Developing pre-and post-event measuring attributes has become a full-time job for many brands," according to *Promo Magazine*. ING, a financial services company and home of the Orange Savings Account, for instance, spent significant time developing a research process to evaluate sports and event sponsorships that it continues to fine-tune. The company's head of advertising and sponsorships said, "We wouldn't be able to justify the sponsorships without some level of effectiveness. We measure every move we make."[12] Figure 9.1 illustrates a process to evaluate sponsorship and event programs.

The good news for marketers is that there are several approaches that go well beyond one-dimensional circulation-type data, approaches that can be applied before, during, and after a sponsorship or event. The type of research a company can do is dictated more by sponsorship size, company budget, and availability of existing sales and tracking data than by a lack of readily available tools. Again, a small- to medium-size company is probably better off not even trying to play on this field than spending the money on research that will likely show no or inconclusive effects.

Start by Testing the Concept

Before they invest substantial time and money in new product introductions, companies have tested new product and service concepts for decades. Given the explosion in the number of global, national, regional, and local sponsorship opportunities (indeed, every organization from the Fédération Internationale de Football Association to your local Little League is looking for sponsors), similar testing can guide sports and event sponsorship investment decisions.

To screen different sponsorship ideas, expose members of the target audience to a sponsorship concept, just as they might be in a new product or service test, and ask them about the event, the sponsoring brand, and brand preferences. For example, study participants

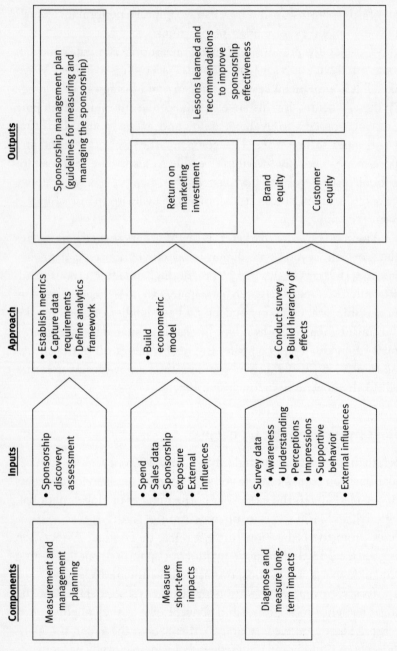

Figure 9.1 Inputs/outputs in Sponsorship Measures.

might read a one- to two-paragraph description of mortgage company Ameriquest's sponsorship of the Rolling Stones tour and afterward answer questions about what they think of the Rolling Stones, how they feel about Ameriquest sponsoring it, and how likely they are to contact Ameriquest the next time they're in the market for a mortgage.

As with traditional concept testing of products and services, the drawback to testing only a few concepts is that the result rests on having picked the best few to test in the first place. Better to test different *configurations* of sponsorships—not just a few concepts individually—in a competitive context and use a battery of measures to capture the likely effects on consumer behavior and, ultimately, ROI. Ameriquest might test three different bands it could sponsor (the Rolling Stones, U2, Green Day), along with four different NCAA sports (football, basketball, baseball, women's gymnastics), five entertainment events (the American Music Awards, the Academy Awards, the network premiere of a Hollywood blockbuster, the Golden Globe Awards, the network broadcast of a Faith Hill holiday concert), and all potential configurations of these to identify the options that have the biggest impact.

Companies can gauge the potential interactions between different options—the effectiveness of the Rolling Stones concert sponsorship, for example, may be enhanced (or hurt by) involvement with the American Music Awards. Although a CMO could employ the more traditional concept test as a go/no-go decision-making tool for an opportunity that's already on the table, the goal with this more sophisticated concept testing is to find the best opportunities *and* lineup of opportunities from the constellation of possibilities.

For many sports and event sponsorships, it is possible for companies to measure the effect on sales, to gauge short-term ROI of the sponsorship, to compare the relative ROI of sports and event sponsorships in terms of sales with other marketing mix elements (TV, magazine, promotions, and the like), and to understand the interactions between sponsorship activity (the advertising that promotes the brand's relationship to the sponsorship) and other marketing investments. A company might discover, for instance, that print advertising, particularly in magazines, complements the performance of sponsorship-related advertising. To do this, "cutting-edge marketers are increasingly turning to marketing mix modeling in order to demonstrate financial proof-of-performance to bottom-line-oriented CEOs and CFOs," says John Nardone, executive vice president at sister company MMA, the marketing effectiveness measurement firm.

Marketing mix modeling is a mathematical representation of a brand or product's business environment that isolates each factor—whether a controllable marketing element or an environmental factor such as interest rates or weather—that has a significant impact on sales (or leads). Marketers can use the tool to look backward to understand the ROI of the marketing factors or forward to forecast future performance. One Fortune 500 health and beauty aids company is measuring the ROI of its NASCAR sponsorship, for instance, to determine how much to spend next year. A major consumer packaged goods company has measured the ROI of its NCAA sponsorship and the interactions between this sponsorship and other media vehicles to optimize its spending across the marketing mix.

To model the short-term ROI of a sponsorship requires three elements:

1. *Weight*. Sponsorship activities should have a significant budget (that is, more than $500,000) and account for at least 2 percent of the overall marketing budget.
2. *Variability*. Sponsorship activities must vary over time. A corporation that has sponsored the same team or event many years in a row will have difficulty measuring the activity's impact.
3. *Quality data*. "There are many moving parts to a good sponsorship program, and you must have data to represent each one," says Nardone. It is essential to identify and gather information from all the potential data sources. These may include event attendance, in-arena promotional activity, event signage, local TV ratings of the event, the media weight that uses the event in advertising, and more.

A marketing mix model enables companies to attribute a percentage of sales to sponsorship activity, define an ROI score, and establish an apples-to-apples comparison of a sponsorship with other marketing activities. These models will also produce data (marginal ROI curves, also known as diminishing return curves) marketers can use as inputs into optimization and forecasting tools to determine the most efficient allocation of the budget across their marketing mix.

One debate in marketing today is whether sports and event sponsorships are sales-building or brand-building tools. We believe that ideally they should improve profitability by increasing both sales and brand equity. Furthermore, given the limited-time nature of most sports and event sponsorships, considering only their short-term effects on different ROI measures provides an incomplete picture of their value.

Brand equity, as we'll be discussing in more detail in Chapter 13, is a number, an overall assessment of the goodwill associated with a brand, which reflects past marketing performance and predicts future sales and profit potential. It has different components that companies can study individually to diagnose their contribution to changing overall equity and market share over time. Knowing a brand's equity relative to competitors' and what drives it enable a marketer to develop and implement stronger marketing programs. By quantifying the direct impact of a sports or event sponsorship on brand equity, marketers have a clear picture of the effectiveness of a particular opportunity as a brand-building tool.

Analyze the Hierarchy of Effects

Having concrete ROI numbers certainly helps demonstrate performance to CEOs and CFOs, but where do marketers go from there? What if ROI is lower than expected? Part of making marketing more accountable and pleasing senior management is being able to explain the reasons for failure and offer a plan to turn around negative trends. Enter pre-post tracking research that analyzes the hierarchy of effects, the chain of events that occurs after buyers are exposed to marketing communications.

In a perfect world, buyers become aware of a sponsorship or event—a NASCAR race or the Sundance Film Festival, for example. Next, they become aware of a brand's involvement, followed by awareness of the message the brand communicates at or through the sponsorship or event. The message positively impacts perceptions and attitudes, and, in the end, their preference for the brand and intention to purchase improve. Sadly, as most marketers have come to realize, the world isn't perfect, and this chain very often misses links.

Say Ameriquest does pre-post tracking research after each of five tour stops on the Rolling Stones concert tour. It asks study participants, among other things, whether they've seen or heard of Ameriquest's sponsorship or advertising promoting Ameriquest's sponsorship (or both); what they can recall about the ad, in particular a message; what they think of the Ameriquest brand; and how likely they are to contact Ameriquest next time they need a mortgage.

Analysis might reveal that—Wow!—Ameriquest achieved record-level awareness of its sponsorship and message, "Not Your Average Mortgage Company." Unfortunately, the message did not resonate with the target; it had no impact on perceptions and attitudes toward the brand, so preferences and intention to contact Ameriquest didn't change. This situation is purely hypothetical, but you get the picture. By pinpointing the problems, marketers get a diagnosis of the problem and can more readily identify the appropriate remedy. In this purely hypothetical case, Ameriquest would know it needs to do some work to develop a more compelling message to change brand perceptions and purchase intentions.

Characteristics of Effective Sponsorships

In addition to different research approaches, marketers also have a vast history of sports and event sponsorships that offer insights into the characteristics of highly effective opportunities. We selected nine cases of sports and event sponsorships for companies in different categories looking for the characteristics of effective opportunities. The companies (who will remain nameless to protect the guilty) represent the banking, beer, coffee, energy supplier, engine oil, fast-food, insurance, and pizza categories. Eight of the sponsorships were sports-related (baseball, football, motor sports, the Olympics, soccer, and tennis), and one was a concert tour.

According to pre-post tracking and sales data, six of the nine had no measurable effect. Three had a positive effect: one on sales but not on brand equity, one on equity but not on sales, one on both. Our analysis revealed the effect of the sponsorship or event was greatest when:

1. There are engaged fans highly involved in the product category. Involvement, as we said earlier, is a characteristic of the consumer, not of the product or service. Some people will spend almost as much time weighing the merits of different toothpaste brands as other people spend choosing a new car. If there's a high concentration of buyers who are involved in a category among a sport's, a singer's, a celebrity's, or an art form's fan base, the sponsorship is more likely to have an impact. Motor oil and NASCAR, for example. Soccer shoes and the World Cup.

2. The event is supported by serious money (that is, substantial investments in activation and promotional activities). According to Sponsor-Click, 33 percent of marketers spend less on activation advertising and promotions that communicate the relationship between the brand and a sponsorship than they do on rights fees. Of the rest, 13 percent use a 1:1 ratio, 14 percent use a 1:2 ratio, 10 percent spend three to five times more activation than rights, 5 percent spend five times rights fees, and 25 percent don't know what they spend.[13]

Although our analysis did not reveal the magic ratio of fees to activation, if a company is not investing at least as much to promote the sponsorship to the target as it spends for the rights to the opportunity, it will see little to no effect of the investment.

3. The company uses the sponsorship to communicate a clear message about the brand to a target excited by the sponsorship and responsive to the brand. Linking a brand to a property like the Olympics or the Sundance Film Festival to build awareness for the brand name only is a poor investment of marketing dollars and a lost opportunity to speak to a group of buyers ready and willing to listen.

Finding a compelling message is as critical to the success of sponsorship and event marketing as appropriate spending on activation. Fidelity Investments sponsored Paul McCartney's 2005 U.S. tour. The tour's theme: "Never stop doing what you love." Fidelity's message: "Let us plan the next stage of your life." For McCartney's predominantly baby boomer audience who are at least thinking about (if not in the process of) retiring, the idea that Fidelity could help them continue doing what they too love no doubt resonated deeply.

4. *There is a clean linkage between the product and sponsorship.* iPod sponsoring the Grammy Awards; Mott's sponsoring the Wiggles, a popular kid's musical group, U.S. tour; Michelin sponsoring Formula One; a "clean, green" energy company sponsoring the concert tour of a musician with a well-publicized penchant for the environment. The connection is pretty clear. But when the connection starts to become more subtle or stretched—a fast-food company sponsoring the Olympics, a breakfast cereal sponsoring NASCAR, a national bank sponsoring the NCAA basketball March Madness tournament—the effectiveness begins to decrease. If it takes longer than five seconds to explain the connection between a brand and a sport or an event, most target buyers aren't going to get it.

Granted, our sample was small, but it illustrates what marketers can discover by taking a closer look at common attributes of effective sports and event sponsorships.

"With more money being invested," said *Promo Magazine*, "the call for return on investment has reached near-deafening levels. Marketers want to know exactly how much bang they're getting for their buck."[14] Clearly, gut-based media selection has a fact-based counterpart that will quickly capture the attention of apprehensive marketers. If marketers use the tools and insights garnered from a growing historical record of sports and event sponsorships not only to report performance but also to improve it, this form of nontraditional media has the potential to be the first in its class that companies can say unequivocally will deliver a return on investment that exceeds expectations.

And as a start on that improvement, here are seven questions top management ought to be asking about the company's sports and event sponsorships:

- How should we define measurable criteria for sponsorship performance?
- How much should we spend on a sponsorship?
- Where should we spend our sponsorship investments?
- What return should we expect?
- Is sponsorship meeting its objectives?
- How did this sponsorship drive both short-term (ROI) and long-term (brand equity and customer equity) results?
- How could the sponsorship's effectiveness be improved?

10

How to Make the Sale Reps Our Friends . . . Really

Over breakfast not long ago, we asked Professor Benson Shapiro, the recently retired Malcolm McNair Professor of Marketing at the Harvard Business School and an international authority on sales management, what he thought was the biggest problem in business today. He said, "The biggest problem is that sales and marketing are in separate fiefdoms. They don't even talk to one another."

This observation was reflected in our recent meeting with a group of marketing executives from one of the world's most successful package goods marketing companies. When we asked about the sales department's involvement in the marketing planning process, the CMO told us that the sales department was in another building and that marketing people had virtually no contact with the sales management or sales reps.

We regard the salespeople as the Marine Corps of a firm's marketing effort. They're in the front lines, engaged with the customers every day. In the United States, the Marine Corps reports to the chairman of the Joint Chiefs of Staff, who in turn reports to the commander in chief. Because sales, in theory, is a component of marketing, the analogy in a corporation should be that the sales department reports to the CMO who reports to the chief executive officer. But as we all know, that is unusual, if only because—as we saw in the study we reported in Chapter 1—the majority of company managements see the firm as sales- rather than marketing-oriented.

Let's talk a little bit about why, what the situation means for companies, and why we think it would benefit both the organization and the salespeople if the situation changed.

A Very Strained Relationship

"The typical relationship between the two is very strained. A lot of friction," says Kevin Moran, the president of MSS Multi-Sponsored Studies. Because Moran has held both sales and marketing positions, he has seen the situation from both perspectives, and in his current position he works with both salespeople and marketing executives. Salespeople tend to believe they know how the market actually operates because they are on the streets, speaking with customers every day. "They typically feel that more control of communications efforts should reside in their hands, that the most effective way to do things is to spend down right at the customer level versus the marketing department, which they feel is not as attuned—at least on a grassroots level—with exactly what's going on and what customers are thinking. The sales information is based on a day-to-day interaction with customers."

Sales executives often feel that because marketing departments are not as close to customers, they are not as well positioned as sales to decide how to spend money on communications as is the sales department. They are especially critical of trade programs deployed to go after consumers. Yet marketing departments do tend to manage these budgets, and as a result sales executives are occasionally jealous because they don't control the money. The dollars they receive are often based on decisions the marketing people have made on what they are going to get and how they are going to get them.

Our associate Chuck Sakany was a sales representative when the company for which he worked at the time was merged with a larger corporation. "My first perception of the marketing department was that these guys were really heavy-handed. To me they were intruding into what I thought were sales-defined areas. I guess from their perspective they were just ensuring accountability. They wanted to understand what effect the money they were handing off to the sales organization to grow the brands was having. But from the sales rep's perspective, it seemed like, man, this guy comes in with a club and just beats you over the head. And, by the way, he's doing it in front of the senior management."

Sakany admits today that his new marketing chief was probably just doing his job. "He is signing off for these funds, which basically the sales organization has complete control over once we receive them. He wants to know what's happening, and what he's receiving in exchange. And of course there's only so much money in the pot for sales or marketing, so there's a little bit of competition for that as well."

At its heart, the sales department/marketing department conflict seems to be one of culture and of mutual misunderstanding. Salespeople (to make sweeping generalizations) tend to be independent, entrepreneurial, self-confident. Marketing people (to make more sweeping generalizations) tend to have more formal education and therefore tend to think they are more knowledgeable about the big picture. ("If you had an MBA like me, you wouldn't have to be out in the trenches every day.") Marketers want to control the process; salespeople don't want to be controlled. Marketers are at headquarters, close to the centers of power; salespeople are in the field, meeting customers. Marketing's contribution to the organization's bottom line has to be explained and justified; sales' contribution is direct and obvious.

The marketing and the sales departments' ultimate goals align closely—both, after all, want to find and retain customers—but the means to the end differ. The sales department tends to focus on tactical activities, and often those are trade-related. The marketing department generally has a more media-related consumer focus to the activities designed to drive the brands forward. Sales is more short-term oriented; marketing is usually more long-term focused. Sales has hard measures: dollars in the bank; marketing deals with softer measures like brand equity, consumer perceptions, and awareness.

The friction—or lack of communication—between marketing and sales departments harms an organization two ways: It wastes company resources and it hobbles profitability. Resources are wasted when the marketing department produces research, collateral materials, and sales training that the salespeople cannot or will not use. Profit suffers when the salespeople are not talking to those prospective customers who are likely to be the most receptive to the organization's products or services and who are likely to be the most profitable—information that comes from the marketing department. (If it doesn't, the marketing department is not doing its job.)

The key disadvantage of leaving marketing and sales in their separate silos is that it often reduces the effectiveness of both. Marketing efforts are not done in concert with the salespeople; the salespeople do not use all the marketing tools available. Often when there are turf battles, both sides become secretive. Salespeople don't want the marketing people to know exactly what they're doing; marketing people don't believe they need to consult with sales before they move forward on marketing programs. All this leads to inefficiency and hard feelings. The slogans within the organization should not be, "We are the sales department!" and "We are the marketing department!" It should be, "We are the company."

We understand the attitude can be difficult to promote. In an industry in which the salespeople work entirely on commission, such as securities brokerage, it is difficult to tell the salespeople they must do this or can't do that as long as what they do is within the bounds of the law. It is a little easier if the company pays straight salary or salary and a small commission. Sales compensation is well beyond the scope of this book, but senior managers who would like to make their organizations more efficient and profitable cannot ignore the subject. All we will say here is that if the company's sales compensation plan is not producing the strategic sales results management wants, it is time to revisit the plan, retrain the salespeople, or both. If there is a disconnect between the company's goal—to have the sales representatives in front of the most potentially profitable customers—and if the salespeople can earn more by selling to less profitable customers, something ought to be changed.

Identify Targets for Salespeople

We believe the marketing function should help segment prospects and customers for the sales force. It should undertake the same kinds of analyses for the sales force that it does for getting the word out. Ideally, the marketing department has an illustration such as Figure 10.1 and can tell the sales force the best targets to go after are segments A and B because they represent the greatest share of potential profitability. You can ignore segment E and place less emphasis on segments C and D.

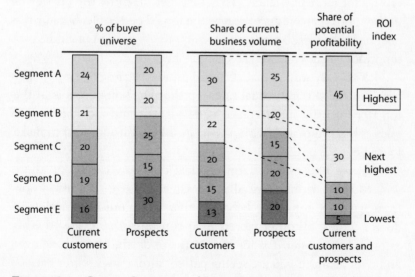

Figure 10.1 Current Customer and Prospect Segmentation for Sales Force.

Also, when you visit customers in segment A, these are the kinds of sales messages to which they are most likely to respond. Prospects in segment B are more likely to react to these kinds of messages because not every message works equally well for every customer.

Occasionally, a client will tell us that the company already segments the sales force's targets. Some salespeople are specialists in discount stores, some are specialists in chain drugstores, and some are specialists in independent stores.

That is the equivalent of saying you have segmented the marketing terms of SIC code or demographics—large, medium, small, for example. You have segmented the market in terms of variables that help you manage your business but don't necessarily help you improve your business. You have segmented the market in terms of the wrong factors. It is the same problem we discussed in Chapter 4: segmenting on the basis of heavy versus light buyers, or women aged 18 to 34. There are better ways to do it, although not everybody has got this word.

In the pharmaceutical field, for example, we have discovered that a common way that companies segment is to look at the prescribing pattern data of physicians that is nationally available in most categories for most physicians. They say, "Let's identify the physicians in the top 10 percentile, or maybe the top 20 percentile, because the doctors in the top 20 percentile account for 45 percent of all the prescriptions written for this class of drug. Let's go after them."

It's an easy way to manage the business because the sales manager can tell the individual sales rep that Dr. Kotopoulos is in the top 10 percentile and his office address is such and such. Make your sales call on him, and, with physicians like him, you need to make four sales calls a year.

But we find every pharmaceutical company calling on those same doctors with essentially the same message. We also know from work in consumer behavior that the more prescriptions a doctor writes, all other factors held constant, the greater the inertia and the easier it is for the doctor to do the same thing over and over again. If you are seeing patient after patient after patient every 20 minutes, it is unlikely that you are going to say, "Let me try something new today." All the sales representatives who sell a given drug call on these relatively few doctors, who are relatively invulnerable to new medications. They are a lousy target.

W. W. Grainger, a Fortune 500 distributor of facilities management supplies—everything from adhesives to tools and test equipment—has apparently decided to segment its 1.5 million customers for unplanned maintenance, repair, and operations purchases (MRO). These are the unexpected and unusual incidents: an elevator button breaks, for example. According to Deb Oler, Grainger's vice president of sales and marketing operations, the firm has begun to move to a more consultative sales model, but that is not so simple to do. Grainger's sales force has product expertise, but it now needs professionals capable of building relationships and understanding a customer's business well enough to match resources to needs.

To deal with this difference, Granger instituted an 18-month training program for its sales force that includes business finance. It also reconfigured the force. Salespeople serving large customers now call on no more than 35 accounts. Salespeople who meet with midsize customers now have 125 assigned to them. Inside salespeople have 500 each. "This model is built around contact frequency so that our sales professionals can best match product, programs, and services to help optimize the purchase of unplanned MRO," says Oler.[1]

It's Not about Price

The issue of price routinely comes up when we talk to or about salespeople. Virtually all sales representatives believe they could sell more if the company just cut its price or at least let the sales rep negotiate (a nicer word than *bargain*).

Unquestionably, a price segment exists. We find one in business-to-business marketing as in consumer marketing. These are customers who do not—within reason—care about delivery times, after-sale service, or company reputation; they just want the best price. They exist, and we just have to live with it.

Although there are customers who care mainly about price, we have found no correlation between this price sensitivity and company size. Many clients know in their gut that the bigger the customer, the more pressure for special prices. The data, however, says this is not necessarily so. Repeatedly, we have found there is almost no relationship between volume and price sensitivity. We have found that "your price is too high" is an excuse prospects give when they don't want to give a real reason for not buying now.

We recently finished a major industry study and could not find any indicator of price sensitivity. You couldn't tell by industry; you couldn't tell by size; you couldn't tell by volume purchases. There are some price-sensitive big companies and some relatively price-insensitive big companies; there are price-sensitive small companies and some relatively price-insensitive small companies. It does not matter how much machine oil, cement, industrial gas, plywood, software, glass, or steel they buy. It's just who they are.

Unlike what many salespeople will say, however, this is not the entire market. It is not even 50 percent of the market. Depending on the industry, price-sensitive customers may represent as much as 40 percent or as little as 20 percent of the total market. Which means that 60 percent to 80 percent of your customers are not fixated on price.

(And those who are, by the way, are often just as happy not to see your expensive sales reps. These customers will buy off the web or over the phone; they're not interested in having a relationship, so you don't have to spend a lot of money cultivating one.)

We do tend to find three other segments in business-to-business marketing in addition to the price-sensitive; two that seem to turn up in most industries are the relationship segment and the technical segment. The companies that are interested in a relationship are open to solution selling. Don't just sell us jet aircraft engines, they say, we want you to provide all the maintenance for the next 10 years. Don't just sell us polypropylene, show us how to design new products using it. Don't just sell us package delivery, help us with inventory control and reducing shrinkage. The solution sale is not for everybody, but there is usually a segment open to it. And sometimes, price-sensitive customers become less price-sensitive when a company offers solutions to their problems. These customers want the end solution. The price customer doesn't care.

The third segment we typically find in business-to-business marketing are the highly technical customers. These are the customers who want to hear about the advanced technology or the latest formula—real technical advice. They don't want to be buddy-buddy, but they are interested in the real science and the technical data. They want a direct line to your engineers. They may not care about solutions, and price is usually secondary. They want value-added, but the added value they want is not service and relationship; it's technical input and advice.

These three segments usually appear in the business-to-business work we do—price, relationship, and technical advice—and there is usually a fourth or a fifth segment, but they depend on the industry or category. We never know what the fourth or fifth will be, but the other three seem to recur regularly.

To recap: We find a general gut impression among business-to-business company executives is that everybody is a price buyer, information that comes from the salespeople. In fact, the evidence shows not everybody buys on price, and employing different offering strategies can reach different segments. The gut impression is that sales reps have to visit customers in person, and the good news is that they don't. Virtually all customers are on the web. We have clients ask, "Are you sure that at the factory they have access to the Internet?" Yes, we've studied it, they all have desktops, and 85 percent say they go online.

Target the Sales Force

Up to this point, we've been talking about targeting consumers or B2B decision makers, the folks who actually buy the company's product or service. In many organizations, it is possible—indeed desirable—to target the sales force.

If you are a major insurance or real estate company or a manufacturer employing independent reps, you don't own your sales force. The insurance company may have 13,000 sales representatives around the country, but they represent other firms as well. When we ask the company to tell us something about their salespeople, they tell us they have data on the rank order performance of all these salespeople. They know the best performers, the top 20 percent or the top 40 percent or whatever. But that's about it.

We ask, aren't these salespeople motivated by different things? Aren't there those who are just looking to increase their earnings? Aren't there those who really enjoy the relationship with the clients? Aren't there those who are just biding their time until they can retire? Could be, but the company executives don't know.

Pharmaceutical representatives are company employees selling exclusively for the company, but the issue is the same. What does the company know about them? It knows how much they sell. It does not know their motivations. It does not know their perceptions of the corporation vis-à-vis the competition. It does not have any insights other than greater levels of financial incentives to get these folks to work harder or better or more successfully.

Most companies know virtually nothing about the folks selling their products or services. Many companies, both business-to-business and business-to-consumer, could do profitable segmentation work to better understand the reps. If the company better understood the motivations, aspirations, and limitations of its salespeople, it could use them more effectively. It is the difference between targeting everyone and targeting the most profitable consumer segments.

When a company has independent salespeople, it also tends to know very little about its ultimate consumers, the customers of the salespeople. The reps do not ordinarily gather the kind of market data we have been talking about throughout this book, nor are they usually willing to share customer information with the company. As a result, few companies provide the reps with targeting data on their customers. Few provide the reps with insights into either the business-to-business or their consumer targets that would help them do a better job.

We are currently doing work for a number of corporations designed to provide the sales force with a thorough description of the segments that they ought to go after. We are providing the salespeople with a script to helping market the product or service with each of the different target groups the company has identified. One key is learning whether the prospective customer is responsive to a sales call at all. Wouldn't the salespeople like to know that this financial services prospect, this purchasing agent, or this doctor is interested in the company's product or service, is willing to talk, and tends to set aside 20 minutes a day for salespeople?

What Marketing Can Do

If you agree that friction exists between the marketing and the sales departments—even if it is no more than poor communication—and if you agree that the organization is less efficient and profitable than it could be as a result, what should you do? How does the CMO make friends with the vice president of sales and the sales force? (We're suggesting making friends rather than a palace coup, which usually leaves too many sullen and resourceful survivors around to do mischief.)

The place for CMOs to start is by looking at the sales department as a client the way they look at the organization's end customers. Marketing should view sales as an internal client and recognize that the salespeople are the ones on the street or on the phones or on the Internet. They are the ones who are touching customers with conversations and letters and presentations and the like, and they are clearly a key source of information that could make the marketing function stronger.

Chuck Sakany has more suggestions to alleviate the adversarial relationship. "Often, marketing folks are coming from another organization, and they lack two things: They lack experience with the brand or brands that they're now responsible for, and, in all likelihood, they haven't had much exposure to—or no exposure to—what the sales force is actually doing."

The first requires some due diligence, studying the brands and their history in depth. The second probably requires getting out of the office. Sakany says that the way to enhance the relationship "is to go out and really get involved with the sales force in a fact-finding way. Just go out and observe what they are doing; what the process looks like. What sort of schedule. Spend a couple of days actually traveling with two or three of the top company salespeople in different regions."

Brian Cohen, senior vice president and CMO of Farmers Insurance Group, which provides insurance management services, says that every new marketing department employee has to spend time selling insurance. "I came in as VP of business development, which was a position where I had to identify new product opportunities for the company," he told *CMO Magazine*. "Before figuring out what to sell, I hit the road, investing a lot of time visiting agent offices and studying their sales processes. You just learn so much." In turn, all Farmers Insurance Group field sales personnel rotate through the marketing department to help them understand the marketing issues they should be addressing in the field as well as the consumer data they can obtain from marketing.[2]

It also would not hurt for the marketing organization to invite the more senior sales management to be a part of the marketing development process. Getting to know each other better would be a big step in the right direction. Knowing each other might prevent the marketing department from, say, developing programs that require more time than the sales force actually has to give. So a good first step is to clearly understand what both groups are trying to achieve and what they are capable of accomplishing given whatever constraints in time, budget, or systems the organization has on them.

Why Sales Should Cooperate

Why should salespeople cooperate with the marketing department? The first question most salespeople will ask about a new marketing initiative is, "Will it put any more money in my pocket?" Salespeople have a good sense of what they are confronted with every day in trying to sell something. They want to know, "Is the marketing department assisting?" The challenge is to convince the salespeople and the sales organization that marketing is assisting, not blocking, not usurping, not hindering, and not taking money that sales believes it could spend more effectively. The best salesperson is the one who really does embrace what marketing is doing and understands it.

Once the CMO has traveled with sales representatives, then what? Assess the goals handed down from the executive level and develop a marketing plan that—again, given the constraints of the market and the sales organization—will meet those goals. If you know you have to grow the revenue by 10 percent and net profit by 11 percent, these are the parameters in which you must work. The marketing task is to develop programs to meet the goals while working within the parameters.

Obviously, a real-world situation is a lot more complicated than this. When the CMO returns to the office, he or she ought to better understand how to communicate with the sales organization and understand the things they are capable of doing. But the company must also do some customer research to understand where there might be shortcomings in the current offerings. The marketing department should not focus so tightly on sales that it loses sight of customers.

When we have investigated client sales efforts, we often find the salespeople are spending an inordinate amount of time on either inappropriate or not as profitable customers as senior management would like. They are missing opportunities. What they are doing is relatively easy. Changing that situation requires altered scheduling, different compensation plans; work with the sales manager to create incentives that actually drive the behavior the company wants driven. It's not a walk in the park.

Adding to the difficulty for a new marketing management is that they are often dealing with salespeople who have been with the organization for 10, 15, or 20-plus years. These veterans have developed a voice within the organization, and they have developed a routine that is comfortable and familiar. It can be very difficult to pry them loose from the way they have been doing things in the past. It works for them, and it has worked for them, but it may not be working for the company. If their compensation is satisfactory, they are happy to continue with the way they have been doing business. We'll talk much more about implementation two chapters ahead.

We worked with an industrial materials company not long ago, and when we looked at the way the sales force was interacting with the customers, we found a different contract in place for every single customer. Essentially, each sales rep was running his or her own little independent business with virtually no regard for the company's requirements. Although the business was marginally profitable, the parent company was considering sale or liquidation.

We did considerable work to understand the customer needs and company products and services that could be developed to meet those needs. We learned—in contrast to the sales reports—that many customers would be willing to pay for services the company could offer but never had. The services could be not only profitable but also would distinguish the company from competitors.

It was a painful process to actually go out with the sales force and help them understand and implement the new strategies. To understand that every customer would not—should not—require a different contract. To understand that price was not the only thing that drove the customer's decision process. It took months of hard work, but the business turned around to become the most profitable division in the corporation.

Obviously, there is only so much a marketing executive can do. If you are a CMO and the senior vice president of sales is in another building, you are limited. You both have your fiefs, your own way of doing things, and that has worked well enough. If the president and CEO tolerates (or encourages) the situation, the odds of it changing are not great.

Although we believe that, as a general rule, the sales function should report to marketing, senior executives do not always agree. For five years, both marketing and sales reported to Kim Schaller, vice president and CMO of Hershey Entertainment & Resorts. In 2004, senior management decided to split the functions, with the head of each group reporting to the CEO. Schaller is not unhappy with the change. "With marketing, I'm in my comfort zone," she says. "I don't have a sales background, and that honestly was a stretch for me. Sales is a very different discipline. You like to do what you're good at, and I didn't feel I was adding value the way someone who understands sales could."

"She's very honest about saying she doesn't know sales," says Tim Bugas, the vice president of sales at Hershey Entertainment & Resorts. "And I'm not a huge marketer. So we decided to learn from each other and make whatever programs we're putting together work." To keep the lines of communication open, Schaller and Bugas have lunch together every Thursday. That is very different from other times in Bugas's career when, he says, "marketing ideas weren't integrated with the sales plan or sales' objectives." In other jobs, marketing had its own agenda and assumed sales would follow through with minimal input. "They would give us their idea about what's going to work and say, 'You've got to sell it.' That's very prevalent in a lot of companies."[3]

Whether sales reports to marketing or both report to the CEO, the company should have a process that brings both camps into the marketing planning and help the sales management and salespeople see that marketing is what is going to drive the brands forward. At the same time, marketing should understand that sales is going to deliver the actual meat and potatoes to keep the financial engine turning. Also, wise CEOs will work to eliminate the perception that there is competition for financial and human resources between marketing and sales. Such senior executives will help both functions see that there is a finite pool of resources and these will be deployed in the fashion most effective for the organization as a whole, not for one department or another.

Making Friends Makes a Difference

We're sometimes asked by skeptical senior executives whether it really makes a difference to integrate the marketing and sales functions. Can we give an example of a company or an industry in which such integration actually improved the business? In fact, we can.

Ten years ago or so, the alcoholic beverage category had virtually no sophisticated marketing. Company success was 90 percent dependent on what you might call the whiskey-drinking salesman. These were the guys (they were practically all men) who would entertain the distributors and entertain the retailers and entertain the big restaurants to make sales. The alcoholic beverage importers and distillers built their businesses on the salesmen.

With some major mergers in the last 7 to 10 years, we have seen a couple of things happening. First, a dramatic net decline in the number of salespeople who actually go from store to store, restaurant to restaurant for the purpose of making a sale or taking an order. Second, an investment by the large alcoholic beverage companies in the quality and training of distributor salespeople in technology and in marketing. They are teaching the salespeople how important it is that, as they represent the products, they assist in building brands that can thrive over time in a very competitive arena. As a result, the industry as a whole has become significantly more efficient.

For example, Diageo, one of the largest alcoholic beverage companies in the world, was formed in 1997 in the merger of Guinness and GrandMet. Its brands include Smirnoff, Johnnie Walker, Guinness, Baileys, J&B, Captain Morgan, Cuervo, Tanqueray, Crown Royal, and Beaulieu Vineyard and Sterling Vineyards wines. The company essentially purged itself of marketing people who were focused on coupons and rebate programs and replaced them with people they recruited from Procter & Gamble, Coca-Cola, KFC—all major consumer goods companies. These are well-educated people, seasoned in marketing techniques and advertising. Diageo's management put in place an entirely different organization focused on developing brands and building them over time versus pushing cases of product through the distribution system.

We believe that Ben Shapiro at Harvard is right. The silos must come down and marketing and sales work together for the good of the entire organization. We expect that mature individuals can accomplish that, but if not, then a firm CEO might have to make changes. If the organization has been doing things a certain way for a long time, and the CMO or the sales manager or both are not receptive to moving things forward, the individuals themselves could be a problem that must be resolved. One way, of course, is to have the sales function report to marketing, although that may not always be necessary.

As steps toward reducing the friction between the marketing and sales departments and improving sales performance, senior management can ask these questions:

- Rather than rely on salespeople to be the main source of intelligence about customers and prospects, have we undertaken an independent study among these targets to learn what they *really* want and how they perceive our brand versus competitors? After all, salespeople are not trained research interviewers.
- Have we given our salespeople a precise definition of key market targets and what messages they should communicate to win more business?
- Have we provided the sales force with the tools to identify the different targets in their sales territories? Sometimes, a company is able to provide salespeople with a list of customers and prospects to call on. Other times, salespeople are given a few questions to ask prospects to place them in a particular market segment for which the script is made available.
- Have we taken the time to provide the sales force with a product and price that will "fly off the shelf?"
- Have we included the sales organization in all key discussions and decisions concerning marketing strategy and plans?
- Finally, do we have a system for isolating the performance of the sales force overall and individual salespeople in terms of return on investment?

SECTION III

How to Finally Make It All Work Together

11

Connect All the Marketing Plan's Dots

At many companies we visit—large and small, consumer and business-to-business—management often shows us a document we would call fantasy fiction. They call it the marketing plan.

Here's an example. One of the largest consumer products companies in the United States invited us to evaluate their marketing planning system for one of their brands, the number-two brand in a major health and beauty aid category. The document looked good: 122 pages in a shiny binder with lots of tables, charts, and graphs, most in color.

The plan opened with reasonably clear sales objectives, followed by a detailed discussion of strategy and tactics, and ended with a profit-and-loss statement. An appendix was loaded with information about the product category, competitive analyses, pending legislative issues, and a ton of stuff you'd expect smart brand managers to be thinking about.

On a quick first reading, we noticed that the plan lacked vision and mission statements, it barely mentioned the web, and it talked too much about advertising. But these were relatively minor blemishes compared to the problems we found once we studied the plan.

Top management had sent down the objectives from on high. Marketing was to obtain a 10 percent increase in sales. Senior management had set this objective without any concern whether it could be achieved or its implications for brand profitability. Where was the 10 percent to come from? The plan proposed more awareness (another objective), but what kind of awareness, and how would it be achieved? All of the marketing inputs looked very similar to previous the year's. Moreover, there was no evidence of how, even if the plan mysteriously posted gains in awareness, these improvements would generate a 10 percent sales increase.

One section of the plan, we realized, had no connection with another. Marketing's strategy was not linked to the objectives. The plan showed no evidence that the recommended strategy was developed with the objectives in mind. The strategic target of 25- to 54-year-old-women was the same target every major player in the category was trying to reach, and nothing about the target or the positioning suggested either could deliver a sizable sales increase, never mind the 10 percent sought by the CEO and CFO.

The strategy and tactics were unrelated. It was not at all clear that the tactics were customized to the target and positioning strategies. Advertising and promotional tactics, for example, were generic and virtually any brand, regardless of strategy, could have employed them. Worse, given the importance of trade dress in this category, the brand's packaging didn't reflect its positioning. It was as if people living in different silos entirely had created the packaging and the positioning.

The tactics and objectives were unrelated. The promotion and advertising budget was the previous year's numbers corrected for inflation. True, the ad copy had performed above average on the basis of copy-testing norms and so did the executions that had run the previous year, but that was also a year during which sales declined by 3 percent. Actual-cash-value distribution had peaked at 90 percent, and share-of-shelf facings were in line with market share. There was nothing new here, and management had done nothing to model the relationship between the tactics and the objectives or to forecast the return on investment (ROI) of the $40 million ad budget.

The profit-and-loss statement was simply made up, piling questionable assumption upon questionable assumption with no basis in fact. We were surprised by this plan's deficiencies, not because the total effect was reading fantasy fiction—we see that all the time—but because the corporation carried such a high reputation for marketing expertise. It was doing as well as it was, not because of its marketing plan but in spite of it.

The Marketing Plan Is a Map to the Future

Everyone reading this understands why a marketing plan is important. It's an essential document for large corporate marketing departments, for medium companies, and for start-ups. It forces the marketing personnel to look internally to fully understand the results of past marketing decisions. It forces them to look externally to fully understand the market in which they operate. It sets goals and provides direction for future marketing efforts that everyone within the organization should understand and support. And it is key to obtaining resources for new initiatives.

The marketing plan is to company success as a road map is to car travel. It can act as a tracking mechanism, to determine the budget, and as a scale against which the company can measure marketing effectiveness. And it is an internal communications tool so that everyone understands where the business is going and how it plans to get there.

Interestingly, we find that only about half the companies we visit in our consulting work have a *detailed* marketing plan. Almost everyone has a sketchy plan and a budget—in some cases a detailed budget. But they do not have a fully developed marketing plan. In our terms, they do not know where they're going. And if you don't know where you're going, it's hard to know when you've arrived.

An even more fundamental problem we see in these marketing plans, however, is the connection between the plan and a market target. What does it mean to say, as many do say, in effect, "We're going after the new environmentalists"? Or "We're going after pizza lovers"? Or "We're going after PC enthusiasts"? What is the connection between the strategy for "going after" those people and what goes into the marketing plan? For many companies, none.

After a section on objectives, the typical marketing plan moves on to include a section on the market climate, a competitive analysis, and then the strategy. The latter includes targeting, positioning, the product line, pricing, communications (mostly advertising), customer service, and sales/distribution. The plan talks about how much money the business will spend on advertising, the media schedule, how that is overlaid with promotion, and distribution levels. If the CMO is very clever, the plan includes a section on measuring marketing performance.

It reads nicely. The CEO looking at it may think everything makes sense. The CEO may think that if the company makes these decisions and spends that much money, it will accomplish the objectives.

Unfortunately, as we've just seen, even sophisticated corporations develop marketing plans with no real knowledge of the relationship between marketing inputs and outputs. Top management sets sales and profit objectives without any clear perception of whether they can be achieved. It is very unlikely, as in the example we described, a brand will obtain a 10 percent sales increase after a year when it has dropped by 3 percent, and certainly not without major marketing investments. Calling it a stretch goal does not make the 10 percent any more realistic or less demoralizing to those who have to try to reach it.

Consider the hypothetical marketing mix model for Zippy Data Storage in Figure 11.1. The two outside columns list all marketing inputs, everything from direct sales to manufacturing/labor cost on the left and brand equity factors to consumer behavior on the right. These

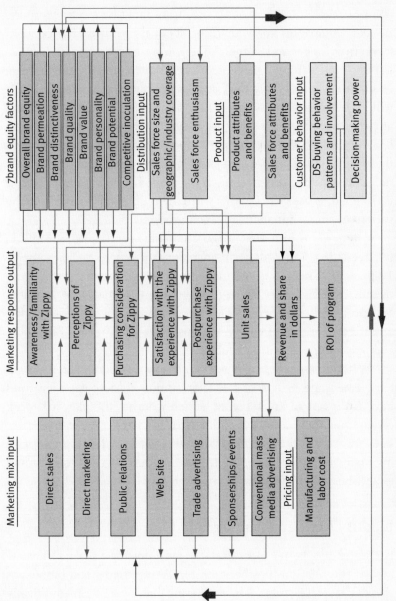

Figure 11.1 Hypothetical Marketing Mix Model for Zippy Data Storage.

inputs vary, depending on the product and the industry. A soft drink, for example, might not have direct sales as an input but will have point-of-sale communications, a significant input for most soft drinks.

Few companies know anything about the relationship between marketing inputs and outputs. They don't know whether increasing trade advertising 7 percent will cause awareness to go up, down, or stay the same. (They hope it goes up, but they don't know if it will.) They don't know whether sponsoring a NASCAR driver has any effect whatever on sales, as we saw in Chapter 9. Let's be clear. Leafing through the typical marketing plan, we find the pages with the objectives, a heavy discussion of strategy, pages dealing with tactics and spending, and nothing is connected. The plan is a fraud. It looks good, is well written, but virtually no one has a clue how the various elements interact with each other.

There is no hint that if the company spends, say, $2 million in advertising, unit sales will increase 6 percent or 2 percent or 10 percent. There is no connection between distribution and the overall objective. No connection between promotional spending and profitability, between sales force size and purchase consideration, between brand equity and customer perceptions. Each plan component operates in a vacuum.

Whether a marketing plan is for a new product or service or an established one, if it does not relate inputs to outputs, companies have little way to know before launch whether the plan will work or whether there are ways to improve it to generate even greater sales and profits. Fortunately, it is now possible to develop a marketing plan that takes marketing inputs and outputs into account and establishes the relationships between them.

Identify Marketing Inputs and Outputs

For want of a better label, we've been referring to plans that establish the relationships between marketing inputs and outputs as *scientific marketing plans*. The marketing plan's core is an empirically based mathematical model that "understands" the connections between each of the market inputs and outputs in a category. This is similar to the customer equity model we talked about in the previous chapter. With it you can say, "If we impact *this* target with *this* kind of positioning and with *this* level of advertising, we can expect to achieve *this* level of sales."

The first step in creating such a model is to identify all marketing inputs and outputs. The company determines some of these elements directly: pricing, advertising spending, promotion spending. Others it can affect only indirectly: the retailer's relationship with his distributor, for example. But even if the company cannot affect the inputs directly (or at all), it is important to identify every one and chart its relationship to the other elements.

Where does the information for the marketing mix model boxes—the two outside columns in Figure 11.1—come from? You need information about your marketing process and the competition's. Some of it will be from syndicated information services. Nielsen or IRI data can tell you about distribution and retail prices. You know your prices and can probably estimate what your competitors are charging, so that will give you a good approximation of retailer markup.

Nielsen or IRI data will also give you a figure for numeric distribution, the number of stores you're in (if you do not have it internally), and for total stock, your share of the display within the stores. You may be in a store but not be well stocked, so it is important to know both. A syndicated service tracks share of conventional media. Public relations includes how much money you are spending or the value of the PR activity you are getting. Trade incentives are just that—how much money you're spending on trade discounts, twofers, and the like.

The left side of the figure shows all the marketing investments a computer company can make, broken into all the significant components. Showing it laid out neatly like this, however, and actually gathering the relevant figures are, we realize, two very different things. Marketing people cannot always lay their hands on the data. What did we spend on NASCAR? I don't know, that's somebody in another building. Well, give him a call. He's out; he doesn't like to tell me; it's politically sensitive.

To make the model function properly, you need to conceptualize it at the beginning of the process, to identify every single input and output. You then need to establish a strategy to collect data on a regular basis over time. This includes defining expenses correctly. For example, some people will call the money the company spends on a race car *advertising,* some will call it *merchandising,* others will call it *promotion.* How the accounting department assigns money may not be the way you would want to use it here.

Assembling the company's own costs can be a chore, but if you do it well you have not only your expenditures but also a fair idea of what your competitors spent. To establish positioning penetration, campaign penetration, consideration, trial, loyalty, and preference figures, you will need a consumer tracking survey. Retailer satisfaction with distributor and retailer satisfaction with the brand comes from a trade customer satisfaction survey that asks consumers if they are happy with this brand, that brand, the other brand.

Therefore, to begin to develop a marketing plan model, you need four and as many as eight sources of information: Nielsen or IRI; Leading National Advertisers; a consumer tracking study; a study measuring buyer readership, viewership, and listenership for media vehicles the company employs; a customer satisfaction survey; a source of nontraditional media spending such as events, sponsorships, merchandising; and public relations. You need the information for your brand, for competitive brands, and, very importantly, for your market target (and if you can get it, the market target impacted by the positioning strategy) over time so you can begin to see cause and effect.

True single-source data, which merges media exposure information with sales data for individual households, is increasingly available. Many companies merge this data into their overall structure for evaluating advertising and, in the process, changing their advertising evaluation system fundamentally.

In the near future, it will be possible for most brands to parse the effects of short-term sales promotions and local store activity to uncover the direct short-term effects of advertising. For those who take a longer-term view, the promise of single-source panel data is the ability to track the longer-term effects of advertising on purchasing loyalty and deal sensitivity.

Model the Relationship between the Factors

The next step in a scientific marketing plan is to do the modeling. This is not something a manager wants to do by herself unless she's skilled at using some sophisticated software like the SAS Institute's enterprise data mining package. What most companies do is turn this problem over to econometricians or statisticians skilled in analyzing marketing concepts and data.

Working with the experts and the data, you learn which boxes are important and the directions of the arrows. We did not know these connections when we started. We *did* know that not every box has an arrow going to every other box, but we had to discover what input affects what output(s) and to what degree for this company in this industry. For example, public relations does not affect everything; in this situation it affects only campaign penetration. Price at retail does not change share of facings; it encourages trial but not loyalty.

How do you model the relationship? How do you learn that in your particular situation that share of facings, not price, affects loyalty? You cannot use your gut instinct. The only way is to study it, to do what we have been recommending throughout this book: rigorous analysis of unimpeachable data.

Do this analysis and you sometimes discover surprising things. Not so surprising after managers reflect on the information for a while perhaps, but so surprising initially that CMOs do not always believe the data. In a number of U.S. product categories, for example, distribution is no longer a driving determinant of market share. But share of weighted distribution is an increasingly powerful predictor. By this we mean the average of all standardized units that one brand or even one model holds in a product category in a market (say, outlets selling PCs). An implication of this is that in many categories in the United States and around the globe, the products are being transformed into commodities.

If share of weighted distribution becomes the single strongest determinant of market share, it suggests the metaphor of a blindfolded buyer. Brand, price, packaging, and shelf talker become less important in the buying decision. The blindfolded buyer simply reaches out and takes what's on the shelf. What she grabs is a function of distribution.

Decision Calculus Can Help Smaller Companies

What happens when you don't have the data or the resources to collect all this information? What happens if you don't have an econometrician/statistician on staff and cannot afford to hire one? You can still employ a stripped-down version of the marketing mix model and use a simple questionnaire with relatively few customers to obtain the information.

Senior management in a medium to relatively small company ought to be closer to the firm's customers than top managers in a Fortune 500 corporation. A smaller company has fewer moving parts than a giant corporation. It is possible to see—and roughly measure—the effect of public relations or a trade advertising campaign relatively quickly and directly. A part-timer with a pleasant telephone personality and a questionnaire or a web site survey (or both) can obtain customer attitudes toward the company and its products or services.

At a minimum, the marketing executive at a smaller business ought to set an objective in terms of the percentage of people in the marketing target area who have ever heard of the company. Set a target of people who have ever bought from the firm, how much business they have given, and whether they repeat or not. With four or five questions, the marketer can compare the firm's sales performance in any six-month period to these survey numbers. We can imagine doing a survey on a continuous basis every day, having people make a couple of phone calls to people in the surrounding area and take them through this two-minute interview.

To estimate the effects of marketing mix changes, a smaller company can employ a decision calculus approach developed by

Professor John Little at the Sloan School of Management at MIT. In decision calculus, we rely upon the judgment of knowledgeable people in a company, sometimes aided by their marketing consulting firm or advertising agency. Their informed judgments, rather than statistical analysis of empirical data, help set parameters of the kind of model we've just discussed.

Assume that we're interested in determining what would happen if we increased our advertising budget. Assume the firm spent $50,000 on advertising last year, and research tells you the brand has approximately a 20 percent share of market. If you double the spending from $50,000 to $100,000, what effect do you think it would have on share? Would it double? Would it go up by 65 percent? 50 percent? Ask other executives who have the experience and background to make an informed estimate to come to a consensus judgment. Let's say that judgment is that share would go from 20 percent to 28 percent.

What if the CEO wasn't so generous and proposed increasing the budget by half, from $50,000 to $75,000? Assume that the consensus judgment is that share would go from 20 percent to 26 percent.

Now, if the CEO gave an infinite amount of money to spend on advertising, what would happen to share? Go through the estimating process again to come up with an average of 39 percent, maybe even 40 percent. What would happen if the advertising budget were cut to zero for the next couple years? Terrible things. What exactly? Share would drop to 12 percent.

A research analyst can now use some nonlinear regression analysis to fit a line that connects those five points. You can apply it to every number. "What if the advertising budget were $55,000?" "What if it were $60,000?" "What if it dropped to $25,000?" In a situation in which you do not have enough data, or cannot collect the data in a reasonable time, you can go through this decision calculus approach. Although what we've just described is no substitute for doing the kind of sophisticated analysis discussed in Chapter 14, it's better than just pulling your ad budget out of the hat. It's using your head rather than your gut.

Experienced marketing executives who know how much money a company is spending on advertising can estimate the level of media exposure (usually measured in terms of gross rating points, or GRPs) the budget can purchase. If you know the GRPs for a year, you can estimate approximate consumer awareness level for a new product or service at the end of the year. If you know the awareness level and if, through testing, you know what percentage of the prospects exposed to the concept are interested in buying it and if you adjust those numbers to account for the difference between self-reports and actual behavior, you can estimate trial (that is, first purchase), assuming the product was distributed everywhere.

Once you have a ballpark figure for trial, you can take an estimate of ACNielsen's all-commodity volume distribution at the end of the year (the percentage of total product category sales in those stores in which the product is distributed) and approximate trial in terms of units. Do this by simply multiplying the trial score by the distribution number.

If you can estimate repeat purchase (the percentage of customers who will buy the product two or more times) based on some research, estimate how frequently these people buy products in the category and how much they buy each time, you can roughly estimate share of units. If you know the new product's price relative to other prices in the category, you can estimate share of market in dollars.

In short, an experienced marketing executive, simply by using the back of an envelope, may say, "I forecast that the market share for this product in dollars will be about a five" and be in the ballpark most of the time. This is not a gut feeling; it is experience using fact-based information.

Use the Model to Find the Most Efficient Path

Companies typically make some statement of the marketing plan's objectives in the opening pages. These objectives may include market share (Achieve a 10% share of the South African soft drink market by December 31), sales (Sell $62 million of our new software product in the first quarter), market penetration (Achieve 600,000 additional credit cards in force in current markets next year), profit margins (Improve our profit margin to 25% in domestic markets in the next year), or some combination of all four.

As an aside, these particular goals, unlike many we see, support the organization's mission, are challenging but attainable (you have to trust us on this one), are measurable, and include a deadline or schedule. They are appropriate goals. Goals that lack one or more of these elements—"To improve profit margins in 2008," for example— are worthless because they are too fuzzy to be helpful.

A common fuzzy objective is, "We are going to build awareness." What kind of awareness? Top of mind? Unaided brand? Total unaided and aided brand awareness? Unaided or aided advertising awareness? Partially aided or fully aided tracer (e.g., slogan) penetration? What about unaided associations of the brand with key attributes and benefits? That's a type of awareness. Or how about some composite of all these measures, which we refer to as campaign penetration? These are the alternative measures of awareness we showed in Figure 8.1.

Assuming advertising managers can answer these questions— and often they cannot—why choose one measure of awareness over another? It's not an easy question, and many advertisers (and their agencies) avoid it by being as fuzzy as they can. When you're really fuzzy, you can't be measured. If you can't be measured, you're not accountable. The days of the marketing department not being accountable, however, are numbered.

The second part of the marketing plan, after an assessment of the current environment, is usually the sales forecast for the upcoming year. It includes sales objectives, a distribution objective, and maybe a consumer objective: total brand awareness, trial, repeat purchase, preference. But usually those objectives come out of the ether. Management simply announces, "This is what I want from you next year." That, as we've suggested, is setting up the department for failure.

The third part of the plan is what the company will do to attain those objectives. What are the programs? We're going to put

X amount of money into trade incentives. We're going to put Y amount of money into heavy merchandising. We're going to put Z amount of money into light merchandising. We're going to have a public relations program. We're going to have this kind of advertising spending, and our price to the retailer will be A. If we do all those things and invest the way we've just outlined, we will make our share objective.

But, as we said previously, with the exception of those companies that have a model, there is no way to explicitly confirm the company will reach its objectives with the spending plan. At most companies, there's no evidence to show that what the marketing department proposes to spend will achieve the objectives.

Top management says we need to increase our market share from 10 percent to 13 percent next year. Fine. What does the company need to do to consumer preference to achieve that goal? What does the company need to do to distribution and to consumer awareness to achieve it? What does the company need to do to advertising to achieve that awareness? This is where customer equity can be useful.

Increasing distribution might achieve the goal by itself. On the other hand, it may be that the company has just about all the distribution it can hope for, so increasing it may be out of the question.

If marketers know the relationship between distribution and sales and the relationship between advertising and awareness, preference, and sales, they can ask key questions (and expect a useful answer). Questions like, "What does it cost the company to gain one share point through advertising as opposed to the cost to gain the point through distribution?"

If the target group and the positioning are all part of this modeling exercise as they ought to be, you can be assured that your strategy and your tactics are linked to both the consumer objectives—like awareness and preference—and to the hard performance objectives—like sales and market share.

This model can save disappointment later in the year. Say, top management wants to increase market share from a 25 to a 30. The marketing department installs its plans and the expenditures, and the model would almost literally beep in alarm because there is no way the plan would reach the goal. The model would predict a 2-point share gain, not a 5.

The model does offer alternatives, however. What if we spent the budget this way? What if we spent it that way? Or, working from the other direction, what do we need to spend to reach the objective? Through trial, you can simulate all kinds of spending plans to see what you can get.

Better, you can do a sensitivity analysis. You can ask, what happens if (for example) we increase heavy merchandising? The model will show that a $10,000 increase in heavy merchandising yields less effect than a $10,000 increase in light merchandising. The sensitivity analysis points a manager toward those marketing activities that offer the best return on the investment.

It seems to us only common sense to connect the dots in a marketing plan; we know it is a radical idea. At this writing, we have seen only a few businesses go through the agony of developing the model of a complete marketing initiative. For everyone else, the pieces of the marketing plan are simply unconnected pieces. Our budget is this. Our sales goal is this. Our share objective is this. Our target is this. With no link between any element. Tomorrow, of course, marketing executives will have an instrument panel in which everything is linked.

Toward a Marketing Instrument Panel

To visualize such a panel, imagine the controls and instruments of a small plane: a throttle to control the engine speed and therefore the propeller's revolutions per minute (rpm); a yoke to control elevators and ailerons, which control how fast you climb, descend, and bank; rudder pedals to change the airplane's direction in level flight. These are your inputs.

On the instrument panel, you have, among other dials, an rpm readout, a rate-of-climb indicator, an altimeter (how high you are above sea level), air speed and ground speed displays, a turn/bank indicator (shows when you're flying straight and level), a compass, and a fuel gauge. These translate your inputs into information about the aircraft's performance.

Move the throttle forward, the rpm increase; release the brakes, and the ground speed begins to increase. When your ground speed is high enough, ease back on the yoke, and the rate-of-climb needle and altimeter show how fast you are climbing and your altitude. Turn the yoke, and the plane begins to bank. Ease back on the throttle, and the number of rpm drops. Ease back enough, and the rate-of-climb needle drops into the "descend" side of the dial.

The pilot, by changing the inputs, changes the aircraft's course, and the instrument panel shows the changes. This is particularly critical at night over water and in overcast weather. Once in the air, the pilot may not be able to see the ground or the horizon and, therefore, have no visual reference on which to depend. She will have to rely on her instruments to show her altitude, her ground speed, her direction, and how much fuel she has left to get where she wants to go.

It would be valuable if brand managers had analogous tools on their desktop computers. They already have a budget (fuel) and a number of inputs they can control: advertising, couponing, sampling, distribution, direct marketing, public relations, pricing, and more.

What they need are a number of gauges that indicate how the brand is doing in the marketplace: absolute sales (units and dollars), share of market (units and dollars), sales by type of store (mass marketer, supermarket, convenience), by time period (last week, last month, month by month, by quarter, etc.). What if the manager had gauges to show, virtually minute by minute, the changes the inputs have on these outputs?

It would be like taking off in a plane: launch the brand with heavy spending on advertising and promotion and watch the sales figure gauge change. Throttle back on the advertising and watch sales level off. Increase couponing and sampling and sales resume their climb.

Of course, the analogy is not perfect. Increase throttle in a small plane and the propeller's rpm increase immediately; push the yoke forward and the plane begins to descend at once. The brand manager does not have such immediate, real-time control. Increase ad spending and it *may* take a month or more for the advertising to appear in the marketplace, although with large media-buying companies this time lag is growing shorter over time. It may take another month before any effect can be seen, although more and more research has begun to indicate that the effects of advertising and other marketing mix components are more immediate than advertising practitioners previously thought, particularly in fast-turnover product categories.

Nevertheless, the goal is to give brand managers the tools to "fly" their brands higher and safer than they can do today so, for example, midway through the sales year you pull the product's current monthly unit sales up on the computer screen: 310,000 cases—a market share of 4.2 percent of units. A few keystrokes and you pull up the current monthly dollar sales figure: $12.4 million—a dollar share of 4.8 because the product is priced at a premium relative to competitive items. A few more keystrokes and you can tell how you're doing in mass merchandisers, in supermarkets, in convenience stores.

You have not only these results at your fingertips in absolute terms, but you can see the trend, a trend line generated by an econometric model built into the software driving the workstation. It shows sales are leveling off in mass merchandisers but continuing to grow in convenience stores.

What about seasonality? How do the sales this week/month/ quarter compare to sales last week/month/quarter? And how do they compare to the same week/month/quarter a year ago? Almost as fast as you can ask these questions the answers appear on the screen.

You now pull up another screen showing marketing investments: a $27 million advertising budget, a $14.3 million promotion budget, and a $7.6 million sports sponsorship budget. You are halfway through the year, so how much money do you have left? The screen says you've spent 66.2 percent of the advertising budget; you have 33.8 percent remaining, or $9.1 million. It is like saying your fuel tank is a third full; how far will it carry you?

In real time, you can take another nonlinear regression analysis of the relationship between advertising and any sales result you care to look at: units, dollars, distribution channel, time period, whatever. The analysis shows a sales curve that suggests incremental spending is probably not going to add much more lift. In fact, it might make more sense to spend less money on a week-to-week basis.

On the other hand, when you look at your promotion spending and sales, there's almost a direct relationship. Perhaps it makes sense to increase that spending. How about sports sponsorship? You have $2.1 million left in the budget, but sports sponsorships have had virtually no effect on sales. Stop that spending entirely. What about the Internet, public relations, direct marketing?

The idea is to put on the screen all the information a brand manager would like to have, including spending data and current sales, and a tool that connects one to the other and suggests what will happen if the manager makes changes. What if you increase advertising by 10 percent, 20 percent, 30 percent? What if you decrease promotional spending by 10 percent, 20 percent, 30 percent? The model automatically forecasts the effect based on current performance.

This instrument panel provides the brand manager with everything she needs to know to make better decisions. Such panels (also known as dashboards) currently being developed are focused on the manipulation of the inputs to help improve brand performance, everything we talked about in the preceding section.

Instrument panels currently at the conceptual stage go well beyond questions about the relationship between marketing investment inputs, sales outputs, and ROI. Although these analyses are indispensable to developing a great strategy, only when a marketer can have at her touch-screen insights into the ROI of alternative strategic decisions will the Cessna become a Learjet.

Consider alternative market targets for a package good: all Americans, all adult Americans, 18- to 54-year-old women, 25- to 49-year-old women, heavy buyers, nonusers of the category, teenagers, and, very important, a target group identified through sophisticated modeling to be financially optimal. Assume that this brand manager, like most package goods brand managers, has targeted her company's marketing efforts against 25- to 49-year-old women. Then all the analyses reported earlier assume this target group. But what if all men and women were the target? Or heavy users? If that were the strategy, what would the ROI be? And what about a financially optimal target? What would happen if our brand manager addressed her efforts to impacting that group?

Today, there are relatively few brand managers in the United States who can answer that question, and they're probably all working at companies that are exclusively wedded to direct marketing, through the mail, the web, and the telephone.

Everything we've said with respect to targeting holds for positioning, the second most important component in the marketing strategy mix. Positioning, as we've said, represents the message we want to imprint in our target's head about our brand and why our brand is different and better. Yet, as we talked about earlier, today the average brand in the average product category is becoming a commodity; it has no positioning. Imagine another dial on your instrument panel that depicts the relative strength of the new product positioning compared to world-class standards. Is the positioning about average, meaning that for all practical purposes we have no positioning at all? Is it one sigma or two sigma above average? Three? What about six sigma above average, which is the goal at many manufacturing companies today? Clearly where you are on the positioning dial, just as where you are on the targeting dial, can have and will have a dramatic effect on your brand's performance.

Everything said here about targeting and positioning applies to every strategic decision that a brand manager has to make: ad copy and execution, pricing, the Internet, public relations, direct marketing, outdoor, sports and event sponsorships—everything. We talked earlier about managers who typically choose ad copy and execution based on its performance relative to copy-testing norms. But as we pointed out, those norms can be dangerous to your brand. An instrument panel, consequently, that includes a dial that enables you to assess the effects of a six-sigma copy or pricing or public relations strategy relative to current practice would be invaluable.

The Development of Expert Systems

The marketing instrument panels we've been describing will be based in part on highly sophisticated marketing mix and simulated test marketing models, sophisticated marketing research, and evolving expert system technology. Expert systems are computer programs that either recommend a course of action or make decisions based on knowledge gathered from experts in the field. Expert systems, which barely existed in 1985, are now being employed in agriculture, business, chemistry, communications, computers, education, electronics, engineering, environment, geology, image, information, law, manufacturing, mathematics, medicine, meteorology, military, science, and space.

Over the past three decades, simulated test marketing and marketing mix modeling technology has evolved from reliable and valid sales volume forecasting tools into a collection of processes that provide targeting and positioning guidance, cannibalization analysis, marketing plan diagnostics, competitive response analysis, and even optimal marketing plans. Marketing plan optimization is at the forefront of existing marketing intelligence, the edge that leads to the kind of marketing instrument panel we've been describing.

Expert systems offer the promise of a transition to expert managers, executives who will pilot their brands to exceptional marketing programs. Because even if a brand manager today had the kind of marketing instrument panel we've been describing, it would still require human judgment and experience to use it properly.

To imagine how an expert system works, think of how a skilled mechanic makes a diagnosis of a car's problem. He asks questions to establish symptoms, history, and indications: "What kind of noise? When did it start? Do you only hear it on cold mornings?" On the basis of experience, the mechanic runs the tests that seem indicated. He applies his accumulated expertise selectively and by trial and error, testing for one thing, then another to rule out possibilities. He may consult with other mechanics or refer to repair manuals to learn more. Out of all this comes a diagnosis.

Skilled mechanics at sophisticated dealerships and repair shops today employ electronic tools that did not exist a decade ago to help make this diagnosis even more reliable. Today, the mechanic can plug the shop's computer into an outlet in the car to learn that the problem is with the third cylinder.

Expert systems typically follow a similar process. The systems represent knowledge in symbolic form, with numeric values reflecting the subjective probability of the information's likelihood or its truthfulness. The expert system's general reasoning strategy (the so-called inference engine) is separate from the domain-specific trial-and-error attempts, models, and facts (the so-called knowledge base). The domain-specific knowledge includes some combination of facts (in a marketing system, these might be something like, "All shipments to Europe originate from our New York office"), rules ("*If* the marketing objective is to stimulate primary demand, *then* the advertising objective is to stimulate category need"), and models and their interrelationships ("To calculate sales-response coefficients, first run a regression of sales on marketing variables").

This separation between inference and knowledge allows the system to use knowledge in a variety of ways. It can select particular elements in the knowledge base and request additional information to solve a specific problem. An expert system can explain the reasoning behind its questions and recommendations by reporting the trials it has attempted and the facts it used to investigate hypotheses and to draw conclusions.

Expert systems will, we believe, lead to expert marketing managers, managers who will design and manage exceptional marketing programs. The kind of marketing instrument panel we just described would be based on an expert system.

The most exciting application of expert systems, however, from our standpoint will occur when they are designed to help marketers create more effective marketing plans. When this happens, it is hard to imagine that marketing mix analyses will not play a major role.

To begin connecting the marketing plan's dots (and to abandon gut feeling and intuition), the questions to ask are something like these:

- Do we prepare detailed plans of each of our major marketing programs each year?
- Do these plans cover objectives, strategy, tactics, costs, and estimates of ROI?
- Are the objectives all separate, realistic, and measurable?
- Have we done modeling to connect the dots in our marketing plans to tie together strategy, tactics, investments, and objectives?
- If we change one element of the plan, can we predict changes in another?
- Has the model been validated with real-world experience? That is, do we collect data to assess and improve the performance of the model over time?
- Do managers use the model to improve their marketing plans?

12

How to Get All These Great Plans Implemented

A while ago (long ago enough that the results are in) a large, multidivisional corporation invited us to consult on the future of one of the firm's divisions. The division's profits and price/earnings ratio had been declining for several years, and it competed in a highly undifferentiated product category that, for the purpose of this account, we'll call bulk chemicals—sulfur, sodium chloride, potassium sulfate, and the like—with relatively low barriers to entry. The market had not been growing significantly, and increasing competition meant that price was becoming the primary basis of competition. Both customers and the division's sales force increasingly regarded the division's chemicals as commodities. "After all," as one salesperson told us, "sulfur is sulfur. Salt is salt. Customers are looking for the best price per ton."

The corporation had invited a major management consulting firm to analyze the entire business, and the consultants had recommended exiting the bulk chemical business entirely. Sell the division to the highest bidder, and if there were no bidders liquidate the assets. Stop throwing good money after bad. The corporation might have taken the advice except that the CEO had come up through the bulk chemical division and felt an emotional tie to it. He decided to explore other alternatives and hired our firm to consider the options.

In an early meeting, we talked about developing a strategy for the business, and one of the executives snorted, "Strategy? We've had four strategies in the last six years. We don't need another strategy. What we need is a way to *implement* the strategy."

Our associate Jim Keiff observes that clients tend to assume that implementation is something they ought to be able to do themselves. In many large organizations, they certainly have the talent pool to do so. We have found, however, that the organization's politics—the power relationships, the threats to expertise, the structural inertia—get in the way of implementation. If the organization does not have some third party who is not deeply involved in politics but who *is* deeply involved in and committed to the strategy to oversee the implementation process, execution often goes off track.

Without the third party to oversee, what results is not necessarily the implementation of the strategy the organization started with but the implementation of a set of joint decisions that are compromises and expediencies independent of the strategy. These compromises and expediencies, which are usually gut decisions, form their own little strategic context. But it is out of context of what the research data told them they should do or what decent logic would suggest is the proper thing to do. As a result, we have begun to talk about guided implementation.

The Guided Implementation Process

The first step to take to increase the odds that the marketing strategy is implemented effectively is to form an implementation team upon completion of the strategy research. This team may consist of people

Table 12.1 Implementation Team

Core Team Membership	Additional Members
Customer service	Legal
Product management	Corporate communications
Safety	Change management
Market-facing organizations	Vertical market managers
Research and analysis	Field sales and inside sales
Marketing	Quality assurance
Customer engagement (logistics, billing, etc.)	Information technology/ management information systems
Technical services	Controllership

from marketing, sales, operations, finance, customer service, accounting, and any other key activity touching the customer. Table 12.1 shows potential core and additional team members. One caution, however: We have found the more individuals on the team, the less effective it becomes. A team with the 16 people named in the figure would be unusual if it got anything done. Although the optimal team's effectiveness is a function of the personalities, experiences, and roles within the organization, we recommend holding the group to five or six. Also, the more creative the team members think they are, the less likely it is that anyone will recognize the plan a year later.

The key to success is to build consensus among the implementation team at the very beginning, says Keiff. You must get the right team together that will work through the entire process in a positive manner. When we are involved, our role is to comanage this effort and facilitate discussion and actions so all groups feel they are fairly represented. In our experience, managers soon realize our only vested interest is to execute the strategy successfully.

A critical objective at the beginning is to establish team (and management) consensus around the marketing research results. What are the market segment profiles? What are the customer need and value drivers? How does the organization interact with the customers in these segments? What are current practices compared to the research findings? What should the organization do differently in sales, marketing, operations, finance, customer service, accounting, and any function that touches customers? What issues should it follow up for analysis or qualitative exploration?

The team's initial focus is on the organization's product/service offering(s). The offerings bring a business-to-business positioning to life for customers as well as for employees. And the organization must design processes to deliver specific product offerings to the most profitable target segments. The exercise requires the team to keep an open mind, to focus on "What is valuable to customers?" rather than "What is best for our processes?"

(As an aside, we find that this is often the most difficult way of thinking to change. When push comes to shove, it's just easier to think of the company and its needs than of the pesky customers and their demands.)

The outcome of this exercise is a report that defines the common understanding of what segmentation implementation means to every area of the company. It also defines where there are differences in what different customers want, will pay for, will value, or all three. These differences form the basis for the next step, which is product/service/price optimization, if required.

During the optimization study, the implementation team identifies the costs associated with the alternative products/services and the costs of changing what the organization is doing today to what it might be doing if it were to implement the various product or service options. Prepared with this information, the team develops a business case for the optimal product/service as defined by the research. This business case also identifies the existing business processes that will have to change to support the optimized product/service for each target segment, the cost of making the changes, and the incremental revenues the changes will produce. The business case also lays out a plan for a pilot program to test the assumptions about the changes that the business case employed.

We find implementation often stalls because senior management is unable to relate to the proposed marketing strategy change. The business case provides a mechanism to translate a good idea into the kind of investment trade-offs the senior managers face every day. Moreover, quantifying the different impacts forces all of the affected functions—sales, customer service, logistics, manufacturing, and the like—to scrutinize the changes thoroughly so, one hopes, there are no unpleasant surprises later.

The outside facilitator then works with the implementation team to execute the pilot program. The goal is to learn whether the new processes and the customer responses conform to the business case. The team carefully monitors what goes on in the pilot so the organization can adjust the processes or adjust the approach to the customer to optimize the new tactic's profitability.

A report from the pilot program identifies how the organization did relative to expectations, suggests any necessary revisions to the business case, and recommends changes to the processes based on what worked and what didn't. The report also contains a revised implementation plan that, depending on the scope and complexity of the new marketing strategy, lays out training programs required, new processes that have to be introduced to the organization, and organizational changes needed to support the strategy. Ideally, it details a program for bringing the organization up to speed on what the new strategy is, why it is changing, and what the changes will mean to everyone affected.

The last phase of guided implementation is to execute the training programs and new processes, to help in the transition to the new organization, and to assist in communicating the new strategy to employees, customers, suppliers, and other stakeholders.

This is the schematic of guided implementation, a process we have seen work effectively. But good as we think it is, we know that it can fail. In the bulk chemical situation, the implementation, even with our participation, fizzled out. But first, more background.

From Commodity to Solution

We found when we went into the field to interview the chemical division's customers and others in the industry that the market appeared schizophrenic. Perceptually, the products appeared like commodities; behaviorally, they were clearly branded. Buyers had good relationships with their suppliers and were not switching vendors every year or six months in search of better prices. Indeed, we found that price was not as important as that company's management—not to mention its salespeople—had previously thought. Buyers were looking for technical services that went beyond cost per ton, although they rarely found them. The perception of commoditization was a result of the homogeneous strategies employed by the company and its competitors for decades. The companies themselves saw their products as commodities and treated them as such in their marketing and sales efforts.

The strategic options had seemed obvious. Because the division was declining in an industry in which profits were also declining, the best option seemed to be to shutter the unit. A second option was to continue to squeeze costs out of the business through downsizing to improve margins. And a third option was to introduce a new strategy that positioned the brand as a provider of high-end chemical solutions and services and not as a manufacturer of a commodity. Senior management decided to evaluate the third option.

The division began by commissioning us to study a national cross section of bulk chemical decision-makers in companies that bought more than $25,000 worth of such chemicals annually. The study assessed the needs, problems, and motivations of these buyers by industry, by type of company, and by several other measures. It looked at customer perceptions of different brands and identified the most profitable segments and, for each, the most compelling sales message. This was the sort of work we discussed earlier in Chapter 4. We followed this study with concept engineering modeling (the sort of thing we described in Chapter 6 with Dunkin' Donuts) to uncover the service configurations that would be the most profitable for the division.

The division developed and pilot-tested a new nationwide targeting, positioning, product, and pricing strategy. The strategy addressed what decision-makers said they wanted: a partner who could help them run their facilities more efficiently, more safely, and more professionally. The division was no longer selling bulk chemicals; it was selling information that its customers wanted and could not obtain as easily, quickly, or authoritatively from any other source. The pilot program was so successful that the organization went national with it, and within 18 months the division had transformed itself from a company that sold commodity products to one that marketed professional services. Brand equity jumped as buyers increasingly perceived the division as a partner in solving their technical problems rather than just another vendor. Two years after the national rollout, the division had become the most profitable in the corporation. But sadly, in another five years, once the initial excitement had worn off, the division slipped back toward mediocrity.

It was a painful lesson to us. This was a situation in which the company management had come to us and said, "We have had marketing consultants in here before, and they have told us what to do. That's not the issue. The issue is we need help—actually taking that strategy and converting it into action." In spite of that appeal, in the end senior management was not willing (or able) to do what was necessary to implement the strategy thoroughly.

Implementation requires senior management's total commitment. If you don't have senior management's commitment to the implementation process, it will fail. We see two dimensions here. One is that senior management conveys to everyone affected that they actually *do* want to implement this strategy. The second is they will take whatever action it requires to do so. On several occasions, we have obtained the first but not the second.

The bulk chemical products division was an example in which we had the first, but we didn't get the second. Senior management was not ready to fire people who weren't willing to participate in implementing the strategy. That becomes a great inhibitor to success. Every organization has some people who just want to continue to do what they've been doing; they resist virtually any change. Many people fear a loss of power or value: losing their jobs or having their experience discounted. They are anxious about learning new skills and sometimes do not see any real need for the change.

In the bulk chemical division case, the sales force was experienced, knowledgeable, and well paid. There were some salespeople who were simply not going to follow the strategy, which required them to sell technical solutions rather than tons of chemicals. They felt their way, the way they'd used for years, was better. The attitude was, "I've been doing it this way for twenty years and that's the way I am going to do it." It had always worked for them, and they saw no compelling reason to change.

We found passive resistance. Not open rebellion, but things were simply not done. Or they were done halfheartedly, and when the results were inadequate the resisters used them as evidence the new strategy was flawed. Senior management was more concerned about alienating experienced, productive salespeople than thoroughly implementing a proven marketing strategy.

The Seven Principles of Implementation

Occasionally, a chief executive will say to us something like, "What you're saying makes a lot of sense, but on the other hand it also sounds like you're telling me you want to do more than just marketing strategy consulting. You want to sell me an extra piece of work, and I'm not sure I want to go that far. All I really want from you is a solid marketing strategy."

The answer is that we can develop the marketing strategy and walk away. And we're happy to do that. But we will tell you that your chances of implementing the strategy completely in the form we give it to you are practically nonexistent. It will not happen. You will pay for the strategy, but unless someone from outside the organization helps you implement it, it is not worth anything to you.

Table 12.2 lays out the seven principles of implementation we have found over long, painful experience. Management commitment means that others in the organization recognize the priorities, they accept direction from the implementation team, and they know management supports their willingness to participate. Without management commitment, employee support is sporadic, employees constantly reexamine the direction of the changes, and they give them low priority.

Table 12.2   Seven Principles of Implementation

---

1. Enthusiastic commitment by senior management.

2. Involvement by all internal and external groups in the development of the strategy, leading to a consensus of what must be done.

3. Sufficient resources, including people, budget, and internal organization support.

4. Clear designation of responsibility and accountability.

5. A mechanism to ensure actions are consistent with the strategy and the plan.

6. A cooperative spirit between the marketing and sales departments and commitment to strategic goals.

7. Agreed-upon metrics for evaluating success.

Without sufficient resources, the implementation team is forced to revise the plan or modify execution. The team must spend time lobbying for resources rather than working on the implementation itself, and the lack implies weak management commitment. With adequate resources, the team—and by extension the organization—is able to execute the strategic plan as designed. The team can concentrate on execution, and the money reflects concrete evidence of management's commitment

Clear designation of responsibility and accountability provides motivation for the people held responsible and accountable. It enables employees in the organization to know who to approach for information, and perhaps more significantly, it enables people to understand who to consult for decisions. Without a clear designation of both responsibility and accountability, there is no motivation to see the execution completed properly. It can be the worst of all possible worlds: those with responsibility are not accountable and those accountable have no responsibility. In this situation, people are confused over whom to approach for information or a decision.

Without a mechanism to ensure actions are consistent with strategy and the plan, it is highly likely, in fact virtually inevitable, that the execution will deviate from the strategy. Obviously, any strategy may be—indeed, should be—modified over time as external conditions change. But those are planned, deliberate modifications. What you don't want are haphazard, unthinking deviations. Deviations from the plan because a key player does not feel like changing behavior. Or does not take the plan as seriously as the marketer. Take Procter & Gamble's (P&G's) first experience with radio frequency identification (RFID) tagging.

RFID allows a company to track products from the factory to the distributor to the retailer's storeroom to the store shelf. In a fall 2005 experiment involving 19 stores of an unnamed retail chain, P&G's Gillette division looked at how the Braun Cruzer electric shaver moved during a special promotion. The shaver, which sells for $55 to $90, was promoted by advertising and a special store display.

With RFID to track movement, Gillette found "a bunch of variability" in the amount of time it took shavers to move from a retailer's back room to a promotional display on the sales floor, says Jamshed H. Dubash, director of electronic product code for P&G. When stores set up the displays as planned, Gillette saw a 61 percent increase in Cruzer sales. On the other hand, some products never left the back room, even after 40 days when the promotion ended.

The test revealed another problem: Some displays were set up and stocked earlier than planned. "You don't want them there much sooner than three to four days before the actual promotion date," says Dubash, "because you could sell out before the promotion hits and now you're going to have an out-of-stock condition." For this test, Gillette "did not try and interact with the system. We wanted to get a good baseline to understand how things were moving. We wanted to see if the store manager would figure it out."[1] Apparently some of them didn't.

Finally, any implementation must have agreed-upon metrics for success. These provide a clear assessment of success or failure, clear identification of the reasons for success, and clear direction for improving performance. Without metrics, there is confusion regarding performance. Managers cannot understand why the performance, good or ill, occurred, nor do they have any direction for future actions.

How to Sustain the Strategy

Every time we talk about implementation, we always talk about sustainability. Clients are always worried that whatever strategy we come up with, a competitor company is going to adopt it and is going to take it away from them. We tell them that we have rarely seen that in our careers. Why other companies don't try to take it away is a mystery, but they don't. Perhaps they feel that if they did not invent the strategy it can't be very good.

But we observe that there are the early adopters of the strategy, then the reluctant followers, and finally rejecters who never embrace the strategy, no matter what it might do for their business. All of which describes what happens in the first couple of years. Take the Mobil Friendly Serve experience.

By the mid-1990s, the retail gasoline market had suffered through consolidation and price competition. In the Los Angeles market, for example, by 1996 the number of stations had dropped 26 percent in 10 years. Retail profit margins had dropped by two-thirds in six years, and with no market growth and little flexibility to raise prices, stations could only try to take market share. But market shares were virtually immutable. "Shell, Chevron, Mobil—you can't tell them apart except they're different colors," said Dave Hackett, a regional supply operations manage for Mobil at the time. "We asked ourselves, what can Mobil do to get to the point that people recognize us?"[2]

Friendly Serve was the answer. It was a marketing strategy that was 18 months in the making and grounded in multiple large-scale research studies. These addressed everything from identifying the most profitable target (as we discussed in Chapter 4), positioning (Chapter 5), service offering (Chapter 6), advertising (Chapter 8), and more.

The research had shown that customers—especially women— wanted clean, safe, and attractive station restrooms. Mobil Friendly Serve stations were to adhere to new, rigorous maintenance schedules to ensure a sparkling appearance inside and out—from neat and orderly driveways, colorful landscaping and enhanced lighting, to attendants dressed in professional uniforms.

Mobil paid dealers part of the cost of hiring attendants to greet customers and pump their gas. According to a Mobil press release, "They greet customers with a smile, direct drivers to open pumps and provide a helping hand, such as cleaning windows, giving directions, and coaching customers on new technology at the pump. They assist in any way possible—at no extra cost. Friendly Serve attendants will be on duty to assist motorists from 7 A.M. to 7 P.M., Monday through Saturday."

The Mobil publicity said that the welcoming atmosphere "makes drivers feel more comfortable no matter what time of the day they stop for gasoline. Close attention is paid to the details that count—attractive, well-maintained (even decorated) restrooms, as well as clean pumps and nozzle handles. Customers really appreciate the personal touch that Friendly Serve attendants provide. If we can make the buying experience faster and more pleasant for our customers, we hope they'll come back again and again. This attention to service has been tried and proven in Florida and California"—two markets in which Mobil had tested the concept with phenomenal success.

The Friendly Serve research and rollout represented a major commitment by Mobil. The company spent thousands of hours training the Friendly Serve participants. Said a spokesperson, "Our goal is to set a new standard for doing business. To achieve that, we need to have the best-trained and most-committed team in the industry."

Two years into the program, however, Mobil reported mixed success. "We've got a great program living inside an average program," said Brian Baker, COO for Mobil North America Marketing and Refining. "In places where we've been successful, we've moved the [market share] needle astronomically. In places where it doesn't work, it truly isn't friendly service." Baker said that in the third of locations where Friendly Serve is considered "well-executed," sales have increased 20 percent (at a time where any market share increase is in the single digits or zero). In the third of stations that show a moderate success in execution, stations have seen an 8 percent increase. In the final third of stations that did not execute Friendly Serve, stations have seen no improvement over last year's sales.

The biggest thing that Friendly Serve has done is differentiate Mobil from the competition. "Customer service is almost nonexistent in our industry," said Jeff Webster, a Mobil official addressing the corporation's annual convention. "There is no competitor— major or otherwise—that has a leadership position in the area of service."

According to statistics released by Mobil and reported by *National Petroleum News*, the company's Friendly Serve strategy appeared to be effective. Overall, year-to-date gasoline sales were outpacing other major competitors by 5 percent. Mobil was making even more impressive strides with its identified, target markets, despite the fact that only 30 percent of the stations fully implemented the strategy. When Mobil launched its plans, it identified six market segments, three of which were defined as Road Warriors (laptop and cellular phone types who did much of their work on the road); True Blues (blue-collar workers); and F3s (fuel, food, and fast). Mobil moved to target those three target segments because they bought more super unleaded gas, drove a lot of miles, and were more brand loyal than other segments. The Friendly Serve program worked as forecast among those segments. Sales to Road Warriors and True Blues were up substantially.[3]

Despite positive reports like these, Mobil was never able to persuade more than a third of the stations to fully adopt the program; another third adopted parts of the program but not the whole thing; and another third never adopted it. The lack of performance became embarrassing for top management. One senior Mobil executive lived in Alexandria, Virginia, where there was a Mobil station between his house and office. After months of waiting, he finally became furious that the station had not embraced the Friendly Serve strategy. He came into the office one morning and announced to the Friendly Serve managers responsible, "When I have people coming from headquarters or analysts or anyone, I want to be able to demonstrate Friendly Serve at that station. It's been six months since we talked about this and nothing's been done. You're going to be looking for new jobs if you don't get them into the program." The station grudgingly took on the program, but it was a halfhearted implementation.

One of Mobil's problems, of course, was that many stations are independent franchisees. Mobil has a detailed franchise agreement but is still limited in what it can force a dealer to do. It can try to persuade. It can try to convince. It can threaten, and, as a last resort, it can disenfranchise, but it is not as simple as firing one station manager and putting somebody else in charge. And even that is not always so simple.

Three top executives in three major corporations have all said to us in the last 18 months in essentially the same words, "One of the biggest problems I have is getting people to do what I want them to do. People just don't do it." Of course, one problem may be structural. The CMO of a giant package goods company told us, "You have to remember that as in a law firm or in a university, people at our corporation have about ten years to make it. If they do everything right, they make it and they become senior brand manager. And if they don't reach that level within that approximate time period, they are pushed out the door. It's like the professor who doesn't get tenure; it's like the lawyer who doesn't make partner."

And how are these junior marketing people evaluated during this trial period? Almost entirely on the basis of their brands' sales performance, not profitability. And certainly not creativity or innovation. At this corporation, profitability is the purview of the finance people, not the marketing people. Marketing people generate the sales, and anything that might detract from the sales goal is unlikely to get implemented because it puts the would-be manager's future in question. As the CMO, with all his experience and authority, says, "I really think that you should try to put more of your budget into digital media . . . or you need to take more money out of the prime time television and put it into something else . . . or we think you really need to change your copy strategy . . . or you really ought to drop that channel of distribution and try to pick up a new channel," the chances are they won't do it.

They will find excuse after excuse after excuse to avoid doing something new because, and these are his exact words, "the organization does not reward you for experimentation." These junior marketers are not lazy or perverse. They simply believe it is not in their best interest to experiment with new things.

Another CEO told us that the MBAs in his organization think they are "more creative and smarter than me. So there is nothing I can give them to do that they think they can't improve. As a consequence, if you check in with them a week later to see what they're implementing, it's not what you have asked them to do."

We find more and more that companies, like people, get bored. After seven years or so in a neighborhood, many people want a new house. After seven years with a car, you definitely need to get a new car. After seven years with a wife . . . , but you get the idea. There comes a time when the strategy begins to change because the strategy is old, boring.

Sometimes change results because people move. After seven years—and usually fewer—there is a new person in the job (the average tenure of a CMO these days is 23 months). And the new boss is usually more interested in making his or her own impact rather than simply continuing a predecessor's programs. In the case of Mobil, even with the halfhearted implementation, the Friendly Serve won kudos all over the world and was going strong in terms of sales and profitability. But the organization took its foot off the gas pedal, and it began to slow down. Not only at the independent dealerships, but at Mobil's own.

It took seven years to roll Friendly Serve out to its maximum levels. During this period Mobil introduced the Speedpass, which is still going strong, and to the best of our knowledge, no other oil company has introduced something similar. But the stations are reverting to the condition they were in before Friendly Serve, perhaps not quite as unkempt as they were before, but they are no cleaner on average than any other company's stations. Mobil has made some standard improvements; they put more lights in the stations, for example. But the Friendly Serve flags are long gone. Friendly service is long gone. It came and went in less than fifteen years.

Questions to Ask about Implementation

Implementation is always difficult. We know as managers in our own company. But we also know that the way many organizations go about it makes implementation virtually impossible. These companies tend to be headed by an autocratic or charismatic leader who decides a change is needed, makes plans behind closed doors, calls a meeting to announce the new strategy, tells everyone where they fit in the plan, brands all those who resist or who question the plan's wisdom as not "team players," and takes credit for any success (and blames underlings for any failure).

To make the implementation of a new marketing strategy at least possible, the most senior management ought to ask several questions:

- Was actionability a prime consideration in developing this new strategy? Did team members talk about, and fret over, this issue throughout the process?
- Was the strategy and its rationale shared with all internal and external groups that might be affected by its implications?
- Have we developed a checklist for each element of the plan that is necessary for success and put a system in place for assuring conformity?
- Do our marketing people have the time to work both on current day-to-day activities and launch something very new?
- Have we developed tools, processes, and software that can help automate some of the mundane processes of implementation to help managers focus on critical issues?
- Have we integrated every aspect of the marketing program? Do our advertising, packaging, web site, outdoor programs, and more all reflect the same targeting and positioning strategy?
- Do we have agreed-upon metrics to evaluate success?

13

Brand Equity—Out; Customer Equity—In

Throughout the 1990s, marketing consultants preached the joys of brand equity. Although we weren't sure at the time what they always meant—and still aren't—marketers and their bosses became convinced that brand equity was important and had to be measured.

Everybody started to measure. There isn't a major company we see that doesn't have some system for tapping into brand equity. It is part of strategic thinking. It is part of advertising evaluation. It is part of advertising tracking. At some companies, where they are using econometric models to evaluate the relationship between marketing program investments and performance, they think of the relationship between the investments and sales as measuring short-term effects and the relationship between the investments and changing brand equity as indicators of long-term performance.

Now in the last few years, the focus has changed. Now companies are talking about customer equity. How many equities does a company need? And what good are they?

Perhaps the place to start this discussion of fairly sophisticated marketing strategy is with the kinds of questions marketers routinely try to answer. These are questions like:

- How much money should we invest to build the brand? Should we spend another $1 million or $5 million on a marketing campaign—advertising, direct mail, samples, a contest, or some combination thereof—to promote the brand?
- How much money should we invest to enhance our product or service? Should we add features? Or cut prices? Do both?
- How much money should we invest in relationship building or in customer relationship management or both? Should we spend $3 million to improve our frequent-buyer program?

Until fairly recently, a gut decision based on intuition and experience was about the best any marketer could do to address questions like these. We didn't have the tools available to construct solid answers. Now we do. Regrettably, this chapter will not give you definitive answers to your own, similar questions—after all, every marketing situation is unique—but it will give you a way to think about the questions and to find the answers for your organization. And let's begin with brand equity.

What Brand Equity Means

The first time we heard the expression *brand equity*, we were not sure what it meant. Fifteen years later, we find that academics and marketing practitioners still talk about brand equity as if it had some common meaning when in fact is has all kinds of meanings: "awareness," "brand bonding," "brand personality," "customer lifetime value," "price value," "product differentiation," "loyalty," "strength of feelings," "user imagery," and more.

To understand brand equity, we have to start with what is a brand. (And if this is too basic, feel free to skip ahead.) The American

Marketing Association defines a brand as "a name, term, sign, symbol, or design, or a combination of them, intended to *identify* the goods or services of one seller or group of sellers and *differentiate* them from those of competition." Professor Kevin Keller at the Tuck School of Business at Dartmouth College says that what distinguishes a brand from its unbranded commodity counterpart "is consumers' perceptions and feelings about the product's attributes and how they perform. Ultimately the brand resides in the minds of consumers."[1]

Some companies define brand equity as the incremental dollar value of the brand name. If, everything else being equal, you can sell your branded bath soap for 10 percent more than a store brand, your brand equity reflects that difference. To the consumer, your branded product is worth 10 percent more than the store brand. But why, if everything else is equal, is it worth more? Because the brand name *itself* has value.

One of our early studies measured attitudes toward 57 brands among a national sample of approximately 1,000 consumers at multiple points in time. We found seven factors that seemed to capture brand equity satisfactorily. These were the brand's permeation, distinctiveness, quality, value, personality, potential, and competitive inoculation.

The brand permeation factor is a weighted combination of brand and advertising awareness and availability. The more consumers are conscious of the brand and the advertising for the brand and the more easily they can find the brand in stores, the stronger this factor.

The brand distinctiveness factor is a weighted combination of measures that indicate brand differentiation, uniqueness, and superiority. Not unexpectedly, the more consumers see a brand as different from, unique, and superior to competitive products, the stronger this factor. (Remember, these are consumer perceptions, not necessarily reality.)

Brand quality is an overall assessment of the brand as a whole and its line extensions in terms of different indicators of product/service quality. The more reliable, trouble-free, and consistent a brand is, the stronger this factor.

Brand value is a combination of perceived and actual price relative to perceived quality/excellence. This is, in essence, a measure of whether the brand delivers what buyers pay for—often known as price-value.

The brand personality factor reflects the extent to which the brand's image is congruent with who the buyer is or wants to be. If the consumer sees the brand as sophisticated and if she wants to be seen as sophisticated, she will feel positive toward the brand. If she sees the brand as a good value and wants to be seen as a canny shopper, she will buy the brand even if it costs more than comparable products.

The brand potential factor reflects the extent to which consumers will pay more for, go out of their way for, or are willing to try the brand's not-yet-introduced new products or line extensions. If, as one example, a consumer has strong positive feelings toward the Sony brand, he is more likely to buy any new Sony electronic product than he will buy another company's similar product.

Competitive inoculation reflects the extent to which the brand is protected against competitive inroads, the extent to which the consumer would stick with the brand in times of adversity or competitive pressure.

You can measure each of these factors by three to five questions embedded in an Internet or personal interview or a mailed questionnaire in which respondents can see and rate brand logos. Out of all these measures, it is possible to obtain a single brand equity number. Our favorite approach is to regress scores for each of the seven measures against market share over time and then weight the measures by their relative importance in a regression equation. You can do this not just for your brand, but also for all major competitors in the category. Brand equity can then be expressed as your share of total equity in a category relative to competitors.

Brand Equity Is Not Market Share

We have learned that no matter how a company measures brand equity—simple measures or more complex—some brands have more equity than market share. Others have more share than equity.

Table 13.1 Brand Equity versus Brand Share*

Higher Brand Equity than Brand Share	Lower Brand Equity than Brand Share
BMW	Lexus
Skol	Budweiser
Mobil 1	Castrol
Pepsi	Coke
Pizza Hut	Domino's
Saks	Neiman Marcus
Subway	McDonald's
Michelin	Goodyear
Target	Wal-Mart
Citizens Bank	Bank of America
Apple	Dell
Dunkin' Donuts	Starbucks

*Based on data within markets in which both brands compete.

Table 13.1 compares the brand equity and market shares of 24 different brands. BMW, for example, has more brand equity than market share, whereas Lexus has more market share than brand equity.

Our research has found that brands with greater brand equity than market share include BMW, Skol, Mobil 1, Pepsi, Pizza Hut, Saks, Subway, Michelin, Target, Apple, Citizens Bank, and Dunkin' Donuts. Brands with greater market share than brand equity include Lexus, Budweiser, Castrol, Coke, Domino's, Neiman Marcus, McDonald's, Goodyear, Wal-Mart, Bank of America, Dell, and Starbucks.

A brand equity measure does provide a useful explanation of brand performance—why some brands seem to do better than similar competitive brands—but it is incomplete. Over a wide range of product and service categories, we have found that brand equity explains about 49 percent of the variance in market share. It explains only 49 percent because so many other factors also impact share: conventional mass media, direct marketing, distribution, public relations, web site communications, consumer promotions, point-of-sale communications, and pricing among others.

Strong brand equity is a goal to which brand managers should aspire because brands with strong equity appear to be more able to convert marketing investment into enhanced marketing performance than brands with weak equity. Strong equity brands are often in the so-called acceleration range of their market response curves. Their owners can do more with less.

We have found, for example, that only 30 percent or fewer of all customers of brands with strong equity are vulnerable to switching; 50 percent or more customers of brands with weak brand equity are vulnerable. Some 60 percent or more of all customers are loyal to brands that have strong equity; 40 percent or fewer are loyal to brands with weak equity. In other words, strong brand equity means loyal customers.

Perhaps our most interesting finding is the ratio of possible incremental business to current business among brands with strong equity is 30 percent to 200 percent (and sometimes even more). That is, these brands have a market potential considerably greater than their current share by expanding their business among current customers, finding new customers for the current product line, and finding new customers for an expanded product line. The same measure for brands with weak equity is less than 20 percent. The weaker the brand equity, the harder it is to grow the business.

Brand equity, like IQ, an SAT score, or a price/earnings ratio, is a number. It is an overall assessment of the goodwill associated with a brand that reflects past marketing performance and predicts future sales and profit potential. When combined with a financial assessment of brand profitability, it provides a more complete accounting of a brand's value to the corporation or a potential acquisition's value. For example, in a situation in which we were involved, the asking price for a beer company was $3.2 billion. The buyer's financial analysis suggested the company was worth $1.1 billion. A brand equity and market potential analysis suggested a value of $900 million. The reason? There was little brand equity and, therefore, little potential for growth.

So if this is brand equity, what is customer equity, and how can you use it?

What Customer Equity Means

In 2000, Roland T. Rust and his associates, Valarie A. Zeithaml and Katherine N. Lemon, published their seminal book, *Driving Customer Equity*. We regard Rust, a professor of marketing at the University of Maryland, as a virtual Isaac Newton of modern marketing science. He recognized for the first time that although brand equity is important, it doesn't tell the whole story. It is really one of three components that drive consumer and business-to-business decision-making behavior: brand equity, relationship equity, and product (or value) equity.

Customer equity, loosely defined, is the financial value of a customer over, say, a five-year period. This financial value of a customer is eclipsing brand equity as a measure of marketing performance.

It is possible to think of customer equity a little like home equity. Home equity is the value of your home less what you owe on the mortgage. Although this value may rise or fall as the neighborhood or the market changes, there are things you can do (or neglect to do) to affect your home's dollar value. For example, you could remodel the kitchen, landscape the backyard, build a family room, update the electrical system, add a deck, or do nothing to the house and buy a new car.

Each choice adds something to the dollar value of your home, even buying a new car. Leaving a new BMW Series 7 in the driveway may give potential buyers one impression of your home's value; a beat-up 1958 muscle car will give another. Assume for the moment you want to make the decision that will increase the dollar value of your home the most. (You may, for example, want a family room so you have a place for your 42-inch flat-screen home theater and you don't care whether it increases the value of the house or not.) How do you make the decision? You study real estate manuals that tell you which of the choices are most likely to increase the value of the house more than the cost of the change—or not.

It is the same with customer equity. You want to choose the strategy that will increase the dollar value of your customers the most; you want them to be loyal, to buy your products more often, to tell their friends about them, and to buy your new products. The organization, however, has limited marketing resources; where would they best be spent? Where can you safely cut back? Advertising? Packaging? Customer service? Which investments on which marketing element(s) will have the greatest positive impact on revenue and, if done right, on profits?

In the simplest terms, customer equity is a measure of how much each customer will spend over time in your market, added up over all the customers in the market, and discounted back to present value. It is a sophisticated concept that takes into account brand switching patterns, Markov chain analysis (there's an explanation coming), demographic projections, life expectancy forecasts, and value discounts.[2]

Although customer equity enthusiasts talk about customer lifetime value, in practice we have found that no one in business is much interested in results for more than five years. Customer five-year value is good enough for most executives. But they *would* like to know what total category sales are likely to be in five years, and they would like to know their piece of that total, given the current trajectory of the brand and how they might obtain a larger piece.

For example, it is possible to do a research study among 500 to 1,000 buyers in a product category and come up with a number for a brand in the category. Ask people in the survey—customers or prospective customers—how many dollars they spent in the category this year. You can then multiply this to obtain a five-year projection (adjusting for purchase frequency and other factors) for individual consumers. Take as hypothetical illustrations: The five-year customer equity value for BMW driving machines is $71,750. The five-year customer equity value for Hartford insurance is $33,192. The five-year customer equity value for Perdue poultry is $1,169. For the Gillette Fusion shaving products, $147. For Tide detergent, $65.

Customer Equity Is More than Current Value

The important point to note right now is that this number reflects more than the current value of today's customers. This current value is what the average customer will spend on, say, Gillette Fusion products and blades in an average year. Customer equity tells you what customers will spend on Fusion products over a five-year period. But that requires several things: an estimate of how many customers will continue to buy at the same rate as they have, how many customers will switch to another brand (or stop shaving), and how many new customers will begin to buy the brand.

Rust and his associates developed a brand-switching matrix that provides insights into where new customers may come from and where current customers may be going. It gives marketers a very good idea of how many customers the company is likely to have five years out and what they are worth over the period.

We modified the Rust model by taking the demographic profile of the current customers, fed it into a demographic forecasting model, and projected the customer profiles forward. It answers the question, "If nothing else changes but the demographic profile of the United States, how many customers will the company have in five years?" Multiply that by what the company estimates they will be worth, and it has a future value. The brand-switching matrix estimates the number of people who are going to drop the brand over the five years and the number of people who will start using the brand at some point over the period.

Five years is an arbitrary period. It is possible to look at longer stretches. If Cadillac were to look at customer equity over a 20-year period, it would notice its customer population is fairly old and growing older. Project that forward in time, and the proportion of people buying Cadillac will shrink.

Demography can be a powerful predictor of future performance. For example, 25 years ago, we hired a University of Pennsylvania demographer to create 64 different demographic segments based on gender, age, occupation, and geography. We then calculated the population percentage of American Express cardholders in each of the 64 cells. We then asked the demographer to tell us how much each cell would shrink or grow over 10 years. We assumed that the percentage of American Express cardholders in each cell would be no different in the future and projected the number of American Express cards, based on changing demographics alone.

More recently, we were again working for American Express, and we decided to revisit the earlier analysis. We used the same 64 groups and assigned all current cardholders to one of the groups. We then assumed that current penetration numbers would be what they were more than two decades earlier and multiplied everything out. The number of cardholders was within 5 percent of the 20-year-old projection. All the success American Express enjoyed over the 20-year period was because the population was getting older, becoming more educated, and becoming richer.

Three Factors Drive Customer Equity

Just as a brand may have more equity than market share, so a brand (or a company) may have more customer equity than current value. Brands with a disproportionate share of customer equity enjoy a number of positive characteristics. Their prospects for long-term growth are strong, their value for acquisition purposes is greater than for companies of comparable size in revenues and profits, and their investments in marketing dollars are more easily converted into incremental sales than their competitors with a lower ratio of customer equity to market share.

As Table 13.2 indicates, Air Products has higher customer equity than current value, whereas Praxair has lower customer equity than current value. CBS has higher customer equity than current value than MTV, and so on.

Three factors drive customer equity: brand equity, which we've just discussed; product equity (our label for what Rust calls *value equity*); and relationship equity. Brand equity is the customer's subjective assessment of a brand, above and beyond its objectively perceived value. Product equity is the customer's objective assessment of a product or service. And relationship equity is the customer's

Table 13.2   Customer Equity 2006–2011

Higher Equity than Current Value	Lower Equity than Current Value
Apple	Dell
Air Products	Praxair
CBS	MTV
IM/Wireless	E-mail
Mobil	Shell
NASCAR	NBA
Sony	Hitachi
Harley-Davidson	Suzuki
Target	Wal-Mart
Hyundai	VW

tendency to stick with a brand above and beyond the objective and subjective assessment of the product or service.

In many large companies, three different executives are responsible for these factors. The advertising manager is responsible for the brand equity, building the brand through advertising and promotion. The product manager is in charge of product equity, responsible for price, quality, and convenience. The loyalty program manager is responsible for the relationship with customers through loyalty programs and community outreach programs (such as sponsoring a Little League baseball team).

Because three different executives or departments are often responsible, there is often competition for company resources. The advertising manager argues for more advertising. The product manager for new features. The loyalty program manager for an improved customer relationship management (CRM) system. They all commission research to prove the case for their proposal. But to understand—and, more to the point, to improve—customer equity, the organization requires only one study.

The same survey among 500 to 1,000 buyers that we used to measure how much each customer will spend over time in the market can—should—also measure the effects of brand, product, and relationship equity on customer equity.

For the purposes of a customer equity measure, brand equity may consist of customer brand awareness (through direct mail, newspaper and magazine ads, or TV ad awareness), customer attitudes toward the brand (it's exciting/energized, caring, technologically advanced, family friendly, and the like), and customer perception of brand ethics (committed to the community, honest and trustworthy). These are similar to, but different from, the seven brand equity measures we discussed earlier.

The three main factors that drive product equity are quality (for example, reliable service, selection, leading technology, appealing aesthetics), convenience (easy installation, on-demand/time-shifting, parental controls), and price (reasonable prices, a variety of clear pricing plans). As we've seen, however, most company managements seem focused on price as a way to raise sales, but, again, only 15 percent to 35 percent of buyers in most product categories consider price as the primary factor in a purchase. Depending on the product and the circumstances, quality and convenience will often trump price.

Loyalty programs, community building programs, and CRM systems drive relationship equity. We find it interesting that the CRM component of relationship equity management is being driven by information technology (IT) people, not by marketing. CRM these days is a good way to tick your customers off in seven seconds—send them to voice-mail jail. Because it costs so much to install a CRM system, senior managements have given them to IT departments to develop and install without any involvement from marketing. But the IT people are not marketers, and they designed the systems to hold down the cost, not to enhance customer experience or boost sales. The unintended consequence is that they diminish customer experience and—over time—cut sales so the money saved at one end is lost at the other.

One of the components of the Rust/Zeithaml/ Lemon customer equity model is a brand-switching matrix that considers the probability that the customer will buy another brand the next time she shops, based on her self-report. As soon as the customer reports the probability of repeating with her current brand, the mathematical program will take various factors into consideration, such as purchase cycles, and make a prediction. This is where we see the Markov chain, where probabilities are repeatedly calculated based on the current situation rather than on history.

For example, any children's game in which the moves are determined by dice is a kind of Markov chain. The next state of the board depends on the current state and the next roll of the dice, and you can chart the probabilities of what the dice will say. This is different from a card game in which, as the number of cards in the pile goes down, the probabilities of drawing any particular card change.

Say the model makes the prediction that in five years T-Mobile's market share will be very close to a 10. The model might also say that Cingular's share will go down slightly and Verizon's will remain essentially the same. That is what the shares would be if everything stayed as it is.

But, we suspect, T-Mobile's CMO doesn't want everything to stay as it is. T-Mobile would like its share to be 20 in five years. What does the company have to change to have the greatest effect? A customer equity model tells you which of the three drivers of customer equity and their separate components have the most effect on the brand.

More importantly, the model provides specific insight into what happens if the company succeeds in changing each of the drivers. Suppose the advertising awareness component of brand equity went up five points, what does the company get for it? Now what is the share of customer equity, which can be converted into dollars? What if the company improves the convenience of its service by five points? What does it get back?

Improving service is a long-term investment. Companies that put money into doing so don't expect the investment to be paid back in a few months. They expect it to pay out over the next five years. Marketers do a customer equity forecast over a five-year period because they know that the market ordinarily does not move that fast. If a technology investment costs $300 million, the corporation may expect only a $30 million increase in incremental revenues the first year, but after five years it's returned $450 million.

Connect Spending to Marketing Results

The difficulty, of course, is connecting marketing spending to the precise change in one of these three drivers of customer equity. At the moment, organizations are using decision calculus: They put the marketing people in a room and ask how much they think the organization would need to spend to move the relationship equity number 10 percent, 20 percent, 30 percent, 40 percent, 50 percent, or 100 percent. How much would it have to spend to move the brand equity needle by comparable amounts? How much would it have to spend to change consumer perceptions or move product equity?

Based on those estimates, the company can develop an equation that provides guidance on what it ought to spend on what strategy. Think of it as a cool approach to giving you some insight into how much emphasis you should place on the product, on the relationship, and on the brand.

Research has found that these three equities—the product, relationship, and brand—act differently in different industries, and, of course, the individual drivers of the equities have different effects on individual brands. For example, brand equity has relatively little impact in the airline industry, considerably more impact in the grocery industry, with the rental car industry somewhere in between.

Relationship equity—primarily loyalty programs and CRM systems—has a major effect on the airline industry, but they are much less significant in the rental car and grocery industries.

Product equity, in contrast, has a major impact on the rental car industry, relatively little on the airline industry, with groceries in between. For example, Avis has a much greater customer equity opportunity by focusing on product equity than by focusing on either brand or relationship equity. The subdrivers of product equity are quality (the most important opportunity for Avis), convenience (significantly less important), and price (even less important). The research has found that different product/service features affect quality perceptions at Avis, with the ability to rent a preferred car having the greatest impact. Other product/service features, in descending order of impact, include having the car ready to go, having cleaner cars, and not having to fill up the gas tank.

A study of the cable television industry found that product equity was the most important driver of customer equity. The subdrivers of product equity were the speed of response to customer problems, the breadth of programming alternatives, and the availability of special events and newly released movies. Among the things we learned was that product reliability was an overriding factor: The Internet connection and TV works through thick and thin, storms, rain, whatever. In fact, reliability was about the only consideration on the Internet side of the business. Customers wanted to know they would never have a glitch, the Internet would always work.

The surprise factor was with the television side of the business. The customer survey statement "I get a lot of interesting information from them in the mail" was very big for the cable/TV business. Customers felt that if the monthly communication they receive in the mail is interesting and useful, if it explains what is going on with the cable service or the pricing or the options, it had a big impact. They wanted to be told what was happening in entertainment and with their TV service every month.

When you think about it, it made a lot of sense. But nobody thought it would come out as big as it did. It was huge. One's gut would have said—like the client's as it turned out—go with a groovy advertising campaign and create excitement. The data said just be really reliable and have a constant flow of information on a monthly basis in an envelope, maybe even a magazine.

We thought the client had a good opportunity for custom publishing, the kind of private magazine we talked about in Chapter 7. It is still not cheap, but come up with handsome magazine and send it to customers once a month. They will love it. The client's gut said no, we want to have 65 percent of our money in TV advertising and the rest in newspapers. That's what we've been doing. That's what's built the company. It just feels right.

In contrast, a study of customer equity for one of the major laptop computer manufacturers revealed that product equity was relatively unimportant. Senior management's gut had told them that price and product features were driving the category, and that's where the company needed to concentrate. The customer equity research told a different story. It showed that 55 percent of the brand share could be explained by brand issues. Prospective customers were more aware of other brands, and more had positive attitudes and perceptions toward them. People reported that competitors were always sending them direct-mail information; they saw competitive advertising all the time; competitive products were endorsed by people in the industry. Surprisingly, the feature-to-feature and functionality comparisons and price had very little to do with the purchase decision; they only explained about 12 percent of product choice. Our client's decision was clear: Either invest in a major advertising campaign and other marketing activities to put the company brand in people's faces. Or don't, and get out of the laptop computer business.

Assess the Costs of Changing

Once company management knows the effects of all three drivers and subdrivers of customer equity, it can appraise the costs of changing performance of each driver over time. Which is why you want to look at five years' worth of data. It might take Avis more than a year and several million dollars to make it possible for most customers to rent their preferred car, an investment in time and money that cannot pay a healthy return in less than five years.

Figure 13.1 is a schematic chart showing various possible management decisions, their effects on equity subdrivers, those effects on the three major equity drivers, and their effect on customer equity.

So to return to the three questions a CMO might be asking:

- How much money should we invest to build the brand? Should we spend another $1 million or $5 million on a marketing campaign—advertising, direct mail, samples, a contest—to promote the brand?

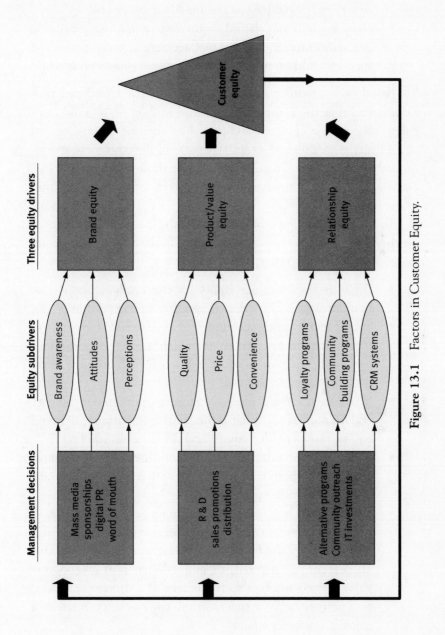

Figure 13.1   Factors in Customer Equity.

259

- How much money should we invest to enhance our product or service? Should we add features? Or cut prices?
- How much money should we invest in relationship building or in customer relationship management or both? Should we spend $3 million to improve our frequent-buyer program?

Based on a careful customer equity study, the CMO can now recommend that the company spend $7.8 million on a brand campaign, raise prices 5 percent and introduce the line extension, and do a loyalty program for the top 10 percent of the customers, spending only $1.3 million. The CMO can make these recommendations confident that their impact and return will be far out of proportion to the investment.

To begin diagnosing customer equity, the questions to ask focus on the three equities: brand, product, and relationship. These are questions like the following:

- What is the customer equity for our product, service, or brand today and how does it compare to competitors?
- How does our customer equity compare to our market share? Is it higher than market share, which suggests opportunities for significant growth, or is it lower, which suggests problems that need to be fixed?
- What are the key drivers of customer equity in our category and for our brand? What is the relative importance of brand equity, product/value equity, and relationship equity?
- Which components of each of these three drivers are most critical? Is it brand awareness? Is it product price? Is it customer relationship programs?
- How difficult is it to change consumer perceptions on each of the dimensions that drive customer equity? What will it cost to change the brand perceptions on each by 5 percent, 10 percent, 20 percent, or more? What is the economic value gained through such changes? If a driver is changed by 5 percent, what is that worth to the marketer in terms of gains in customer equity?

- What is the best use of limited marketing resources in terms of the customer equity framework?
- Where can we safely cut back? That is to say, on which dimensions is it safe to say that no further expenditures are required or are valuable?
- Finally, what is the best mix of marketing resources to produce the maximum gain in profitability to changing customer equity?

14

Yes, You *Can* Measure Marketing ROI

Recently, we sat down with senior management from McDonald's Corporation. They had invited us in to talk about marketing return on investment (ROI), the measurement of which was a mandate from the corporation's CEO. We learned that the firm had some very interesting systems in place. They measured sales for every one of their more than 2,000 stores. They had an advertising tracking study in place, which measured awareness, familiarity, messages communicated, consumer attitudes, and customer behavior on a monthly basis. They had been collecting that data for about three years. And they had a separate brand equity project measuring consumer perception of their brand versus major competitors. All this was good information, but it was not good enough for the CEO.

The CEO wanted to understand the links between marketing investments and sales and, ultimately, the return on those investments.

What are the effects of advertising on television, radio, print, and other traditional vehicles McDonald's has been using forever? And how do these effects compare to nontraditional vehicles such as digital billboards, Internet advertising, an entertaining and informative web site, simulated word of mouth, and a host of other nontraditional vehicles? If the corporation were to increase the marketing budget, say, 10 percent, how would that affect sales? Would the incremental sales cover the increased expense and then some? At the time we talked, no one knew, although McDonald's was hardly alone. Very few companies have systems in place to measure the effectiveness of their marketing programs. Even fewer are able to accurately assess ROI or identify a financially optimal way to allocate the marketing budget.

Ed See, the chief operating officer of Marketing Management Analytics (MMA), says that "what was a basic black-or-white decision— do I advertise on TV or in print?—has become far more complicated. Marketers now confront a dizzying array of choices from digital, to product placement to sponsorship to cable to network TV and wireless, among other new media. And with so many options, failure is that much easier."[1]

Senior executives are demanding measures of marketing's impact on financial returns, and more and more of them are getting it. A joint research study by Lenskold Group and MarketingProfs found that "the ability to link brand measures to incremental sales and profits has increased over the past year. Marketers reporting their ability to make this brand measure link as 'a real source of leadership' or 'as good as it needs to be' increased from a combined total of 6 percent in 2005 to 15 percent in 2006."

The study found that marketing organizations that calculate ROI, net present value, or other profitability metrics to assess marketing effectiveness report high CEO and CFO confidence and a strong perception of accountability. According to the researchers, "26 percent of the marketers surveyed indicated that their organizations calculate ROI or similar financial metrics for at least some portion of their marketing campaigns. Of this segment, 31 percent [that is, only about 8 percent of the total] reported that their CEO and CFO were very confident that their marketing investments were profitable."[2]

One reason for direct marketing and Internet marketing's growing popularity is the clear connection between the effort and the result. It is relatively simple to calculate the cost per impression, the cost per click (what it costs to have an advertisement clicked), and the cost per order on the Internet. But what is the effect of a prime-time 30-second television commercial? What many companies need is a comprehensive marketing mix model that quantifies the return on sales—and on brand equity.

Preparing for an ROI Analysis

Marketing organizations are increasingly seeking to improve the efficiency, effectiveness, and accountability of marketing efforts. Those that orchestrate and optimize marketing resources—and close the gap between data and timely insights—will outperform their peer group in revenue and profit performance and create significant competitive advantage. Sophisticated marketers are looking beyond sales and profits and asking questions about brand equity (and, ultimately, customer equity). They realize that brand/customer equity is not only an indicator of the *long-term* effect of marketing spending but also can cause marketing spending itself to be more effective. Brands with strong equity tend to enjoy a much higher level of market response than brands with lower equity; it's as if equity is an accelerant in the ROI creation process.

To do this, a marketer must assemble a great deal of data, preferably over three years or more. The more data, the stronger the analysis. It's best if this data can also be disaggregated into regions of the country, individual markets, or even individual channels of distribution (that is, the McDonald's on the southwest corner of Maplewood Avenue in Gloucester, Massachusetts, or the Stop & Shop supermarket in the East Gloucester Shopping Center).

Imagine that McDonald's has weekly data available for 2,000 stores for three years. That's 312,000 data points to examine (2,000 stores times 52 weeks times 3 years). Sometimes the data is quite limited. For example, a marketer may have only four quarters worth of data for just one year, and this data can be disaggregated into nine U.S. census regions. That gives 36 data points to work with (4 quarters times 9 regions), not nearly as many as an analyst would like, but enough to give some insight into the links between inputs and outcomes.

Marketing investments are then estimated for each vehicle type (prime-time television, drive-time radio, outdoor, web advertising, sales promotion, public relations, etc.) for each time period for the smallest unit of geography possible. Generally speaking, a consumer marketer can estimate investments in most cases for individual markets, but direct marketers can make these estimates at the ZIP code, block or even household level.

It is critical to include in the data-collection process insights on the distribution of the product by channel, by time period, and by geography. In a given market, for example, what percentage of all the stores that sell products in our category carry our brand? How often was it on the shelf available for sale? For an individual store, how many shelf facings did we enjoy for every time period being measured? What was the product's price during each period? Equally important, what was the price compared to competitors' prices? In a given period for a given store, was there a price promotion? Were there changes in the price that took place over time? Were there changes in product quality or packaging? It is important to gather on a consistent basis any information about the brand and its competitors.

Many ROI modelers ignore the effects of competition because it is often extremely difficult to gather. But if it can be obtained (such as in automotive or pharmaceutical sales), it should be included. After all, if a competitor increases or drops its price, introduces a new product, changes an ad campaign, or dramatically ups or drops its television ad spending, the move can have as much effect on your brand as anything you do in the market.

At the same time, marketers need to conceptualize what other variables—often called *exogenous variables* because they are beyond the organization's control—may affect marketing investments and sales. Month-by-month unemployment numbers by market are important, but so, too, are the number of days of rain or snow.

All the variables we've been discussing are, in technical jargon, the *independent* or *predictor* factors. They are the variables that theoretically cause sales changes to occur. Sales-related variables, survey variables, and measures of customer equity are the *dependent* or *predicted* variables. For the purposes of measuring ROI, the most important of these are sales measured in standardized units (such as, 12-ounce equivalents of soft drinks or individual PCs), revenues, and market share in units and dollars. As we mentioned earlier, we'd like to see this data collected for as many time periods as possible for as many geographic areas as seem appropriate. For a package good, this could be an individual store or market. For a PC manufacturer, this could be a market, a ZIP code, or, better yet, an individual retail outlet. For a financial services company, the data is most typically collected on a market-by-market basis.

Going beyond Short-Term Sales and Profits

Another set of variables has to do with the effect of the marketing program in the heads of individual buyers or decision-makers for the consumer or industrial product or service. Companies usually collect this kind of data in the tracking surveys we've talked about before and assess measures such as awareness, familiarity, messages communicated, attitude changes, predispositions to buy, and actual behavior, sometimes on a daily basis and often reported on a quarterly if not monthly basis.

This survey-based data has a very important role. Its job is to help interpret why the marketing investments had the effects revealed through the analysis. Or, as is often the case, why there were no effects. Did the marketing program generate awareness of the brand and its advertising but little else? Did the marketing program surprise management with its strong effect on awareness but little conversion in attitudes and behavior? Did our spending impact everything except buyer behavior? Often, the survey-based measures are examined in sequence in what researchers refer to as a *hierarchy of effects* model as shown in Figure 14.1. Awareness comes first; sales and customer equity come last.

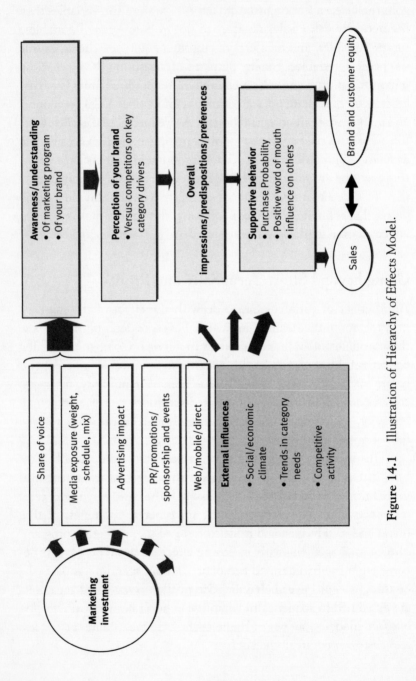

Figure 14.1 Illustration of Hierarchy of Effects Model.

Another job for hierarchy of effect modeling is to help set objectives for the marketing program and anticipate likely results. A new products marketer may say, for example, "Our objective by the end of the year is to generate 50 percent total brand awareness [a typical number] of the new product, 30 percent trial [that is, first-time purchase], 60 percent repeat purchase, and a 10 percent market share." Assuming that these objectives were set using historical data rather than gut instinct, measuring the performance of the new product over time as compared to the objectives is a very useful exercise because it provides real benchmarks.

Sometimes, the company obtains measures of customer equity and its drivers—brand equity, product equity, relationship equity— from the tracking study, but often it obtains them from an independent piece of research. Many marketers regard the effect of changes in investments on sales as indicating short-term effects, whereas the effects of changes in investment on customer equity indicate more enduring, longer-term effects. Measuring both sales and customer equity, therefore, are related but different.

Once a marketer has assembled all of the data capturing the independent and dependent variables, everything from marketing investments and distribution through sales and awareness and buyer behavior to customer equity, the task of analysis can begin. Although it is beyond the intent of this book to describe these analyses, we can say that econometric modeling using linear and nonlinear regression analyses is employed to assess the relationship between every independent and every dependent variable over time. Companies usually use such modeling to measure the extent to which changes in predicted variables (top line dollar sales, unit sales, and the like) are associated with changes in the predictor variables (marketing investments, product and price, competition, seasonality, external drivers, and the like).

The point of all this is to isolate the ROI of each aspect of the marketing mix/spending to identify which dollars have the greatest effect. For example, do daytime television commercials have a greater effect on sales than prime-time? Do ads in shelter magazines have a greater effect than ads in news magazines? Do drive-time radio spots have a greater effect than quarter-page newspaper ads? The goal is to provide a reliable (true over time) measure of the volume return or elasticity (or both) for marketing vehicles such as TV, print, radio, consumer promotions or events, and direct mail as well as base sales drivers such as price, distribution, competition, and the like.

The first step is to identify all the key brand-related metrics that the company believes are important and therefore captured in the firm's tracking systems. In the case of McDonald's, the company could identify sales by region, by store, by part of day, by menu item, by individual customer receipt, and more. A company needs to identify the key metrics of the business, such as awareness, positive image, trial, repeat business, and loyalty. These are exceptionally useful insights in their own right. With this, the company can determine the paths and interrelationships of the variables. For example, some marketing investments drive sales but don't enhance brand awareness, image, or personality. Other investments drive both sales and brand health measures. Certain investments will increase new users; others will foster greater loyalty among current customers.

As a result of all this work, the company will have a complete model such as the one in Figure 14.1 with the company's marketing investments on the left and sales and customer equity on the right. Note that share of voice, media exposure, advertising impact, public relations, and web/mobile/direct investments affect awareness and understanding of your brand. External influences, over which you have no control, affect customer perceptions, overall impressions, and customer behavior. In the end, sales affect brand and customer equity, and they in turn affect sales.

Once the company has such a model, it is possible to quantify the percentage of sales due to each element, the elasticity associated with raising or lowering its support level, the financial ROI of each, the geographic and channel differences of each marketing element's response, and any seasonal opportunities for increased efficiency. It is also possible to quantify the effects of the responses on each other.

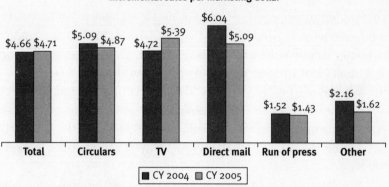

Incremental sales per marketing dollar

Figure 14.2 The Effect of Investments on Sales.

For example, a credit card company may learn from its model that there are only small synergistic effects between its TV advertising and direct mail. Figure 14.2 illustrates the effect of marketing investments on sales. Last year, direct mail alone accounted for 47 percent of incremental sales (sales above doing nothing at all), television alone accounted for 24 percent, magazines for 22 percent. The TV/direct mail synergy accounted for only 4 percent of the incremental sales. (Other marketing activities made up the difference.)

The model shows the effect of investments on sales and, with historic data, compares one year to another. In 2006, for example, the credit card company generated $4.71 in incremental revenue for every $1 it spent in marketing, up from $4.66 a year earlier. Television was the most efficient vehicle, returning $5.39 in incremental sales for every $1 invested. Direct mail, which had returned $6.04 in sales in 2005, was less efficient in 2006, returning $5.09 in sales for every $1 invested.

With these results, of course, management can spot trends, identify weaknesses, and know when and where to make changes.

Learn What Drives Customer Equity

Management can also collect the interim effects of campaign penetration, brand perceptions, unaided awareness, and more to permit a special analysis of customer equity. As we discussed in the previous chapter, customer equity has three major elements: brand equity, product equity, and relationship equity. Again, knowing a brand's customer equity—*and what drives it*—enables a manager to develop and implement stronger marketing programs.

We have been able to show that marketing investments produce gains in customer equity as well as in sales and market share. Also, gains in customer equity will, in turn, enhance the effectiveness of the investments themselves. Yes, you can measure marketing ROI.

You can measure ROI in the context of a senior marketing performance evaluation designed to address five critical questions:

1. How are we doing in meeting our objectives in terms of key measures of performance (that is, sponsorship awareness, affinity, customer equity, ROI)?
2. How will we do? Based on our current trajectory, will we achieve our end-of-year objectives?
3. How are we doing compared to competitors? What are the strengths and weaknesses of our programs?
4. Can we do better? What can our analysis tell us that will improve sales and customer equity performance?
5. What's the ROI of our overall program and its individual components?

Make Decisions on Facts and Analysis

As we said at the beginning of this book, we believe with Peter Drucker that nothing in business is as important as marketing. Yet, as we see in our daily work, too many marketing programs waste precious time, money, and company resources. Too many marketing executives make decisions on hunch, instinct, and gut feeling rather than on facts and analysis.

Part of this we know results from the pressure to make quick decisions. The speed of business does not seem to allow time to develop careful marketing plans or implement marketing programs. As a result, too many CMOs pick a market target in a blink. They make a positioning decision because intuition tells them the message makes sense. They write a marketing plan in 6 weeks; create, test, and produce a new TV campaign in 12 weeks; and implement the whole thing within 90 days. This is not the way to treat a new product or service you want to be profitable.

Every senior executive in every industry has good reasons why decisions must be made immediately, the product introduced next week, the program set by the end of the month. They are lashed by a sense of urgency; making decisions quickly is the intuitive thing to do. Corporations reward fast decision-making and frown upon taking pains. (And at the other extreme—it can be equally dangerous—making no decision when one is required. So-called analysis paralysis is a real disease.)

Nevertheless, it usually does not matter whether the company introduces its marketing campaign in September or January, delays the new web site by four months, or pulls all advertising until the last quarter. Marketing managers need time to consider alternatives and weigh options. When they have the time—which is most of the time—the thoughtful approach is to do it right. This means undertaking rigorous analysis of alternative decision options based on hard data using criteria related to profitability.

We have tried to show that marketing decisions made with your head are, on balance, better than the ones based on your gut. At the same time, you do need creativity and judgment. You need to distinguish between a situation in which your gut is leading you off target and one in which your judgment is adequate. The multimillionaire CEO of the hotel chain who decided the firm's target market were people much like himself had flawed judgment. The tire company marketing executive who decided not to air the animated 42-second commercial had good judgment (and a certain amount of courage to say the production investment was almost a total waste).

Creativity and judgment are fine, but they must be balanced with rigorous analysis of unimpeachable data. Only with both the data and the analysis can one hope to make decisions—strategic and tactical—that, if not optimal, are close to it.

Connect every marketing plan input to its output. The average marketing plan contains a discussion of the marketing climate, the elements of the marketing strategy, the specific goals and objectives of the marketing program, and the tactics the company plans to employ to reach those goals, but they're not connected to one another. As Chapter 11 described, they can be.

But most marketing executives do not really know if the company spends $1 million on advertising whether sales will go up, down, or stay the same. Their gut tells them sales will go up, but they cannot be sure. For many companies, it is often a surprise when things turn out well or badly or the same. Everybody hopes the new product (service, advertising campaign, promotion, price) will do well, but they don't really know whether it will or not.

Today, it is possible to create scientific marketing plans that tie inputs to outputs. The technology is available and can help you steer your brand, products, services, or company confidently. Turn up the advertising, turn down the promotion, increase share of distribution, launch the new product, and see the effects before you spend serious money.

We know it is hard to do this when you have fires to put out every day. People are working harder than ever, and, because they are working so hard, they don't have time to step back, think, consider, reflect, and implement properly. It just seems more realistic to go with your gut.

Even when a gut decision turns out to be a good one, companies continue to have difficulty with implementation. We've seen banks, package goods companies, automobile manufacturers, hardware and software firms, Internet companies, credit card companies, utilities, agribusinesses, telecommunications companies, and pharmaceutical businesses develop strong strategies only to watch them fail in the marketplace because of poor implementation.

Sometimes, the quality of the implementation is handicapped by the fact that the marketer does not control all the points of contact with the end user or customer. Mobil Corporation, as we've discussed, developed and implemented the most powerful, transformational strategy in the gasoline service station industry when it launched Friendly Serve. But Friendly Serve could have been even stronger because Mobil was unable to persuade all of its dealers to participate fully and enthusiastically in the program, even when it was in the dealer's best interest to do so.

Mobil's problem is not unique. Insurance companies have major problems implementing marketing programs to consumers through independent agencies. Food marketers have difficulties implementing marketing programs in supermarket powerhouses. Brokerage companies, computer software companies, toy makers, appliance and consumer electronics manufacturers have difficulty in breaking through and gaining the cooperation of the middlemen who stand between them and their customers.

Successful implementation not only requires enlisting the support of dealers, independent agents, brokers, and retailers, it also requires motivating every person in the organization who has contact with the customer—and every external partner (the ad agency, package design firm, PR agency, everyone)—to buy into the strategy. It generally requires genuine cooperation between the sales and marketing departments.

This is not easy. People resist change, and many people don't want to be pushed into implementing someone else's ideas. But it has to be done. Sometimes, it requires an intemperate drill sergeant. More usually, it takes the hard work of an inspired CMO who is willing to get down in the trenches and do whatever is necessary to persuade the troops to follow. And sometimes it takes the CEO knocking a few heads.

U.S. business, as always, faces an uncertain future. Led by financially oriented managers during the 1980s, 1990s, and to date, a frenzy of mergers and purges, acquisitions and divestitures, expansions and downsizings resulted in a new business landscape. The dot-com bubble grew and burst, and the remaining firms have a better idea of what a business requires.

Financial wheeling and dealing, searching for the magic bullet in reengineering, portfolio analysis, self-directed teams, total quality management, value chain analysis, and a balanced scorecard have had their run. Responsible chief executives recognize the overwhelming, overarching power of marketing to grow their businesses.

As we've said many times before, developments in marketing are changing the fabric of industry, extending the limits of what we know, and separating winners from losers. The exceptional marketing organization stays abreast of these developments, capitalizes on new thinking and new discoveries, and stakes out the frontier as its own. The exceptional CEO and CMO understand these developments, trends, and ideas and play a leading role in implementing them in their companies.

The bold leaders are committed to developing and implementing transformational marketing strategies. By "transformational" we mean strategies that change brand trajectories, career paths, sometimes entire companies, and occasionally even industries.

They are wise enough to follow the lead of the late Peter Drucker, who said, "Our job is not to defend yesterday but to invent tomorrow." They are wise enough to know that their heads are smarter than their guts.

Notes

Chapter 1

1. Janet Adamy, "Half a Loaf: At Giant Baker, Freshness Project Takes Sour Turn," *The Wall Street Journal*, September 23, 2004, eastern edition, A1.
2. Reed Abelson, "Maker of Twinkies and Wonder Bread Files for Chapter 11," *The New York Times*, September 23, 2004, C5.
3. The Interstate Bakeries story is based on Janet Adamy, "Half a Loaf: At Giant Baker, Freshness Project Takes Sour Turn," *The Wall Street Journal*, September 23, 2004, eastern edition, Al; Reed Abelson, "Maker of Twinkies and Wonder Bread Files for Chapter 11," *The New York Times*, September 23, 2004, C5; Jennifer Mann, "Problems Pile Up, Overwhelm Kansas City, Mo.-based Interstate Bakeries," *The Kansas City Star*, September 26, 2004,

NA; Janet Adamy, "Snack Foods' New Marketing Sweet Spot: Grown Ups," *The Wall Street Journal*, April 12, 2005, eastern edition, B1.

4. Gary Hamel, "When Dinosaurs Mate," *The Wall Street Journal*, January 22, 2004, A12.

5. "Mastering Innovation—Exploiting Ideas for Profitable Growth," Deloitte Research 2006, http://www.deloitte.com.

6. The American Consumer Satisfaction Index, http://www. theacsi.org/.

7. http://www.cmomagazine.com/read/070104/manifesto.html.

8. Sarah Ellison, "Focus Group—P&G Chief's Turnaround Recipe: Find Out What Women Want," *The Wall Street Journal*, June 1, 2005, eastern edition, A1.

9. Pat O'Halloran and Patrick Mosher, "Marketing: Underrated, Undervalued, and Unimportant?" *Human Performance Insights*, no. 6 (September 10, 2003): 1.

10. Theodore Levitt, *The Marketing Imagination* (New York, Free Press, 1986), 153.

Chapter 2

1. Curves International information based on personal conversation with Gary Heavin, April 4, 2006.

2. Brian McCormick, "Curves Attracting Notice," *Crain's Chicago Business*, August 4, 2003, 1.

3. Barbara Mikkelson, "Curves," http://www.snopes.com/business/ alliance/curves.asp.

4. Joy Keller, "The 30-minute Formula," *IDEA Health & Fitness* (June 2003): 62; John W. Kennedy, "Rolling with the Curves," *Christian Reader* (January–February 2004): 30; Brian McCormick, "Curves Attracting Notice," *Crain's Chicago Business*, August 4, 2003, 1; Eve Tahmincioglu, "Easy Does It for a Giant of Gyms," *The New York Times*, August 31, 2003, 3.2; Kelly Pedone, "Ahead of the Curves," *Texas Lawyer* (August 2, 2004).

5. Rachel Donadio, "The Gladwell Effect," *The New York Times Book Review*, February 5, 2006, 12.

6. Larry Kubal, "The Power of the Blink," *Venture Capital Journal* (August 1, 2005): 1.

7. Felix Dennis, "Books: Outgrabing Lewis Carroll," *Management Today* (April 7, 2005): 33.

8. Richard Posner, "Blinkered," *The New Republic*, January 24, 2005, 27.

9. Imara, The Wisdom Light, http://www.thewisdomlight.com/.

10. Marci McDonald, "Psst! Want a Hot Tip? Try a Crystal Ball," *U.S. News & World Report*, January 8, 2001, 37.

11. Ruth Shalit, "The Return of the Hidden Persuaders," September 27, 1999, http://www.salon.com/media/col/shal/1999/09/27/persuaders/.

12. David Kiley, "Shoot the Focus Group," *Business Week*, November 14, 2005, 120.

13. Olson Zaltman Associates, http://www.olsonzaltman.com/oza/zmet.html.

14. http://www.salon.com/media/col/shal/1999/09/27/persuaders/index.html.

15. Gerald Zaltman, "How Customers Think," *Fast Company*, February 2003, 45.

16. http://www.businessweek.com/magazine/content/06_23/b3987083.htm?chan=search.

Chapter 3

1. Regina Lewis and Rebecca Mardula, "Re-Concepting the Dunkin' Donuts of the Future" (paper presented at AMA Strategic Marketing Conference, Chicago, IL, May 2005).

Chapter 4

1. Marakon Associates, "New Global Study Finds Companies Struggle to Understand Customer Needs, Hampering Organic

Growth" (New York: Marakon Associates, November 17, 2004).

2. Daniel Yankelovich and David Meer, "Rediscovering Market Segmentation," *Harvard Business Review* (February 2006): 122.

3. Gina Chon, "Chrysler's Made-Up Customers Get Real Living Space at Agency," *The Wall Street Journal*, January 4, 2006, B9.

Chapter 5

1. Sarah Ellison, "Brewers Plan Image-Enhancing Campaign: 'Got Beer?'" *The Wall Street Journal*, November 7, 2005, B1.

2. Al Ries and Jack Trout, *Positioning: The Battle for Your Mind* (New York: McGraw Hill, 1981).

3. Philip Kotler, *Marketing Insights from A to Z* (Hoboken, NJ: Wiley, 2003), 136.

Chapter 6

1. Clayton Christensen, Scott Cook, and Taddy Hall, "Marketing Malpractice: The Cause and the Cure," *Harvard Business Review* (December 2005): 74.

2. Regina Lewis and Rebecca Zogbi, "Re-Concepting the Dunkin' Donuts of the Future" (presentation to the 2006 Senior Marketing Executive Roundtable, The Conference Board, New York, April 2006).

3. Mark Koestnere, "Dunkin' Donuts Launches Experimental Store in Euclid, Ohio," *News-Herald* (Willoughby, OH), March 10, 2006, 1.

4. Boston.com, "Dunkin' Donuts to Offer Hot Dogs, Other Foods beyond Breakfast," http://www.boston.com/news/local/massachusetts/articles/2006/08/23/dunkin_donuts_to_offer_hot_dogs_other_foods_beyond_breakfast/.

Chapter 7

1. Kris Oser, "Fortune 500 Marketing Chiefs to Increase Online Spending," *Advertising Age*, January 5, 2006, 1.

2. Online Publishers Association, http://www.online-publishers.org.

3. Randall Stross, "Someone Has to Pay for TV. But Who? And How?" *The New York Times*, May 7, 2006, 3.

4. Brian Steinberg, "TiVo's Latest Viewing Option: Commercials," *The Wall Street Journal*, May 8, 2006, B3.

5. Magazine Publishers of America, *Engagement: Understanding Consumers' Relationships with Media*, New York, 2006, p. 2, http://www.magazine.org.engagement.

6. Ibid., p. 6.

7. For a detailed report on the television study and its implications, see Kevin J. Clancy and David W. Lloyd, *Uncover the Hidden Power of Television Programming* (Thousand Oaks, CA: Sage, 1999).

8. Dan Ephron, "The Pizza Offensive," *Newsweek*, May 29, 2006, 30.

9. Nat Ives, "New Food Title Serves Up Product Placement in Edit," *Advertising Age*, July 18, 2005, 8.

10. Steve McClellan, "For a Whole New DRTV Experience, Call Now," *Adweek*, September 5, 2005, 10.

11. Robert Berner, "I Sold It through the Grapevine," *Business Week*, May 29, 2006, 32.

12. Willow Duttge, "Don't Blink, You'll Miss It," *Advertising Age*, June 12, 2006, 1.

Chapter 8

1. Sheree R. Curry, "Dump the :30 Spot and Embrace On-Demand," *TelevisionWeek*, July 25, 2005, 60.

2. Gina Chon, "Toyota's Marketers Get Respect—Now They Want Love," *The Wall Street Journal*, January 11, 2006, B1.

3. For a detailed account of this study, the methodology, and the findings, see Kevin J. Clancy and David W. Lloyd, *Uncover the Hidden Power of Television Advertising* (Lanham, Maryland, Sage, 1999).

Chapter 9

1. Mike Reisman, personal interview with the author, January 1, 2006.

2. SponsorClick, *Sponsorship Marketing Global Report*, http://www.sponsorclick.com.

3. Julia Chang, "High Scores: Get More Out of Your Sports Sponsorships," *Sales & Marketing Management*, August 2005, 10.

4. Promotion Marketing Association, *Event Marketing Council 2002 Intellitrends Survey*, http://www.promomagazine.com/research/industrytrends/marketing-major-event.index.html.

5. Jo Wrighton and Jathon Sapsford, "For Tire Makers, an Expensive Battle at the Racetrack," *The Wall Street Journal*, October 27, 2005, A1.

6. New Century Marketing Concepts, http://www.insmkt.com/fund.htm.

7. Julia Chang, "High Scores: Get More Out of Your Sports Sponsorships," *Sales and Marketing Management*, August 2005, 10.

8. Betsy Spethmann, "Buzz Gets Louder," *Promo Magazine*, April 1, 2005, http://www.promomagazine.com/research/industrytrends/marketing-buzz-gets-louder/html.

9. Becky Ebenkamp, "Out of the Box: Now, a Blur of Our Sponsors," *Brandweek*, October 4, 2004, http://www.brandweek.com.

10. Karla Ward, "The Derby by Yum Brands and the Chick-Fil-A Bowl," *Lexington Herald-Leader*, February 2, 2006, NA.

11. Mike Reisman, personal correspondence with the author.

12. Patricia Odell, "Promo Exclusive: By the Numbers," *Promo Magazine*, January 1, 2004, http://www.promomagazine.com/research/eventtrends/marketing-promo-exclusive-numbers/html.

13. "Sponsorship Research," http://www.eventmarketer.com.

14. Patricia Odell, "Promo Exclusive: By the Numbers," *Promo Magazine*, January 1, 2004, http://www.promomagazine.com/research/eventtrends/marketing-promo-exclusive-numbers/html.

Chapter 10

1. "Grainger Takes a New Look at Unplanned MRO Purchases," *Purchasing*, September 1, 2005, 53.

2. Constantine Von Hoffman, "Culture Crash," CMO *Magazine*, July 2005, http://www.cmomagazine.com/read/070105/culture_crash.html.
3. Ibid.

Chapter 12

1. "P&G's End-to-End RFID Plan," *Baseline*, June 28, 2006.
2 Jill Leovy, "They're Not Just Gas Stations Anymore," *Los Angeles Times*, May 4, 1996, 1.
3. The information on Mobil Friendly Serve is based mainly on company statements (*Business Wire*, May 23, 1996); Jill Leovy, "They're Not Just Gas Stations Anymore," *Los Angeles Times*, May 4, 1996, 1; Angel Abcede, "Mobil Puts on a Happy Face," *National Petroleum News*, December 1996, 58.

Chapter 13

1. Kevin Lane Keller, *Strategic Brand Management*. Upper Saddle River, NJ: Prentice Hall, 2003, 4.
2. Readers who are interested in a far more comprehensive discussion of customer equity should read Roland T. Rust, Valarie A. Zeithaml, and Katherine N. Lemon, *Driving Customer Equity: How Customer Lifetime Value Is Reshaping Corporate Strategy* (New York: Free Press, 2000); and Roland T. Rust, Katherine N. Lemon, and Das Narayandas, *Customer Equity Management* (Upper Saddle River, NJ: Pearson Prentice Hall, 2005).

Chapter 14

1. Ed See, "Bridging the Finance-Marketing Divide," *Financial Executive*, July–August 2006, 50.
2. Jim Lenskold, "An Executive Summary of the Marketing ROI and Measurements Trend Study," *Lenskold Group*, http://www.lenskold.com/newsletters/Execsummay_June06.html.

Index